MACBETH IN HARLEM

MACBETH IN HARLEM

Black Theater in America from the Beginning to *Raisin in the Sun*

CLIFFORD MASON

RUTGERS UNIVERSITY PRESS

New Brunswick, Camden, and Newark, New Jersey, and London

Library of Congress Cataloging-in-Publication Data

Names: Mason, Clifford, author.
Title: Macbeth in Harlem : Black theater in America from the beginning to Raisin in the sun / Clifford Mason.
Description: New Brunswick : Rutgers University Press, 2020. | Includes bibliographical references and index.
Identifiers: LCCN 2019040028 | ISBN 9781978809994 (hardback) | ISBN 9781978810006 (epub) | ISBN 9781978810013 (mobi) | ISBN 9781978810020 (pdf)
Subjects: LCSH: African American theater—History—20th century. | United States—Race relations—20th century. | Race in the theater. | African Americans in the performing arts. | African Americans—Race identity. | Theater and society—United States—History—20th century.
Classification: LCC PN2270.A35 M37 2020 | DDC 792.089/96073—dc23
LC record available at https://lccn.loc.gov/2019040028

A British Cataloging-in-Publication record for this book is available from the British Library.

♾ The paper used in this publication meets the requirements of the American National Standard for Information Sciences—Permanence of Paper for Printed Library Materials, ANSI Z39.48-1992.

www.rutgersuniversitypress.org

Manufactured in the United States of America

CONTENTS

To Margaret

MACBETH IN HARLEM

INTRODUCTION

Let's talk character and plot. The American character is the hero. He fights off the world and wins in the end. It doesn't matter what the odds are. He comes out on top. It follows, therefore, that the American plot has only one real conflict. *War!* The American character can only become the American Hero if his ultimate challenge is war. And the harder it is for him to win the war, the better for the drama, since he will, ultimately, win at all costs. This both permeates and is emblematic of the American culture at large. During the Cold War, a football coach famously got his "troops" ready for combat by telling them that the other team were the Chinese Communists, and when the coach's team scored a touchdown, they were scoring one for *our* side—the American side, the American way.

Since the American drama is complicated, it also follows that no matter how sophisticated we become in both our plots and our heroes, in the end, the result must be the same. Any American character must be a hero, and his victory must reflect the superiority not only of who he is but of the culture he represents: American culture. In this context, where do we put the Black American hero and the Black American conflict—and, just as important, the Black American plot? That takes us back to the sixties and Carl Reiner for an opening line: *"Enter Laughing"*!

Not only does the American hero, Black African version, have to laugh, but he's always had to laugh. Heywood Broun, one of the great theater critics of the twentieth century, said of Bert Williams in his prime, "Because Bert Williams was a Negro he had to be funny." And James Weldon Johnson said of Black plot, American African version, that lovemaking was forbidden because it made white audiences uneasy to see Negroes making love onstage. We can take that even further. A Boston critic said of a Black musical of the twenties, which had become too sophisticated for his taste, that when he succumbed to the surreptitious desire for the broad tang of "nigger" humor, he wanted no disturbing atom of intelligence busy-bodying about. In other words, "Don't think, just dance, sing, and tell watermelon jokes." To be clear, we're not talking about a mild form of censorship, such as what Chekhov experienced in Czarist Russia when an early collection of his short stories was too irreverent for the censor. Or when Shakespeare's plays ran afoul of the Lord Chamberlain's censor, the Master of the Revels, because of the many times the Bard committed regicide: *Macbeth, Richard II, Julius Caesar*. No, these inestimable gentlemen were operating in a system where they had the freedom—indeed, the wholehearted support and enthusiasm of a devoted following—to give rein to their artistic imaginings in any manner or form that their genius could create, despite annoying setbacks that did nothing in the end to diminish that genius. That freedom made their men and women "universal" because they spoke truth to the human spirit, a truth that can be understood in any language and any age. The problem with such universal truths is their need to be unfettered in the telling. They don't have to encompass the whole realm of human endeavor to be universal. They can deal with the smallest of plotlines, the most parochial of landscapes, but within that minute microcosm, *they must speak a truth*. And general audiences, certainly the ones who pay good money to see "good" theater, *know* that truth when it's on the stage. They react to it the way they always have. They make it immortal in the context where theater lives. *A Streetcar Named Desire, Death of a Salesman, Long Day's Journey into Night*. Popular entertainment truth, watered down truth, musical comedy truth must all hit a chord somewhere in the psyche of the audience to be successful.

Which brings us to the dilemma of the Black American truth: there isn't any. At least not in the context of the American experience. The critics raved about Richard Wright's *Native Son*, when it was a play on Broadway, calling it "the biggest American drama of the season" and "a vivid evening in the theatre, a tragic case of a morally mangled victim of society and circumstance": "In comparison, all the productions of the current season seem dim and ancient chromos. The theatre, that slumbering giant, tears off its chains in this production. From the theatrical point of view it is a technical masterpiece." And Orson Welles, the director, was hailed as one of the best influences the theater had, whose talent was abundant and inspired "as contrasted with the pussyfooting and the pseudo-intelligence and the feminism that has crept into this theatre of ours." In spite of all this enthusiasm, *Native Son* had a plotline and a hero that would chill the liver of any commercial producer of the present period. Not only does Bigger Thomas (Wright's "native son") understand that in his America, he can only speak *his* truth, but he explodes at the state of his oppressed soul by killing. And kill he does to release the psychic pain that's killing him morally and spiritually—not once, but twice. And the critics bought it!

Now that's truth with a dagger through the heart. But why must the Black American version of the truth be so harsh? Well, I need not go through a litany of the pain and the genocide, the trail of sorrow and tears, the unending brutishness that the American spirit has shown toward the African, Black American version. It's not necessary for me to repeat the horrors of killing men and women born in this country, who in a time of peace were treated as if they were caught in a time of war committing treason. The cause for the sadistic violence didn't always have to do with the often trumped-up charge of "rape," as if the idea of a white woman being attracted to a Black man was an unheard-of phenomenon. The Irish gang riots of 1863 were against the idea of a "nagur war." And what war were they talking about, pray tell? The Civil War. The Irish in New York, Manhattan specifically, rampaged through the streets in wolf packs seventy strong killing anyone Black they could find, hanging many on lampposts, most often in the vicinity of Fourteenth Street, because they refused to be conscripted to fight the Confederacy just to free "nagurs." They even burned down an orphanage. Lincoln had to send in the army to restore "Law and Order."

The question that follows is what has happened to this truth. Except for Canada Lee, who played Bigger Thomas, expostulating it in splendid anger 144 times on Broadway *ca n'existe pas* (which is French for "Are you kidding me?"). You know why. The Shuberts tried to close it but couldn't. The producers closed it even though it was still doing good business. It was not only a truth that lived but one that proved it could pass the ultimate test of the Broadway producer: it was good box office. So its death must be put down to a cultural prejudice rather than to an economic necessity. And this explains how Black theater (you know the version) has existed for all of the twentieth century and two decades into the twenty-first without speaking that truth. Only a brilliant act of legerdemain could have created it whole cloth out of such a leaking vessel.

It's almost as if ole Shakespeare was able to create great tragedy using only Falstaff for a character. Or as if a Jewish German who wrote about the 1930s did so without mentioning either Hitler or the holocaust. I'm not saying it couldn't be done, but no matter how compelling the narrative, it would be a hollow truth at best. A prefabricated one constructed to please an audience *that didn't want the real truth*, only a version of it that would cause them no discomfort, since that is what they are paying for—a *Night at the Opera*, Marx Brothers truth, or a *"Master Harold"* . . . *and the Boys* truth, where Master Harold spits in the face of the boys and did so on a Broadway stage night after night and did good business. I know firsthand, since I sat in the audience and saw Danny Glover and my good friend Zakes Mokae take the spit. And Zakes Mokae, a South African actor, had been one of the many members of his acting fraternity who helped Athol Fugard "write" not only *Master Harold* but *Blood Knot* and some of his other plays as well. So Zakes was an actor and author who still ended up taking the spit.

Black truth can only exist in a version that is denigrating, and the real truth, the one that has been burned into the Black soul, "break the heart of me" in all its rage and horror, can only exist beneath the grin, the feckless offering of pretending that Black men can beat up on white men the way white men beat up on Black men in the real world of American coexistence. If the Black American wants to eat of the humungous pie of the American theatrical plentitude, he must do so with a pair of false teeth. No racism can be essayed, or at least not a racism that bites. Poor suffering Black people that white people have to rescue or whose demands are so modest that no one with a human heart could deny—these can pass muster. But that's all.

It's odd that people can be so generous, so giving, when they are forced to react face-to-face to the human suffering of a fellow creature, but once that suffering becomes the topic of general discourse in an open forum, their hearts can become as hard as a rock, resisting any hammer. Frederick Douglass experienced the phenomenon when he was on the run after escaping from slavery. He said that no matter what door or window he knocked on, whether Democrat or Republican, Quaker or Catholic, none would deny him a crust of bread, a glass of water. Yet every one of them would probably support the Fugitive Slave Act.

And that's what the American version of Black theater, African style, has become: a vast Fugitive Slave Act. It is not the purpose of this commentary to do The Black artist has had to survive as best he can if he intends to thrive at his craft as opposed to becoming a shoe salesman (if he can get the job). Nor do I hold the white audience solely responsible for the way in which it has demanded that the Black character, the Black plot—indeed, the Black story—be a version on the public stage that would shame anyone in any other country who saw their reality so ingeniously distorted. It's a cultural problem that is as innate in its existential reality to the American character, the American experience, the American custom, the American way of life as peanut butter and jelly.

It is the Black saga, after all, that has described to us who we are as a people. Having lied about *all* men being equal, having made Black people the footstool, the public joke, the violent, lazy, chicken-eating, stealing denizens of rat-infested neighborhoods, it would seem unconscionable to then let that miscreant represent the American hero who has to win the war if he's to be a hero, American style. To let his story be the iconic example of the nation's culture would be folly when he has a story to tell that puts a lie to the very suggestion that America has been a paragon of virtue, of manly heroism that is a lodestar for a torn, tired, tormented world to look to for succor and comfort, for surcease from pain, for the balm of Gilead, the Resurrection that, once found again and held on to, will make America great again, as it has always been.

In conclusion, let me add that the men and women I write about here were fighting against the odds, not giving in to them. The stands they took and the battles they fought will, if only half remembered, in some small measure make their sacrifices and their deaths a triumph, even when those deaths took place in the most abject of circumstances. How and why they lived transcends the way they died.

Hotel Greystone
New York City
August 2019

1 · THE BEGINNING

On April 14, 1936, an all-Black production of *Macbeth*—directed by Orson Welles, produced by John Houseman, and funded under the Federal Theatre Project of the Works Progress Administration of Franklin Delano Roosevelt's second term—opened in Harlem at the Lafayette Theatre on Seventh Avenue, just south of 132nd Street. Every major newspaper in the city covered the event, and Eleanor Roosevelt lent her august presence to it, accompanied by Mayor Fiorello La Guardia and Hallie Flanagan, head of the Federal Theatre Project. A ten-block square area was cordoned off, and more than ten thousand people stood in the streets just to witness the arrival of celebrities.[1]

Inside, all 1,300 seats were filled. The Monarch Lodge Band #450 of the Black Elks led a parade down Seventh Avenue that started two hours before curtain time. They were called the Improved Benevolent and Protective Order of Elks of the World to distinguish them from the white Elks, who maintained a strictly segregated policy in those days and were known as the Benevolent Protective Order of the Elks without being improved. But this was only one band. There was another one—110 musicians strong—that had been giving a concert inside the theater for an hour before curtain time. The evening was by all accounts an event, the last big event for Harlem that would see the whole city and beyond come to its doorsteps to join in celebration and pay homage to its importance as a cultural center. Harlem didn't disappear after 1936; it's there now. But those glory days when the Federal Theatre actually sent shows from Harlem to Broadway and across the entire country lasted but a little while—a scant three years, in fact—and then were to be no more when Congress, in an act of vindictive folly, killed the entire Federal Theatre Project, Black and white, in June of 1939.

Theater in Harlem never recovered, although there were at least two other triumphs during the war and after that rivaled the achievements of the *Macbeth* production. But that was almost afterglow and proved, if anything, that the strength of Harlem as a theatrical force had grown so large that it had life left in it even after it had been killed. The two plays were *Anna Lucasta* and *Native Son*. Both went to Broadway: *Anna Lucasta* from the American Negro Theater and *Native*

FIGURE 1.1. Ira Aldridge as he appeared when he received the Gold Medal of the First Class for Art and Sciences from His Majesty King Frederick IV of Prussia in 1853. Art and Artifacts Division, Schomburg Center for Research in Black Culture, The New York Public Library.

Son from Orson Welles and John Houseman, who had headed the Harlem unit of the Federal Theatre. *Lucasta* was an amazing box-office hit, running up over nine hundred performances on Broadway alone at the Mansfield Theatre. In addition, it was playing in Chicago for a year and a half at the same time. *Native Son* was the last collaboration of Welles and Houseman's stormy decade-long partnership. They used the great Black actor Canada Lee, who had been their Banquo in *Macbeth*, for the lead role of Bigger Thomas. *Native Son* was both an artistic and a commercial success that went on the road after opening on Broadway at the St. James Theater.

But brief as Harlem's triumph was, it had been a long time in coming. And the odyssey of the thousands of Black men, women, and children who had taken the journey from the old fort at the tip of Nieuw Amsterdam in 1606 was a long one. By foot, horse, carriage, boat, and train, they passed through every major section of the city, stopping along the way to make settlements here, settlements there, each time to be pushed and buffeted farther north, each time being forced to move on again, to finally, exhaustedly, get to Harlem three hundred years later. It was a trek that had exacted a heavy toll in suffering and in human effort to arrive at the day and time when the high and the mighty, the makers of taste in art, would come to Harlem to see Black actors do Shakespeare.

Black actors do Shakespeare! In 1936! Burnt cork—minstrelsy's blackface—was hardly dead. Fay Bainter, that illustrious lady of the screen who played so many mothers and aunts of the better American family in the forties (she was Bette Davis's Aunt Belle in *Jezebel*), had appeared in pigtails and *in blackface* as Topsy the teenage wench in *Uncle Tom's Cabin* just three years before. She was forty at the time. And Topsy's Southern plantation, darkie[2] negro accent would have shamed any minstrel man. She's described in Scriptnotes as "A wild and uncivilized slave girl [who] gradually learns to love and respect others by following the example of [little] Eva," who is white. And Black plays of the thirties still had the type of dialogue in them that would make any self-respecting member of the Urban League die of shame. Here's part of a scene from *Meek Mose* by Frank Wilson, whose career spanned over half a century in New York and Hollywood as a paid actor, writer, and sometimes producer. He had dozens of Broadway credits to his name, not least of which was the premiere of the preeminent Theatre Guild's production of *Porgy* on Broadway in 1925; he played Porgy. Here's part of a scene from *Meek Mose*:

NATHAN: Mr. Mose, doan you depen on dis white man. Dese folks are evil, I tell you.
MOSE: I knows dat, but dese white folks ginus a certain 'mount of money and built dese shacks. We took it, now what else is dere for us ter do?
NATHAN: Mr. Jenkin, yo sho is a quiet livin' man.
MOSE: I live according ter de Bible (solemnly). I follow God's Commandments. I wuz raised ter do dat fum a baby, an I never inten to do anything else. His words says, "Love you enemies. Do good ter dem dat hat' you." An "Unto him dat smittith you

on one cheek, turn de odder. De Jews . . . Who's any mo meek and humble den de Jews; de never fight, and dey get ebey thing?"³

You'd think dialogue like that would prevent either the writer or what he wrote from ever being heard from again. Alas, such was not the case. Not only was *Meek Mose* performed on Broadway in 1928, but Wilson's *Walk Together Chillun* opened the Federal Theatre Project's three-and-a-half-year tenure at the Lafayette. It was the peculiar concept of the Black actor as cultural phenomenon that made such drivel possible. The Black writer may have written it, but he was encouraged to do so, even got produced only because he was willing to do so. Realistic portrayals of Black life in that period would have been met with as cold a reception on the commercial stage as it's met with at the beginning of the twenty-first century. Noncommercial and off-Broadway theater may have their share of Black reality from time to time, but not Broadway.

Shakespeare, God bless him, was not new to the Black actor, even in 1936. The drama critics of such esteemed journals as the *New York Times*, the *New York Herald Tribune*, and the rest may not have been overly impressed with what they saw and heard Black actors at the Lafayette do with "Out, out damned spot," and "She should have died hereafter," but these actors, many of them well known in their day and after, did not do a minstrel-show version in darkie dialogue. It was cut, but it was not bowdlerized. Jack Carter as the Thane used traditional stage speech, and his ability as an actor who could handle the classics was proved not only by his performance here but later, when Welles and Houseman used him in their Mercury Theatre production of Marlowe's *Doctor Faustus* in the role of Mephistopheles. For any actor, Black or white, to have been able to say that in his lifetime, he played on Broadway in a Mercury Theatre production in a leading role of a classic and got good reviews on top of it, is to have gone to the pinnacle of success in the actor's art. Then there was Edna Thomas as Lady Macbeth. *Fortune* magazine, *Time*'s sister and hardly considered a bastion of liberalism, said of her, "Edna Thomas turned in one of the season's great performances as Lady Macbeth."⁴ She had trained as a classical actress ready, willing, and able to do the part. And do it she did.

But the daily drama critics, in their aggregate wisdom, must have gotten ague or some similar debilitating disease over the sight of so many Black faces staring across the footlights at them all at one time, trying to do Shakespeare, that immortal Englishman. Cultural shock took over from critical judgment in all probability, and what the eye saw, the mind could not comprehend. Even down to today, Black speech has a special place in the artistic conception of most white writers. In *Roots*, part 1, poor whites spoke like Yale School of Drama graduates, but every Black actor had an accent as thick as down-home gravy no matter how long he or she had been in "de house" instead of "de cotton patch." But if the critics thought that Black actors doing their own style of Shakespeare, even under the august tutelage and direction of Messrs. Welles and Houseman, had to be suspect on the face of it (literally) in 1936, imagine what confusion the fourth estate was thrown into in 1821 when an all-Black company was not only doing Shakespeare in New York but doing it under its own auspices—without any benefit of white help, control, guidance, or funding.

In that year, in Greenwich Village, a group of Black actors formed what they called the African Grove Theatre and made *Richard III*, *Othello*, and *Macbeth* the heart of their repertoire.[5] James Hewlett, the first actor of the group, was, in fact, considered to be one of the leading performers of his day. What were Blacks doing in Greenwich in 1821, and what were they doing there doing Shakespeare, you ask? Greenwich Village was then the center of the Black community in Manhattan and had been for over fifty years, having moved uptown from the Five Points area, in what is at present city hall. This community had many prosperous and successful Blacks in it, most of whom had attended the African Free Schools, founded in 1787 to educate Black children who had been denied the opportunities that other children had. The African Free Schools were in fact the precursors to the New York City Board of Education, which came into being in 1840, incorporating the work of the Free Schools into its system. Prior to the African Free Schools, no such concept of free education existed in New York for anyone Black or white.

Three men are crucial to the story of African Grove: its producer, its star, and one of its minor players. The star was James Hewlett. The producer was an ex-seaman named William Alexander Brown, born in the West Indies, who bought a house on Thomas Street in 1816 and turned the back into a tea garden where he put on theatrical entertainment. And the minor actor who would go on to fame and fortune in Europe, becoming one of the Continent's most successful tragedians, was Ira Aldridge. (More on him later.) The tea garden was so successful that Brown built a theater on Mercer Street that could hold between three and four hundred people. And his tea garden following became his theater audience. It was here on Mercer Street that Brown, Hewlett, and his fellow actors pioneered Black theater in America. Most of what they accomplished is lost to history or known only to the historian or the student, which is unfortunate because before they were through, they had made history, even if it has been buried and forgotten.

Hewlett started out as an entertainer on the summer resort circuit, primarily Saratoga, interspersing his act with songs. By 1825, he was being billed as "one of the most astonishing phenomena of the age . . . who, notwithstanding the thousand obstacles which [color] must have thrown in the way of improvement has . . . risen to a successful competition with some of the first actors of the day."[6] Granted, it's just an ad. But the comparison with top white actors proves not only that he was actually a professional with a public image, who was recognized as such by the theatrical community, but that in having done all that two years before slavery was even abolished in the state, he was the first star of Black theater in America.

He, Brown, and the rest had to endure every form of ridicule, calumny, abuse, and victimization at the hands of both the law and the press that a body—, any-body, singular or plural—could take. The *National Advocate*, a leading daily of the period, ran this editorial in August of 1821: "Among the number of ice cream gar-dens in this city, there was none in which the sable race could find admission and refreshment so they opened their own. . . . The little boxes of this garden were filled with black beauties 'making night hideous.' . . . The gentleman, with his wool nicely combed, and his face shining through a coat of sweet oil, borrowed from the castors; cravat tight to suffocation, having the double faculty of widening the mouth and giving a remarkable protuberance to the eyes."[7] A month later, it was reporting the opening of *Richard III* thus: "These imitative inmates of the kitchen and pantries [have resolved to set up a play]. . . . Richard III . . . was agreed upon, and a little dapper, wooly-headed waiter at the City Hotel personated the royal Plantagenet."[8]

The leading theater of the day was the Park, which was located across from city hall. In 1821, it had just reopened at a huge cost and with 2,500 seats that had to be filled. An Englishman named Stephen Price was running it. He bought many an English actor to America at great expense so as to corner the market on theater in New York. The great Edmund Kean himself played there in 1820. It was unfortunate for African Grove and for Hewlett and Brown that they were giving Price a run for his money. They even found themselves with more whites in their audience than they knew what to do with. So they set off a section just for them (Blacks were segregated at the Park, having to sit in the balcony with the whores) because, as Brown explained it, they didn't know how to act when they were in the presence of Black ladies and gentlemen of quality. That coupled with the fact that the newspapers, as we've seen, were having a field day ridiculing them (but, in so doing, were giving them a hell of a lot of publicity in the bargain), meant that they were making their mark.

That made them a threat, and not just to Price but to the gentlemen who had sunk all that money into rebuilding the Park theater, a couple of fellas named John J. Beekman and John Jacob Astor. Still, such healthy competition in the marketplace may have been endured if for no other reason than to prove that all men are created equal. But alas, the sable thespians didn't know their place. They committed the ultimate act of folly: having had to move the company to a bigger theater at Bleecker and Mercer Streets, Brown realized he was now too far away from his core audience of free Blacks. So he built a theater near to them—but that was also nearer the Park. That was bad enough, but when Price brought over the English actor Junius Brutus Booth to play Richard III, Brown rented a hotel next door and put on his own production of *Richard III*, with Hewlett playing Richard.

That was it. Beekman–Astor–Price did what is still being done to Black Ameri-cans today; they called the police. But they needed a reason, so they hired some hooligans to go into African Grove and break up the performance. This the white toughs did. When the Black actors fought back, the cops showed up, said *they* were disturbing the peace, not the white hooligans, and carted them off to jail. Still, the actors persevered. Sometimes even finishing the scene in jail, albeit for their own entertainment. But eventually, they were broken, and their theater permanently closed.

How good were these productions of *Richard III* and the rest? It's hard to tell because the reviews were really only intended to lampoon: "Richard had some robes made up from discarded merino curtains of the ballrooms; and from a paucity of actors, some doublets occurred, as these: King Henry and the Duchess Dowager were represented by one and the same person, while Lady Ann Catesby were [*sic*] sustained by another."[9] When they weren't indulging in something like that, they were reveling in the supposition that Shakespeare would have turned over in his grave at the sight of *Richard III* being performed by an actor as Black as the ace of spades. But that our sable thespians were making their presence felt, there can be no doubt. Said the *American*, "We have heretofore noticed the performances of a black corps dramatique in this city, at their theatre, the corner of Bleecker and Mercer Streets. It appears that the sable managers, not satisfied with a small share of the profit and a great portion of fame, determined to rival the great Park Theatre, belonging to Messrs. Beekman and Astor."[10]

And Hewlett himself had become an accepted name by the time he dropped from history. Said George C. Odell, a theater historian of the period, "The first week in March [brought at the Chatham Theatre in New York] no less a celebrity than the Negro Hewlett . . . listed in the *American* as 'the celebrated tragedian' and elsewhere as 'the Star of the West.'"[11] Hewlett had even gone to England; whether he was able to perform there is not actually known, although evidence of his being there for that purpose is quite solid. Nor do we know why he suddenly disappeared from sight in 1831. But we do know that both he and Brown gave them something to remember them by for their last production.

Not only was Brown the producer; he was also a writer and an actor himself. And he's credited with having written the first play by a Black writer performed in America, *The Drama of King Shotaway*, based on a Black Carib insurrection against the British in 1795 on the island of St. Vincent—an insurrection with which Mr. Brown seems to have had firsthand knowledge. And the boys put that play on as their swan song at African Grove in 1823. Hewlett played King Shotaway, and we can only guess at the reaction of the power brokers of the city to such "sable" temerity. New York may not have been a plantation, but the proslavery lobby was flourishing, not because they cared about having slaves in New York but because they were the financiers and the chief profiteers of Southern slavery. They built the ships and insured them; all the cotton picked by Black hands that never saw a penny of the profit passed through the port of New York. So a play about a slave rebellion, played by an all-Black cast in the midst of that kind of mainstream marketplace robustness, must have ruffled not a few feathers. Say one thing for African Grove: the boys went out with a bang.

Three things happened in 1823–1824, while Greenwich Village was still the center of the Black community in New York City, that would have an effect on Black theatrical activity for the rest of the century, with residual shock that has lasted well into the twenty-first. The first was the destruction of the Black theater movement in New York, a movement that had been started by Blacks, financed by them, and controlled artistically by them. One in which they chose to match their abilities against those of the best of the lot. Not only did African Grove do Shakespeare, but they included other plays that were part of the classical repertoire of the period: *Pizarro* by Sheridan, *Bertram* by an obscure parson, and probably *Oroonoko*, a popular eighteenth-century relic by Thomas Southerne.

The second important event of that year was the introduction of the plantation darkie in *The Tailor in Distress*. The white English actor Edward Forrest created the character, and not being able to get a white actress to play opposite him in similar blackface, Forrest had to start out by using an elderly Black woman. White actresses soon overcame their squeamishness, however, with the success of Forrest's character. Indeed, the plantation neegrow became so popular that he gave birth to a tradition of theater that saw only grinning and bootlicking coons who spoke an absurd dialect that was interspersed with even more absurd attempts at being sesquipedalian. This type, who was in fact a complete fiction in the sum total of all his moving parts, always got drunk, always stole chicken, always had a knife fight, and was never allowed to be romantically associated with a woman. His descendants have lived right down through to Lillian Hellman's *Little Foxes* where a Black servant, as a full-grown man, can't take a simple telephone message without dissolving into utter confusion. At first, Blacks performing these roles were not even allowed to have lines. This eventually gave way to "talking Negroes." But this only happened after white performers, starting with Forrest, dominated burnt cork for a good fifty years, allowing Blacks to finally caricature themselves after the Civil War. Which was their only option even then, if they wanted to make money in theater.

And for the long night of three-quarters of the nineteenth century, gone was any trace of African Grove or the tradition that it had created, or had attempted to create. And the only man who still had a bit of the torch in him, Ira Aldridge, took it to Europe, where he kept it alive and where it burned brilliantly through his amazing gifts. But it has been a lamp that has shown only obliquely in his native land. Before he died, he rivaled the great Edmund Kean, and that is no wild exaggeration, as we shall see. Aldridge's departure in that fateful year, 1824, never to see native land again was, of course, the third event.

ALDRIDGE IN EUROPE

Is it possible that an American actor could have conquered the capitals of Europe as long ago as the middle of the nineteenth century and done it by playing the leading roles of the Shakespearean repertoire? In America, most of our Shakespearean actors were still coming from England. Is it also possible that he could have been so brilliant in cities like Vienna and Berlin that he was given the most prestigious awards in the arts and sciences that those venerable capitals of royalty and privilege had to offer, that he was given them personally by emperor and king alike? Is it possible that he could have been so popular in Russia and was asked back so often that he spent five years touring the provinces, introducing Shakespeare for the first time to cities like Odessa and Zhitomir after he sold out in St. Petersburg and Moscow? Is it conceivable that he could have been the first person in history to perform Shakespeare in both Serbia and Turkey—and that in the case of Serbia, his became the official method for doing Shakespeare for the rest of the century? Even more, is it possible that because he was one of the few actors around popular enough to make a living doing classical repertoire that no other actor will probably ever play the major roles of the Bard in live performance more often than he did? Well, Ira Aldridge accomplished all this and more in the forty-three years he spent playing Shakespeare in England and on the Continent. A chair in his honor sits in the Shakespeare theater in Stratford-on-Avon to this day. I know because I checked.

When the African Grove closed, Aldridge saw the handwriting on the wall and caught the first boat out for England, never to return to native land. He was seventeen. He signed on as a steward, but by the time the ship landed, he had become the valet of English actor Henry Wallack, who was also on board. Wallack introduced him to the manager of the Coburg—a minor London house then, now the well-established Royal Court, and he was ready to take the plunge. Having solved the problem of a booking, Aldridge solved the problem of anonymity by assuming a new name: he called himself Mr. Keene, drawing from that of Edmund Kean's but changing the spelling. Then he made himself the son of an African prince from Senegal and opened at the Coburg in the title role of *Oroonoko*. He's eighteen! John Philip Kemble originated the role at Covent Garden. It was the sole property of the patent houses (Covent Garden and Drury Lane were the only two theaters with a license to do legit theater); that's how much it was prized as an acting vehicle. But it's a Black part. Oroonoko, not just the son of an African prince but a prince himself, is captured in his homeland, sold into slavery, and shipped to Surinam. Aldridge scored an immediate success and was held over for seven straight weeks, doing five different plays.

Even though the audiences were delighted and he sold out doing Black parts that leading white actors had had success in, when the seven weeks were up, he had to retire to the provinces because the press was not ready to take him seriously. There is a downside to Oroonoko, however. The prince, it turns out, is only opposed to slavery when it enslaves him. The first review comes from the *Times*:

> The appetite for theatrical novelty seems to have spread rapidly. . . . At the Surrey there's a man who plays a monkey, and at the Coburg they have brought out a genuine nigger to play Oroonoko. . . . His features, although they possess much of the African character, are considerably humanized. . . . Owing to the shape of his lips it is utterly impossible for him to pronounce English in such a manner as to satisfy even the unfastidious ears of the gallery. . . . It appears . . . that this gentleman, Aldridge, is one of the principal ornaments of the African theatre in New York, and for his own sake we regret that he did not stay there.[12]

The final complaint of the *Times* is that "although he is black, he's not dark enough." Aldridge was not the only "minority" to be thus flattered. The *Times* also managed in the same review to castigate a Jewish performer for eating raw beefsteaks, saying, "He usually got his bread by selling sealing wax; yet he ate the undressed beefsteaks as well as a natural born savage."

Said *Drama* magazine, "Mr. Keene, it is whispered, was a servant to Wallack. He is tall and tolerably well proportioned. His features are not very negroish. His voice is weak, so is his conception. Theatricals we suspect will never be profitable to him."[13] Outside of London, he gets a better review from the *Brighton Gazette*: "[We found in him] an actor of real and undoubted talent. He exhibited an acquaintance with the stage . . . that would not have shamed the tragedians of our own country, and, with few exceptions, are not to be found amongst us in the present day. . . . His style was perfectly free from extravagance. . . . He was received with great applause and on the fall of the curtain shouts of 'bravo!' were kept up for a considerable time."[14] And finally the *London Morning Post*: "In the intellectual ability which Mr. Keene has manifested in his several personations here, much good perhaps may result to the sable brethren, inasmuch as they have afforded a powerful illustration that blacks as well as whites may be equally fashioned by education—and that to education principally is to be ascribed that mental superiority which the latter have too often endeavored to persuade themselves that they exclusively enjoy."[15]

1825 was over and young "sable" thespian Ira Aldridge (known also as Mr. Keene, and later as the African Roscius, after the famous Roman actor of the same name) has proven—to the *London Morning Post* at any rate—that Blacks can be made the intellectual equal of whites if they have the advantages of education. However, the critic in Brighton also said he wasn't yet ready for Shakespeare; Aldridge realized he had a lot of growing to do and must, as a consequence, return to the drawing board.

A fellow Black American from his Greenwich Village days, James McCune Smith, was in Glasgow studying medicine, so it is there that Aldridge goes to develop the intellectual side of the actor's art. It will be another two years before he makes a reappearance on a stage, this time in the Midlands. When he does, he stays on one until he dies. The theater is his only means of livelihood throughout his lifetime. He supports two wives and raises five children, all from his earnings as an actor. Six years after his Midlands reemergence, he's in Dublin where he meets Kean for the first time. They both do *Othello* with the same supporting cast, and Kean becomes a fan. He even writes a letter of introduction for Aldridge to the theater manager at Bath. When Aldridge leaves Dublin and plays Bath and then Glasgow, he's come full circle. It had been eight long years since they heaped insult and racial abuse on him. Now that he'd fought his way back to London for another chance to prove himself, not just in any theater but at a principal one in the West End, he expected the chance to come because he had something he didn't have before: reviews that all but crown him as the next king. Said a critic in Glasgow, "He reminded us of Kean in many of his best passages, and when time may have deprived us of that great master, the African Roscius will not be an unworthy successor."[16]

He finally gets the call from the patent house itself, Covent Garden, to play Othello. He opens on April 10th, 1833. The season was in high gear. Macready was at Drury Lane in Macbeth, his best role. Sheridan's School for Scandal was at the Haymarket. Tyrone Power, our Tyrone Power's great grandfather, alternated with Aldridge at Covent Garden where Kean had made his final farewell in Othello two weeks before. Aldridge uses the same supporting cast.

The reviews were both vicious and racist. The *Times* was out done by *Atheneum*, which would years later try to make amends for sinking so low. Said the *Times*,

An experiment, and not a remarkably successful one . . . was last night essayed here. The tragedy of Othello was performed, the part of the moor by an individual of Negro origin . . . who calls himself Aldridge. . . . His accent is unpleasantly, and we would say vulgarly foreign; his manner, generally, drawling and unimpressive; and when by chance (for chance it is, and not judgment) he rises to a higher strain, we perceive in the transition the elevation of rant, not the fiery dignity of soul-felt passion. . . . It is, however, our duty to state that Mr. Aldridge was extremely well received. He "fit audience found, though few."[17]

And *Athenaeum* followed with this:

On Wednesday, this establishment . . . aimed another blow at its respectability by the production of Mr. Henry Wallack's black servant in the character of Othello—Othello, forsooth! This is to be presented in an English national theatre by one whose pretenses rest upon two grounds, of his face being of a natural instead of an acquired tint, and of his having lived as a servant to a low-comedy actor. We have no ridiculous prejudice against any fellow creature because he chances to be of a different colour from ours; and we trust that we have good taste enough to take our hats off to genius, wherever we find it. But in the name of propriety and decency we protest against a decent girl like Miss Ellen Tree being subjected by the manager of a theatre to the indignity of being pawed about by Mr. Henry Wallack's black servant, and if this exhibition is to be continued, we protest against acting being any longer dignified by the name of art.[18]

Aldridge was married twice. His first wife, Margaret, was nine years his senior. They were devoted to each other and remained so throughout her lifetime. He wrote in his diary on his birthday, two years after her death, "In good health, thank god. Dream pleasantly of my Margaret." His second wife, Amanda Paulina von Brandt, was a dancer. She lived in the house Aldridge bought for her and the children for forty-eight years after he died, dying herself in 1915. But long before the end, she had been cheated out of most of what he'd left her by the executor of the estate who even had the precious medals he'd been given melted down and sold for the gold.

He has to abandon Covent Garden for the friendlier confines of a minor house, the Surrey, in the face of the threatening nature of the reviews of his performance as Othello. He does and sells out for a month, which indicates to some extent that the audiences, left to their own devices, didn't mind the "genuine nigger" half so much as the press did. Four months later, he's back in the provinces, still selling out.

Since he refuses to die, they have to kill him. The following item appeared in several papers, as if by *chance*: "Death of the African Roscius. A melancholy and fatal accident occurred to Mr. Aldridge last week. He was returning in his carriage from Llandillo when one of the horses took fright. This occurred at the brink of a precipice. Mr. Aldridge, the postilion and the horses were all dragged over the edge to their death."[19] However, Aldridge's memoir, which he wrote and published himself, assured the world that rumors of his death "were greatly exaggerated." But he has to remain in the provinces for the next fifteen years.

When he returns to London in 1848, the reviews are quite good. But alas, it is at the Surrey again and not in the West End, and the West End does not beckon. So he has to remain a minor house actor, even though he's accumulated this impressive list of patrons: His Majesty Leopold, King of Belgium (Queen Victoria's maternal uncle); the Duke of Wellington; Sir Walter Scott; Prince Esterhazy (the Austrian ambassador to the English court); and the novelist Sir Edward Lytton Bulwer Lytton. You'd think with that kind of power behind him, he could get into any theater anywhere. But he couldn't, not in England. He tries again in 1852 to break the London barrier by appearing at the Britannia in *Othello* and *Titus Andronicus*. And even though the press hails him as "a star of the first magnitude," the West End does not offer an engagement. At this point, he has two choices, other than suicide. He can go back to America, or he can go to the Continent. There were rumors throughout his career that he would return to America for a tour, but his wife was adamantly opposed to it. So he chooses the Continent and sets sail on the fourteenth of July.

This first tour is such a success that he can be said to have quite simply conquered most of Europe. 1852 is only four years after the revolutions of 1848 that brought an end to the age of Metternich and the forces of reaction that held sway for over thirty years following the fall of Napoleon at Waterloo. Europe was ripe for change, and what better symbol of change than a Black actor doing Shakespeare? This is when he gets the Cross of Leopold from Franz Joseph, the last emperor of the Holy Roman Empire, and the gold medal first class from the King of Prussia, Frederick IV. He played Brussels, Aix-la-Chapelle, Elberfeld, Cologne, Bonn, Baden, Basel, Leipzig, Frankfurt, Vienna, Saxe-Coburg, Berlin, Hamburg, Dresden, Prague, Budapest, Danzig, Heidelberg, Berne, Zurich, Munich, and Cracow—and that's not a complete list. He was even in Lithuania briefly.

He was probably at an emotional high point. He knew that he had been kept out of the West End, through uncivilized race prejudice at first and later through jealousy and fear. The reviews he gets in Europe are so good that they almost defy credibility. If he hadn't left England with rave notices, they might even be suspect. But he's at the height of his powers, and nothing can stop him.

In Potsdam, he made 520 pounds sterling for four performances. In Budapest, he made such an impression on one Matilda that she advertised in the *London Times* for a position as governess so that she could see her "grand Aldridge." In Dresden, he makes a fan out of Jenny Lind, the Swedish nightingale, and they become lifelong friends. Years later, she told Aldridge's daughter, "You must always call yourself 'Ira' Your father was the greatest Othello of them all. I am proud to have been his friend." While he's performing in Austria, he learns through an item in the newspaper that a Black family had escaped from slavery in Baltimore to New York, only to be caught and jailed under the Fugitive Slave Act and sold off piecemeal. Aldridge sends the money to purchase their freedom.

In 1858, he's in Saxe-Meiningen, where he gets an honor that has special meaning because it's more than just a medal from royalty, but it comes from a royal house of Europe, one that was instrumental in the development of modern theater. The reigning duke was Bernhard, brother to the queen consort of England (Adelaide, wife of William IV). Together with his son, George, he modernized set design, introduced the split level, detailed rehearsing of crowd scenes, and costumes made with more attention to historical accuracy. The Meiningens influenced the young Stanislavski at the Moscow Art Theater and Antoine's Theater Libre in Paris. Aldridge wasn't just getting a medal because he'd given a good performance. He was being given something that would make him a part of theatrical history. The *Illustrated London News* reported the event.[20] Aldridge was the only actor, native or foreign, to be given the Saxon Cross of Gold and the credentials that authenticate those medals, and could therefore sign his name for the rest of his life as the Chevalier Ira Aldridge, KS (Knight of Saxony).[21] And he did!

In 1858, he only has another nine years to live. He spends most of them in Russia. He was paid sixty pounds a night, received free quarters, and an equipage was put at his disposal for his entire stay in St. Petersburg, which lasted from November 1858 until late spring of the following year. The sixty pounds a night was four times what an average actor would earn in a month! Why were the Russians so generous? His reputation in Western Europe certainly helped, but in much the same way that 1852 was good timing for a tour of Western Europe, 1858 was good timing for an "invasion" of Russia. Russia had just lost the Crimean War. The loss was blamed on the backwardness of the country, which many thought was the result of the nobility's refusal to abolish serfdom. It was to be one of the great events in the history of man. Twenty-three million men, women, and children, who had been tied to the land, who couldn't get married without their masters' consent, who had no legal claim over their own children, but who were, nevertheless, part of the same ethnic group as their masters, would all be set free. Alexander II, czar of Russia, proclaimed the emancipation a month after Aldridge's arrival, so again, the political climate couldn't have been more perfect if Aldridge had produced it himself.

Whether or not he had enough "nobility" to even attempt any of the major roles of the Shakespearean repertoire was a constant, often burning issue. It was stated emphatically almost every time he appeared in the role that a Black man shouldn't play Othello simply because he was Black any more than a fat man should play Falstaff simply because he was fat. Here's Theophile Gautier, who was traveling in Russia at the time, on whether or not he was "noble" enough to play Lear:

> The following week he played Lear. . . . We considered him better in the role of the old king . . . than he was in the Moor of Venice. His outbursts of indignation and anger were superb, but at the same time there was a feebleness, and senile trembling . . . such as one would expect from an old man on the verge of his eighties. One surprising fact which showed how much he had himself under control; although robust and in the flower of manhood, Aldridge, during the whole evening, did not make one single youthful action; his voice, step, and gestures were all those of an octogenarian.[22]

He completely transformed the Russian method of acting, sending *them* back to the drawing board to discard their artificial school of external poses and declamation. He brought actors out of retirement and so won over the acting troupe at the Imperial Theater that they united to a man to pay him tribute and give him a massive gold bracelet on which was inscribed, "To Ira Aldridge, the great interpreter of the immortal Shakespeare, from the Russian artistes, St. Petersburg, 1858." When he left the city, they all came out to see him off. He sent them a letter afterward, which said, in part, "In my person you have shown your sympathy and love for my oppressed people."[23]

When the monopoly was finally broken, both the Haymarket and the Lyceum were elevated to patent house status—in the West End. That still remains all-important. He has one more piece of business to settle in England. He plays the

Lyceum and gets his lengthiest review to date from the *Times*. It is not a good one. He made the mistake of listing his medals and other honors, as well as some quotes of reviews from Europe. This led the man at the *Times* to say, "Heralded by such unmeasured and inconsiderate laudations, it might be imagined that Mr. Aldridge was a much worse actor than he really proves to be."[24] The West End would have none of him, no matter what.

So Russia it has to be, and Russia it is. From 1861 to 1866 he made several long tours. In Zhitomir, the entire Jewish community, headed by the rabbi, came to the theater to thank him for his interpretation of Shylock. For the first time, they said, Shakespeare's Jew was portrayed as a human being instead of a monster.

He's back in England in '64 and a guest of honor at a dinner celebrating the three hundredth anniversary of Shakespeare's birth. This marks one of the few times that he's recognized officially by his fellow English actors. An account of the evening from Tallis's *Illustrated Life in London*, one of the leading publishing houses of the day, said in part, "It is perhaps some consolation that this exponent of the great bard, who has been so much honored in every country but Shakespeare's—his presence on the English stage being just now, it seems, out of the question—was thus enabled to participate in the festival to the honor of him he has done so much to make popular."[25] His de facto exclusion from the West End, in spite of the occasional invitation, was an open secret. Nevertheless, a year later, he's invited to perform at the Haymarket. Madge Robertson, later Madge Kendal and finally Dame Madge Kendal, was his Desdemona. She was seventeen; he was fifty-eight. This time, he is finally well received in the West End! Well, sort of.

Said *Athenaeum*, "Mr. Ira Aldridge was reluctantly accepted at the West End.... He plays with feeling, intelligence, and finish. We were glad that he was well received on Monday, and that his merits were acknowledged by a numerous audience. We may claim this black, thick-lipped player as one proof among many that the Negro intellect is human and demands respect as such.... Altogether we have seldom witnessed a representation of this great tragedy which pleases us more."[26] Another newspaper said, "It may indicate a decay of the prejudice against color that he was received by the audience with applause and that this performance was a legitimate success."[27]

No matter how late the date, after finally triumphing in the West End, if you can call it that, he has no more worlds to conquer. In 1863, he becomes a British subject so he can own property and buys several houses in London, including the one that his second wife lived in until she died. He goes to France, where he also received good reviews, and after France, Poland. He had already been to Krakow; now he goes to Łódź, which was then the most important industrial city in the country. He's invited by August Hentschel, owner of the leading hotel and the local German theater, to perform beginning July 25. The year is 1867. He dies on the seventh of August, in the midst of rehearsing and overseeing the production.

Brutus says, in act 2 of *Julius Caesar*, that "in the spirit of men there is no blood." And then continues, "O, that we then could come by Caesar's spirit and not dismember Caesar! But, alas, Caesar must bleed for it!" Well, in Aldridge's spirit, there was, indeed, blood, and those who hated and feared him well knew it. In order to destroy his spirit, they had to kill it. In order to kill it, they had to make him bleed for it. And he still bleeds. And will bleed throughout history and throughout time, until both the spirit and the blood have been put back and he takes his rightful place as one of the greatest Othellos of them all.

2 · THE LONG NIGHT OF THE NINETEENTH CENTURY

We take our leave of Ira Aldridge, for it's time to return to native land—although we do so reluctantly because it is not a pretty place for the Black actor or his tribe in 1867. But as critics have so often said, "Art must imitate life, not copy it." So we will imitate the events between 1824 and 1890 by extracting the substance of our story rather than copy those events with a deadening cataloging of all the ills that were. Before we do, one point of comparison between the life that Aldridge lived in England and on the Continent and the life he would have lived had he stayed in America needs to be made. Although the *Chicago Tribune* carried his obituary as a front-page story, at the very same time that Aldridge was playing Covent Garden, he would have been hanged in Virginia or North Carolina if he was caught trying to learn how to read. There was a law against it at the time—against a Black man learning how to read, much less act on a stage.

*   *   *

The three decades between the death of African Grove and the publication of Harriet Beecher Stowe's amazing creation *Uncle Tom's Cabin*—amazing primarily because of its unimaginable success and worldwide influence—were years that produced nothing of consequence for the Black man in American theater, with one or two notable exceptions. What Aldridge was accomplishing in Europe was unknown in his native land except to people like William Wells Brown, the first published Black playwright, and James McCune Smith, the doctor from Aldridge's Greenwich Village days. General American theater was not, at large, interested in any aspect of the Black reality that could be exhibited as public art unless that act was degradation.

America had a Black reality of its own that it was having fun with, nurturing carefully, bringing to full growth, turning into a being of monstrous proportions that would in time subsume all other beings, theatrical or otherwise, until like a

UNCLE TOM'S CABIN AS IT IS.   517

UNCLE TOM AT "HOME."

FIGURE 2.1. "Uncle Tom at 'home.'" Schomburg Center for Research in Black Culture, Manuscripts, Archives and Rare Books Division, The New York Public Library Digital Collections.

giant id in a science fiction fantasy, that reality could not be destroyed. The beast still lives in part in the second decade of the twenty-first century. He started life as Sambo or Coon or Boy or Darkie and remained that way right through the Second World War. Since then he's become, until recently, exclusively Comic or Second Man or Pimp in Boots or Street Nigger or Bro trying to find an identity after being on the North American continent one hundred years before the May-flower. What he's never been, again until recently, is himself—the protagonist, the centerpiece of the drama of his time and place in the general marketplace, the way

FIGURE 2.2. "Cassy ministering to Uncle Tom after his whipping." Rare Book Division, The New York Public Library Digital Collections.

all other such male animals have been. White actors and actresses were weaned on the size of his lips and the shade of the color of the white of his eyes. Black actors found themselves unable, even in death, to shake off his terrible grip. He became their only reality on the boards, which in turn reinforced his reality of them. And this reality became the only form in which the Black character as actor, dancer, singer, author, or whatever could exist.

In what was the most exciting era of the century of the Civil War—and the most volatile, except for the fighting itself—what passed for the "state of the art" came either from dearre olde England or from some preadolescent fairyland that existed in the mind of the general public. However, it had no reality that justified its creation—certainly not a reality that was in any way connected to the events of the day in the way that history and the times usually provide the subsoil for the drama. The struggle to keep the legal system of slavery workable and at the same time have it represent the thinking of every group in the society at large (those who wanted slavery, those who didn't, those who had to decide which they wanted before they could gain statehood) resulted—because of the enormity of the issue of suddenly freeing millions of people into the very midst of the society—in turning the entire nation into a giant stage for grand theater. All the world may not have been a stage in the years before the Civil War, but all America certainly was. The Lincoln–Douglas debates actually took place on a huge outdoor platform. Antislavery societies held gigantic outdoor meetings on platforms. Escaped slaves, former slaves, as well as free Black men—lawyers, doctors, editors, full-time abolitionists, and others—were all standing up in front of thousands of people, all across the country, sometimes even in the slave South, and talking, preaching, inveighing against the evil of man, calling on God or the

Engraved by J.C. Buttre

Wm. W. Brown.

FIGURE 2.3. William Wells Brown in an early photograph around the time he published his first book in 1847. Photographs and Prints Division, Schomburg Center for Research in Black Culture, The New York Public Library.

gods to come to their aid, demanding an eye for an eye. Insisting that as men, they should choose to die free rather than live not free.

White men joined them with all the intensity and passion and complete commitment that the importance of the issue demanded. Many of these men died in the process for their Black fellow man. Kansas "bled" because of it. Missouri went up in flames because of it. Nebraska was torn apart because of it. Henry Clay almost became president because of it. Daniel Webster had his greatest hour because of it. John Brown died because of it. Preston Brooks, the senator from South Carolina, physically attacked Charles Sumner, the senator from Massachusetts, while he, Sumner, was sitting in his chair in the Senate because of it (a beating that Sumner never recovered from). And all the while, the fellow who was the cause of it all, he, the Black man, could not exist in a public theatrical context that was in any way connected to any of it. And he, the white man, who was bleeding side by side right along with him, couldn't even make that page of supreme heroism and nobility out of his book of life a cultural reality on the stage. Not that any real flowering of theater takes place "out of the headlines." It is quite easy to speculate on what should have been written at the time 170-odd years later. Certainly, the chaos of the period was unsettling enough to make an artistic statement difficult. But even more repressive, as an effect on the Black character, was the fact that it was impossible to explore this rich vein of artistic inspiration without humanizing the Black persona that was the cause of it all. Since no one was either willing or able to do that, the persona had to go by the boards rather than on them, or be relegated to the vision of Harriet Beecher Stowe, or end up as blackface.

Theater cannot exist where it does not exist. A play is not a play on a printed page. It only becomes a play when it is actually performed on a stage. When it's not on a stage, it's just a script. What happened on a stage when a script was transformed into a play—that phenomenon—became, as arena, the most repressive region in the entire society for Blacks, even more repressive than a Georgia plantation. On a plantation, a slave had time to eat, sleep, be a man for a night, sing songs, pray, have an occasional social gathering, and at times, "get married" in public, even if that only meant "jumping the broomstick." He could even escape it all—run away, as Douglass had done, and Harriet Tubman, and many others. It is said—and there is tremendous documentation on the subject—that between 1820 and 1860, close to one hundred thousand Black men, women, and children escaped to the North and to Canada from the dark night of Southern slavery. But on the public stages, there was no escape. Not a single Black man, woman, or child was allowed once during those years before the Civil War and after the death of African Grove to portray a character of any substance that did not in the end vilify the entire race by making the most egregiously degrading statements about the ethnicity of Blacks. Whatever exceptions did finally surface after 1865 certainly were not of enough force and substance to counterbalance the prevailing preferences of the theatrical fads of the day and of what had gone before.

Reality, in terms of not only what could happen but what was happening, certainly offered a much more varied choice, socially and politically, for even the most vaguely aware dramatist to draw on than what was actually attempted. It has been observed, for example, that neither the saga of the white man destroying the Indian that Cooper made the basis of his work, nor the New England character that Hawthorne and Emerson essayed, nor the Virginia plantocracy of Thackeray—none of these was the true romance of America. The true romance of America was the romance of the fugitive slave. Of Box Brown, who showed up in a packing case in Philadelphia, having had himself shipped from Richmond by white Underground agents to other agents, who were waiting for him when his "box" arrived. Of Anthony Burns, who was reclaimed for slavery by his master under the Fugitive Slave Act after he had escaped and who was only taken back to Virginia when James Polk dispatched two thousand federal troops to Boston to uphold "the law." And of countless thousands, hiding in the night under a bush or in a tree, trying to throw off the scent of dogs, or forging a stream, sometimes in the cold of winter, sometimes when and where it was so treacherous that the other side became only a dream deferred, permanently. Many slaves survived the professional slave catchers, the bloodhounds, the mantraps that crippled and maimed for life, and the nights of hunger and cold spent out under the moon and the stars to reach "Jordan," to tell their story in narratives, autobiographical sketches, and the rest. So much so that they were said to have added a new form to literature, the slave narrative. The old slave spiritual was never more apt: *And before I'd be a slave, I'd be buried in my grave and go home to my Lord and be free.*

In addition to all of this, the Black man was cutting a very impressive figure on several fronts throughout the period. African Grove had been no freak. As early as 1800, two Black men, Absalom Jones and James Forten, had petitioned Congress to abolish both the slave trade and slavery. These were free and prosperous men who not only understood their legal rights and recourses but used them to their best advantage. Harriet Tubman, who died in her bed in her home in Auburn, New York, at the ripe old age of ninety-one, had returned to the South nineteen times after she escaped herself to get others out. She was so successful as a fighter against slavery that a price of tens of thousands of dollars was put on her head. But no one ever collected. This, even though it was during the time when men would abduct women and children on a street corner and sell them in the South under the pretext that they were runaway slaves, no matter how free they were or how much documentation they had to prove it. There were achievements that went beyond the issue of fighting slavery, as all-important as that was.

Benjamin Banneker was the key figure in leading the actual construction of Washington, DC, as it stands today, after the Frenchman Pierre Charles L'Enfant gathered up all his plans and left in a huff and went back to France, leaving Banneker to pick up the pieces and actually do the job. The huge downtown plaza in present-day Washington is of course named after the Frenchman and not the native-born Black American. There was Crispus Attucks saving the day at the

Boston Massacre by actually precipitating it—a point made very clear by Webster. Jean Du Sable who founded the city of Chicago before Lewis and Clark crossed the Mississippi. Before the Alamo, before Texas was a state, a Black man, an ex-slave, was president of the territory, and he abolished slavery there. That man's name was Vicente Guerrero. In 1876, Nat Love, the original Deadwood Dick, won the championship of the West as rider, roper, and revolver shooter at Deadwood, South Dakota. There was one Tony L. Far, another ex-slave, who had real estate holdings in Mississippi in the eighteenth century worth half a million dollars. In San Francisco, the first man to sail a steamboat on San Francisco Bay was Black: Alexander Leidesdorff. And it was his own boat. In addition to him, there was Mifflin Gibbs, who opened the first shoe store in that city.

The Black man did many things in the first half of the century. He owned property; wrote plays, novels, poems, essays; fought and died in every war waged for the republic; voted in many states; called publicly for armed rebellion in others; was cowboy, journalist, preacher, scientist, and sage—all before the Civil War. What he was not or could not become was cultural animal. The most popular form of entertainment, the minstrel show, even while it showed him as baboon, did not allow he himself to play the baboon. The de facto censorship surpassed any real censor's dream in terms of strict enforcement. That what happened in the real world in America between the 1820s and the 1860s—the drama of actual achievement, the exploits that bucked the odds and made heroism an almost everyday occurrence—was in no wise being considered on the remotest level as material for the drama of formal theater meant that the Black man was functioning as cultural animal but denied the formal license. Even so, when he could, he fashioned himself on his stage quite differently from the way he was being fashioned on America's stage. The minstrel show, the foundation for the Black man's presence on an American stage, didn't start out as blackface caricature. Like so much of what Black America has given to the culture of the country without getting anything in return as a thank-you except ridicule and slander, the minstrel show was the Black man's form of entertainment of and for himself, to give succor, surcease, escape from his life as human chattel and to remind himself that he was a man and not a beast of burden.

The history of the ridicule was a three-step process: from Forrest's plantation darkie, to the Jim Crow Jumper who appeared in the 1830s, to the blackface minstrel who held sway from 1843 right through to the early decades of the twentieth century. There are conflicting versions of how Jump Jim Crow came to be, but there is complete agreement that one Thomas Dartmouth "Daddy" Rice was the progenitor. Rice saw a young Black kid dancing in the street (there's confusion as to whether the city was Louisville or Cincinnati). His routine went something like this: "Wheel about and turnabout, an do jist so. An' ebery time I wheel about I jump Jim Crow."[1] Rice knew a good thing when he saw it. Not only did he copy the boy's routine and with it became an overnight hit; he even added a four-year-old Black youngster named Joseph Jefferson to the act: "Rice brought him on in a sack slung over his shoulder and, stepping down to the footlights, sang: 'Ladies and gentlemen, I'd have you for to know that I've got a little darky here that jumps Jim Crow.' With which he emptied little Jefferson from the sack, made up in rags, blackface and all."[2] And Jim Crow "jumped" into national fame. The popular impersonation gave rise to new terms: *Jim Crow cars* and *Jim Crow laws*, which later meant Black segregation in law as well as in practice. How odd. Steal a man's culture, ban him from it, and then use his very words and the ideas they embody to make him a pariah in a land he never wanted to come to in the first place.

With the instant success of Rice and the others who came after him, the 1830s, '40s, and '50s were boon years for white show business. And it was all based on the idea of the Black character as three-fifths of a man—an idea that came right out of the Constitution before it even had amendments. It took another ten years after the advent of Rice for the white minstrel shows to appear. In the same way that the routines Rice "borrowed" had existed in the Black culture for decades, so too was the minstrel show an amalgam of forms that existed on most plantations in the South that Southern Blacks had developed to entertain themselves: "Every plantation had its talented band that could crack Negro jokes and sing and dance to the accompaniment of the banjo and the bones."[3] The first appearance of the blackface minstrel show was a quartet of white men headed by Dan Emmett, calling themselves the Virginia Minstrels. They opened in New York City in 1843.[4] Appearances on the printed page to the contrary, the effect of all this was a vulgar caricature of the Black character. The audiences for blackface minstrelsy were, obviously, all white. Just imagine these white audiences watching white actors dressed up in the cork, with white lips painted and wide, a wig of black hair, eating watermelon greedily, and chicken, and guzzling gin with gusto, shooting crap, laughing loudly, flashily dressed and doing it all nonstop for a good quarter of a century before Blacks were allowed into the act. All of which gave rise to the idea of the Black man as shiftless, lazy, spendthrift, and loudmouthed. That's what white America was doing with the only popular art form that it had at its command, that the three-fifths of a man had given it. On top of that, there "ware too much gold in them thar hills" for old massah not to hog it all for himself. And besides, he didn't have anything like it in his repertoire from Merrie olde England to draw on. None of the other folk traditions from whatever part of Europe he might have come would do in the land of the free and the home of the brave, so why not take the nigra's jig: copy it, use it not only to make fun of him in the bargain but to have a gay old time entertaining folk with it as well. After all, everyone knows how good the nigra is at dancing an' singing.

Whites in blackface started out imitating the plantation neegrow but soon ran out of material on that score. After all, they had never been slaves, they weren't from Africa, and many of them knew nothing about what a plantation was like. The plantation was made up of two kinds of people primarily: the white owners (owning enough property to have land and more than two or three slaves was not easily come by) and the Black slaves (house and field) with occasional white workers such as a foreman or an overseer thrown in. White song-and-dance men, having nothing in them to draw on, soon had to abandon the plantation roots of minstrelsy. In a desperate attempt to find new wine for their old bottles, they began to do such things as turning Donizetti's *Lucia di Lammermoor* into *Lucy Did Lam a Moor* in blackface, no less. But so successful was this newfound form that these white pretenders made a killing during the 1840s and '50s no matter what they did, as long as they covered their face with ham fat, put on the black grease-paint, and whitened the lips and made only the most passing pretense at being a coon. It was the coon concept that gave the whole thing it's winning angle, its gimmick, its shtick. Once you had on the mask and you rolled your eyes, then you had already said to your audience that the two of you (performer and audience) were in on a private "joke" that you had to be American to appreciate—making fun of the nigger. No matter how pervasive was the control over 4.5 million people, it still would have been difficult to get Blacks to make fun of themselves in exactly the right way to make the bawdy joke explore all its obscene possibilities. Certainly, in the hands of Black performers, this art form took on one effect, and in the hands of whites, it took on another. But because Blacks were not allowed to perform in the shows and were also not even allowed to see them at first, the white performers soon lost the invaluable aid of the continuous flow of new ideas from Blacks. In other words, through their own prejudice, they cut themselves off from the source of their theft. Which is certainly one reason why they had to resort to such absurdities as Lucia Di Lammermoor in blackface.

THE BLACK ACTOR GETS INTO THE ACT

But Blacks were performing on stages here and in Europe, many out of blackface, as early as 1815. Andrew Allen, a free Black man, was making a living as a balladeer in the North. It was only the minstrel show itself and the Jim Crow Jumper that was kept as a white preserve. A long list of other white troupes followed Dan Emmett, all tremendously successful, all a "hit." They were also all male and all white. It wasn't until three years after the Civil War, a good quarter of a century later, that Blacks themselves were allowed to get into the act. Lew Johnson's Plantation Minstrel Company was the first. They followed the tradition of the burnt cork. Another Black group, Charles Hicks's Georgia Minstrels, was so successful that a white manager took it over so that it could make real money. Whites just didn't do business with Blacks on any meaningful level in those days, a custom that is still quite prevalent. The Georgia Minstrels and their white manager toured the country and then went abroad. Two Black men who came out of that group, Billy Kersands and Sam Lucas, deserve extra mention.

Kersands gained dubious fame as a consequence of the size of his mouth—he could fit an entire cup and saucer inside it—and his excellent dancing skills. In 1911, when he was playing the white vaudeville circuit, he danced with two billiard balls in his mouth. He said if God wanted to make his mouth any bigger, he'd have to move his ears. (It was reputed to be bigger than Joe E. Brown's.) He was so popular in London that he taught British royalty how to dance. Sam Lucas had a career that actually spanned the entire era of blackface minstrelsy and lasted into vaudeville and, finally, silent film. He was the first Black actor to play Uncle Tom on the stage and the first Black actor to play him on the screen, which ended up killing him. In 1915, while filming the silent film version, he agreed to actually jump in the river to save Little Eva. During the filming of this scene, he contracted an infection that killed him a year later.

In addition to finally getting on the stage, the Black song-and-dance man in the minstrel show itself brought with him all the originality, talent, and most of all, vitality that is his limitless birthright. As a result, new dances, new songs, and new comedy routines entered into the "repertoire." Dancing was actually modernized by these new styles: the stop-time taps, the sand, the soft shoe, and the Virginia essence, as was the vaudeville monologue, which Charles Cruso created as early as the 1870s as the "Man Who Talks." Another minstrel man, Billy Windom, helped introduce the falsetto voice. He was billed as "the singer with the child voice."

But in their desperate attempt to stay alive, Blacks had been pushing ahead in every manner conceivable outside of the minstrel show. There was the singing Luca family, who performed in the North before the Civil War (see Hughes) and a lithograph that has survived shows them as a dignified, well-dressed quartet. James Bland wrote not only "Carry Me Back to Ole Virginny" and "Oh Dem Golden Slippers!" but over two hundred other songs, only fifty of which were published. He was born free on Long Island in 1854. He graduated from Howard University (his father had graduated from Oberlin in 1845) and had a lifelong career as a minstrel singer and banjo player that included going to England, where he stayed for twenty years and gave performances for Queen Victoria and the Prince of Wales. Toward the end of his career, he was able to perform without the burnt cork. Elizabeth Greenfield (dubbed the "Black Swan") was born a slave in Natchez in 1809. In 1853, she debuted as a singer at the Winter Garden Theater (also known as Metropolitan Hall) in New York and, the same year, gave a command performance, also before Queen Victoria.

Of course, in order to keep step with the times, to cash in on themselves, there were, as the Black blackface troupes sprang up, such billings as Miss Hattie Delano's Original Alabama Pickaninnies. But as long as 4.5 million men, women, and children continued to live under the grinding enslavement of a two-hundred-year-old system, all the James Blands and Elizabeth Greenfields and families like the Lucas could do was try desperately to hold on to what little dignity they were allowed and put a brave face on the degradation of their people.

UNCLE TOM'S CABIN AND WHAT CAME AFTER

Perhaps Harriet Beecher Stowe's novel would have been a *Gone with the Wind* of its time (it actually outdid the Margaret Mitchell book in sales) no matter what. It's hard to tell. But that it was the right book at the right time in terms of its practical value—in winning over the hearts and minds of not only a general American populace but the whole world—is not open to the slightest doubt. And that the several versions of plays derived from it revolutionized American theater isn't the slightest bit hyperbolic. It ran continually for ninety years! It was produced in foreign languages from Czech to Polynesian and ran almost as long in England as it did in America. As a play, it started the practice of a single performance of one play as an entire evening's offering for the first time. Matinees, popularly priced tickets, spirituals (not just coon songs), and the long run were all born with *Uncle Tom's Cabin*.

But what inspired the inspiration? The whole phenomenon of Germans in the thirties not knowing about the concentration camps and being nonplussed or dumbfounded afterward when they sat through a performance of *The Diary of Anne Frank* certainly had somewhat of a parallel in America in the 1850s. In the same way that Jews were despised en masse by many Germans, Blacks were certainly despised en masse by most whites in the nineteenth century. But the plantation, the cause of it all, belonged not only to the Deep South almost exclusively but also only to a small portion of that population. This point was brought out by Southern critics long before the Civil War, who warned that the future of the region lay in free labor, not that of slaves.

So the hold on the mind of the South that spread nationwide was essentially a cultural one, but the rank cruelty of the thing itself, not the economic issue, was what Mrs. Stowe brought to the general consciousness. She tapped a vein, struck a chord that, once it had been sounded, seemed to reverberate endlessly. It could very well be that the nation's conscience, which had been pretty well stifled, almost permanently repressed on the matter, had finally been released. Once that sense of guilt was out in the open, there was no end to the sympathy. The constant thirst for more and more and more performances and revivals certainly fed a need much deeper than just "entertainment." The fact that the play ran in one version or another for—again!—*ninety years*, as amazing as that is, isn't as amazing as is the number of different productions that were going on at the same time in all parts of the world.

The book sold more copies than any other except the Bible, and the play(s) was no less popular.[5] What was this hideous monster locked in the closet of the national superego that, once it was let out into the light of day, held a fascination for the multitudes that made it a wonder of the modern world? The thing itself was hideous enough, and the evil had existed long enough for the general population to need expurgation—but only within the safe confines of theater. The

Black in public and private life received very little positive fallout from all of the national weeping over terrible Simon Legree "whupping" poor ole Uncle Tom for everyone to see (or read about). Yet however incomprehensible it may seem from the vantage point of the twenty-first century, the common citizen—who might have seen whole groups of slaves walking miles and miles (women, children, and the elderly included), chained to a huge log called a coffle; or witnessed a beating or a lynching; or read about such things—didn't cry out or weep or in any other manner demonstrate compassion for the suffering of the victim or go so far as to find the whole thing despicable until Mrs. Stowe wrote her novel and until that novel was adapted to the stage. Which certainly proves that literature in general, and the drama in particular, is a form of magic. It releases the parts of our other mind that we only use under special circumstances. That is usually when the all-too-well-ingrained repressions of society are not at play. Sometimes this release is personal and voluntary. At other times, it has "official" sanction, as in the case of Mrs. Stowe's work.

There had been no strong tradition of playwriting by Blacks in the formal Western sense before the twentieth century. Although James Hatch gives Aldridge credit for writing *The Black Doctor* and puts a date of 1847 on it, it was simply a translation, as Marshall and Stock point out in their biography of Aldridge.[6] So William Wells Brown gets the first honors with the publication of his *The Escape, or A Leap for Freedom* in 1858.[7] Poetry and prose are well represented throughout the nineteenth century, but not the drama. Theater can't exist without the playwright. African Grove had Shakespeare and the other nineteenth-century "classics" that used Black characters, and that one play of Mr. William Henry Brown's, *The Drama of King Shotaway*, which he presented when the end was near but that has been lost to history. By the time the Federal Theatre was born in 1936, there were, of course, several Black playwrights who had contributed to the creation of a body of literature that could form the basis for a Black Theater. Alas, very few of them are worth remembering. What made the Black playwright such a rare bird? Certainly, the nonexistent prospects for seeing his script become a play was one factor, but throughout history, that has never really been a real prohibition where a strong compulsion has existed. Where there's a will there is usually some kind of way. Edith Isaacs, in her slim but excellent volume *The Negro in the American Theatre* (New York: Theatre Arts, 1947), offers some theoretical groundwork for this dearth:

> To perceive the significance of the Negro in the American Theatre, it is well to remember that a native art grows only on native roots. The Anglo-Saxon founders of American life were stern-minded folk to whom the theatre was nothing less than the "ante-chamber of the devil." . . . Gradually, plays [from England] found an audience and new men came from other . . . lands who brought their theatre with them. These struck roots in American soil, and this borrowed theatre—English, French, German, Spanish—is the base of our American commercial theatre. . . . That our

commercial theatre has grown so skillful . . . as it has, with so few native roots, is remarkable enough.[8]

She continues,

Our Theatre has never learned what painters and sculptors . . . and musicians [learned] generations ago,—that every art must go back to the soil for refreshment from time to time. That is why today's theatre is so undernourished. We continue to build on a base with little folk foundation, and almost no peasant drama of the kind from which a "cultural" theatre would normally grow. And that is the main reason why, in music and dance, in rhythm and comedy and pantomime, we borrow so freely from the Negro theatre which has been developed from the earth up.[9]

Certainly, the need to express the spirit in artistic form was finding a strong outlet in dance and song. Africa had a long tradition of theater, albeit an oral tradition that was closer to ritual and storytelling than to three acts with an intermission. But Western theater is a fairly recent animal and not as imitated in the world at large as is the African model. I'm not suggesting that Asia—China, Japan, Korea, India, and other giant, very ancient cultures—"borrowed" their theatrical forms from Africa. I wouldn't be so bold. But the African and the Asian model are closely allied. The Black man didn't learn a new language the way an Italian or a German did, with the freedom and encouragement of the society at large to improve himself, and he didn't have the benefit of the great works of his culture in translation or in the original to shore up his sense of self. He was killed on many occasions just for trying to preserve his language, his culture, and his native tongue. If he had been allowed to develop in theater, not out of any falsely construed sense of humanitarianism but simply because, in the best tradition of the American spirit, you get what you earn—if only on that level, he had been allowed to strut and fret his hour or two upon the stage—then things would have been quite different. Black theater would not have had to wait another hundred years after the death of African Grove to come to life. White America had not reached that level of sophistication in the 1850s that Edith Isaacs talks about a hundred years later. Our American drama, like our novel, was still suffering under Emerson's reproach that England was too much with us. However, we had reached the stage as a nation where we were suspicious of native-grown art but didn't have any real sense of what it would be if it were not a cheap imitation of England's, and that sense of inadequacy helped stifle it. But there were other problems in addition to the low level of our national self-esteem.

Beauregard couldn't become the Alabama version of the Earl of Devon because it just didn't translate. America was not a small place made smaller by caste and class and custom. It was a big, sprawling place, made wide and open by nature's bounty and filled with fury, the unknown, and a dramatic plotline that never stood still. Shakespeare's people, for all their diversity and all their differences of locale and time, had one consistency—royalty, nobility, that universal family of the king and his retinue, where each successive majesty carried with him his literary personality as well as his specifically dramatic one that made him as familiar as the man next door in the context of theater. In the wasteland of that combination of an innate sense of inadequacy and a milieu that took away the parochial environment that drama seems to feed on, there was a need (and one that was certainly in this case deep-seated) to find a native art form—to fill that most dramatic of all spaces, a bare stage, with the new experience of the new land in a way that was not only uniquely American but also effective on its own terms.

That the minstrel show did this, fulfilled the need, filled the space, there can be no doubt. That it was taken much more seriously than just as a sideshow and that it became the reigning form of "popular" entertainment that satisfied the hunger of the wasteland, on at least one level, is proven by the exclusion of the creator from the creation. Had it had less meaning, it would not have had to be private property. It was more than just greed, just primeval tribal hate that kept Blacks from doing blackface minstrelsy until well after the Civil War. There was, in addition, the decision to make it a private affair, to keep it for the citizenry only. This even though desperation had dictated using the Black persona—the Black mask. The act itself was no mere imitation for a joke and all in fun. It filled the void. There was the one large hunger that Europe hadn't satisfied. It was all very well and good to read Jane Austen and Defoe and Dickens and the rest (although in time, that too had to share its space with homegrown art). The rabble had to be satisfied in the same way that they too were satisfied by Shakespeare and Ben Jonson 250 years earlier.

But there was also confusion about the thing itself. The Puritan hegemony had made theater a sin, as Isaacs points out. The guilt that in turn created certainly helped make the device of the mask a freeing one. So two things were combined to produce a "winner": a Black beat, with the rhythm and force of the pounding of the heart, on the one hand, and a sad, tragicomic reflection on the world as it is on the other. Both were joined with a disguise so that the son of the father who had intoned moral prohibition could, in wearing the disguise, the mask, escape censure from his tortured self and be free to plunge fully into the river of his new-found theatrical flood. How wonderful it would have been if America had taken the gift with graciousness and gratitude instead of giving in to a degraded need to ridicule and dehumanize the giver of the gift. What America actually did in not taking the Black man's minstrel show seriously was to rob it of its heart and leave only the empty outer form, the shell. Unfortunately, America had not reached that level of intellectual development where it could take anything that Black America had to give seriously. That would have created instant embarrassment and self-ridicule. That's how far apart the two races were. Black America didn't have a Shakespeare or a Shaw or a Chekhov to offer white America to steal, ridicule, or make fun of; nobody on this side of the water did. Whenever we were used in theater other than the minstrel shows, it was always as servant or forgiving Black, and it is only when we write our own drama (which, in the case of the nineteenth century, meant *one* play, in effect) that some semblance of the total man emerges.

Other than William Wells Brown, there is one other exception to all of this: Victor Sejour, a Black writer born in Louisiana to Creole aristocracy, who went to France and became a secretary to Louis Napoleon. Sejour lived from 1818 to 1874, and before he died, he wrote over twenty plays, most of which were produced in French in France. All neat, well-made pieces that emulated the models of Victor Hugo and the newfound school of French naturalism in the second half of the nineteenth century. He became, like Alexandre Dumas, a well-respected member of Paris literary society, and also like Dumas, he left the problem of race behind him, not choosing to make it a part of his work.[10]

While his plays can be light and witty, the material is thin when they are good and simply dated when they're not. Sejour paid such a high price for "surviving" in the one culture that he could—and indeed, was allowed to survive in—that whatever real talent he had was probably repressed by the trauma of fear: the fear of rejection by his adopted homeland if he did, indeed, confront his Parisian peers with the anathema of race. But there was a time when such "cultural" accomplishments were so hard to come by that he was praised for his "Black achievement." Hughes certainly praised him. What Sejour lost or had to give up in order to survive was the one thing essential to Black cultural survival: the uniqueness and the power of the Black cultural pulse that centuries of slave masters tried to destroy, to tear root and branch out of the Black soul. When that cultural pulse is at play, the magic can work. When it's not, forget it. But its appeal is so universal because it's as basic as the heartbeat. Indeed, it is the heartbeat.

The *beat* came over on the boat. Like the Black mind and body that brought it, it too survived the Middle Passage, that infamous journey from the west coast of Africa to the West Indies or the eastern coast of the United States. By sail, the journey took as long as six months, with as many as six hundred souls packed into the bottoms of a ship from upward of twenty out of twenty-four hours of each day. Many of them were dead by the time they got to the New World. Dead from heat, exhaustion, malnutrition, disease contracted because of the filthy conditions in the hold, where bodily needs had to be emitted on the spot. There were several revolts during these crossings—and suicides. There is even a record of a group of slaves who committed suicide, en masse, jumping into the Atlantic, chains and all. "And before I'd be a slave," et cetera.

What happened to the beat after it got here is easy to trace. The myth that as long as the slaves were singing, they were content was prevalent throughout the South. That psychology had the advantage of leaving Blacks free to not only continue their songs but refine and use them for purposes other than emotional release or as a means of soothing their battered souls. "Steal Way to Jesus" and "Swing Low, Sweet Chariot" were as often used as signals either that the Underground Railroad was ready to pick up a "passenger" or that there was going to be a big party that night. Eventually such parties were given official sanction, and many white travelers through the Old South have left records of closely observed dances and "shouts" that they were allowed to attend. Slave owners would in many cases prefer to watch their own slaves entertain them while entertaining themselves over going into town for "professional" entertainment. But for all of this benign intercourse between master and slave, the Protestant influence on Black music and dance and ritual was a particularly destructive one. With their heightened sense of sin, not only did the Protestants discourage the vigorous interpretation that Blacks gave to Christian worship, but they also laid a strict taboo on anything they considered "pagan" or "voodoo-like." So much of what was allowed to develop in both secular and religious form was boiled down to a pale version of what it could have been.

Still, the beat survived. It survived in the church, which eventually became the safest repository for it. It survived in the secular songs that were a part not only of festive occasions but also of the innate sense memory of every possessor of African ancestry. And because it was one of the few pursuits left to Black men and women in America as slaves, it survived most of all as almost a sum total of all self-expression. There were many Blacks who had a lot of time on their hands. Certainly, the wastefulness of the system was one of the early nonhumanitarian arguments against slavery. Since a Black child or adult was so severely circumscribed in terms of what he or she could or could not do, the list of do's being a small one, the singing and the dancing were constantly being reinforced. There was also the release, the opportunity for expression, for a renewing of the sense of self—a sense that said, after all, that one was not really a beast of burden but a human being, feeling, thinking, dreaming, imagining, waiting for the day of judgment and revenge and the rest of it. All of those needs, coupled with the age-old ability to use song and dance to refine them to a high form of artistic expression, created something akin to Epic Theater (not, obviously, in the Brechtian sense) in New Orleans, in what was called Congo Square, sometime after the first years of the nineteenth century.

Not only was Louisiana Catholic and therefore more liberal in its attitude toward such "sinful" pursuits as hand clapping and shouting and all the intricate artistry of the dance. It also had a large Black Creole population that was very influential, had wealth, owned property, and did all the things that French mesdames et messieurs did, such as duel, hold masques, go off to Paris to be educated, live in magnificent homes, and even have slaves themselves. New Orleans was one of the most sophisticated American cities of the nineteenth century. Far more sophisticated than most cities of the Midwest and East Coast. Since Creoles were Black—that is, by American standards, and certainly by the standards of Blacks in America, who claim as their own any and all who have been conversely rejected by the more that says one drop of Black blood, et cetera—whatever they did can be claimed as part of Black history. One of the most elegant and most grandly produced bits of theater in the history of nineteenth-century America was the Quadroon Balls of the New Orleans Creole society.

The African drum, which had been banned throughout much of America (in all of the South), was allowed in New Orleans. This made the Congo Square dances much more effective as an art form than the shouts and breakdowns that had to pass muster with the slave master and the white public at large. There was, of course, no general communication among Blacks in the several parts of the country as to what direction either song or dance should take. The white entertainers, on the other hand, had the freedom of observing not only what Blacks did but what their fellow whites did and, most importantly, how a paying audience reacted to it all. This was even more important at a time when the country's nascent art forms were just coming into being. Itinerant Black performers moved about here and there, but for the most part, what was learned was usually indigenous to a state or region. The Deep South plantation style that hardened by the 1820s was as far removed from the Congo Square vibrant unleashing as a drawing room comedy is from a piece of street theater. Not only because plantation Blacks were not allowed any instruments, except an occasional banjo, but also because they had been molded by both circumstances and censorship to be more sorrowful, more full of pain and suffering, more the creators of the blues in their tragic side—and to be more happy-go-lucky and loose, making sure that gaiety was never contaminated by thought, in their comic side.

What would have happened to the minstrel tradition or to theater in America in general if Black dance Congo Square style, as well as all the other intricate rhythmic patterns and concepts of movement and sound, had been given the freedom to develop that jazz was later on? We'll never know. The spirit that intoned Shango—the god of war, as well as a lot of other things—was not allowed to grow on American soil as observed formalized art. It had to lay buried within the subconscious layers of the psyche until both time and place would allow some hybrid form to emerge. And only what white imitators could absorb was allowed to become formalized as art and have an objective theatrical life of its own.

Here's what it was like in Congo Square before the sun went down, deep in the heart of Dixie, when cotton was still king and it was illegal for a Black man to vote; marry a Caucasian woman; learn to read, except a copy of the Bible; or sing "The Star-Spangled Banner" in a public place:

> Boudoum!, boudoum! The giant hollow drums reverberated through the . . . Sunday stillness, played by men who sat astride them and pounded with hands and feet. The sound of sticks hitting smaller drums, the clanging of triangles, and the thudding, pounding echo of hundreds of bare feet slapping the hard earth; these sounds, intermixed with the roar of a wounded bull, the screech of circus baboons; the panting dissonance of the Indians playing a wild game of a racquette; these were the sounds of Congo Square.[11]

The Calenda, Bamboula and Congo. Bras de Coupe. Marie Laveau. Voodoo. St. John's Eve. Bayou St. John. Cordon Bleu. Gens de, couleur. Early morning dueling and bullfights. Bienville and Andrew Jackson. The Spanish, French and Americans. Creoles and Cajuns. The Mississippi River and Lake Pontchartrain. Ragtime and Jazz. Cotton and sugar cane *and the drum*! (italics mine)[12]

But that not only the beat survived but the intricacy of its rhythm as well is attested to by some famous white observers of the day. The spirit may have been expunged on one level, but like the miracle of the morning sun, there was enough left over to give seed to Miss Isaacs "native soil" concept of what must be if a real art form is to emerge from indigenous roots. As Langston Hughes reports in *Black Magic*, a friend of Edgar Allan Poe said, "There is no such rhythm as this in Greek poetry [meaning Black dance rhythm]—nor in fact in any other nation under the sun." And Sidney Lanier added, "Here is music in its rudest form, consisting of rhythm alone . . . the most curious noise, yet in such perfect order it furnishes music to dance by . . . I have never seen its equal in my life."[13]

Even though some slaves, and certainly many Blacks who were free, did make their own instruments, obviously many more were without the wherewithal to do so. And so, bereft of instruments, they devised the patting juba, which would have existed anyway but took on an added importance given the force of circumstances. Again, the quote is from Hughes: "Patting juba became an accompaniment to a whole series of intricate dance steps whose rhythms fascinated even the poets of the 1800's. . . . The Negro custom of creating rhythms for dancing without instruments became a part of the white minstrel routines—'striking the hands on the knees, then striking the right shoulder with one hand, the left with the other—all the while keeping time with the feet and singing.'"[14]

WILLIAM WELLS BROWN

And now more of William Wells Brown.

Brown, after he himself had escaped from slavery, wrote *The Escape, or A Leap for Freedom* partly as a parody of *Uncle Tom's Cabin* and partly as his own independent, artistic statement. He had a distinguished career as a writer, producing not only two plays (though some sources insist there were three) and a novel but travel books and essays as well. The second play, *Experience, or How to Give a Northern Man a Backbone*, written in 1856, was unpublished and is no longer extant. In 1867, he published what was the first history of Black Americans in the Revolutionary War. He saw Aldridge in London and thought his Hamlet superb. After seeing Aldridge in Othello, he wrote,

> The following evening I went to witness his Hamlet, and was surprised to find him as perfect in that as he had been in Othello. . . . The whole court of Denmark was before us; but not till the words, "Tis not alone m inky cloak good mother" fell from [his] lips that the general ear [was] charmed, or the general tongue arrested. . . . In the last scene of the second act [when he] mounts into a paroxysm of rage and

WM. WELLS BROWN, M.D.

The Colored Historian.

FIGURE 2.4. William Wells Brown late in life. Schomburg Center for Research in Black Culture, Manuscripts, Archives and Rare Books Division, The New York Public Library Digital Collections.

calls the King "Bloody, bawdy villain! Remorseless, treacherous, lecherous, kind-less villain!" he sweeps the audience with him and brings down deserved applause.[15]

And he took Carlyle to task for racist remarks that the Englishman made when he admonished the Blacks of the West Indies that they "should be taught that if they will not raise sugar and cotton by their own will, Quashy should have the whip applied to him."[16] The man was really quite phenomenal, this first Black American playwright.

He started a bank in the West that thrived for a while and he was a licensed doctor in the state of Massachusetts. Unlike Frederick Douglass and others, Brown knew the ins and outs of the slave trade intimately. He'd been forced to work for a trader in his late teens, and he documented all the tricks of that "trade" in his autobiography: How Blacks were beaten if they didn't laugh and act happy when they were brought before prospective buyers. How the older men and women were spruced up, with shoe polish used to cover their gray hairs. And how infants were left by the road to die when the slave "driver" of the coffle—the huge log to which Blacks were chained—was in too much of a hurry to get to a slave market and refused to stop long enough to let the mother feed the child or tend to its needs in any other way. Or to let her rest when she became too weak to carry both the infant and the part of the log that she was chained to.

Brown managed to get a passport from the State Department in 1849 to attend the Paris Peace Conference, which was chaired by Victor Hugo. He took the world stage for a brief moment, creating an international stir in the bargain. In violation of a rule that prohibited any delegate from making any direct allusion to any issue of the day, such as a peculiar institution way down south in Dixie, Brown declared, before eight hundred delegates from every major country in Europe and beyond (twenty from America), that slavery as practiced in America created a ceaseless state of war and continued a spirit of war in the world. He then went on to say that while slavery had been abolished in every other nation in Europe, America was the single most effective proponent of war by continuing it. He concluded by pointing out that since slavery itself creates a state of war between master and slave, abolishing slavery would be a giant step toward abolishing the spirit of war in the world. He died in 1884 at the age of seventy.

Although he did give readings of it at abolitionists' meetings, Brown's play wasn't performed until the 1970s, in college productions, which proves the old adage that "justice delayed is justice deferred." Deferred or not, it is a much cleverer reading of the slave experience than the work that was extrapolated from Harriet Beecher Stowe's novel; the Black man's version of the world is somehow not worth much.

The reasons for this are fairly obvious. The history is so brutal that the public at large is not interested in hearing the victim's telling of the story. There's enough guilt in the body politic, let's not make a bad situation intolerable by giving the man who has been beaten the chance to talk about the beating. Let's do it for him. That will at least make it more palatable. And besides, how can we really trust him to be fair? He'll probably overstate the case instead of just letting the "facts speak for themselves." Nobody wants a polemic, not from the Black man certainly.

Of course, *Escape* was not a polemic, but it did give slavery a serious beating. That most revered of Southern institutions that nine million Deep South Southerners sacrificed everything in life they had for—family, material possessions, their total economy and the very means to make a livelihood—and finally even died for. That's what *Uncle Tom's Cabin* was about beneath the hand-wringing and the bemoaning of how poor Old Uncle had suffered and the rest of the weeping and wailing. Not only had it been illegal to teach a Black man to read in Virginia just twenty years earlier; Blacks were even being portrayed in leading magazines with tails and heads that resembled lizards, and that doesn't do justice to the full list of degrading images. So there was an embarrassment at the thought of what was being done at the very same time that there was a stated conviction that Black ability in something as elevated as writing a play was simply a cultural contradiction. It was difficult for *white* men to write a successful play, after all.

By the time Brown's play was published in 1858, Mrs. Stowe's novel was six years old, as was the script from it that was the most popular, the one by George Aiken.[17] (Aiken had used the serialized version of the novel, which had been published earlier, for his adaptation.) Other versions of the play had also been around for four or five years. Certainly, with all the world reading the novel, we can be sure that Brown read it and also saw the play—maybe on both sides of the Atlantic. That *Escape* is both satire and spoof of *Uncle Tom's Cabin*, there can be little doubt. In act 1, we meet the Gaineses, Dr. and Mrs. He starts off by telling his wife that he expects more diseases in the neighborhood, so business should be very good soon. He wishes for an epidemic of yellow fever because he thinks he has a cure for it. He doesn't think he'll get that lucky, because of the climate, but there's a good chance of cholera. His wife, the religious one, sympathizes. Says she, "Yes I would be glad to see it more sickly here, so that your business might prosper. But we are always unfortunate. Everybody here seems to be in good health, and I am afraid that they'll keep so. However, we must hope for the best. We must trust in the Lord. Providence may possibly send some disease amongst us for our health."

Cato, the character that some notable Black critics objected to, is Dr. Gaines's house slave. His English is Black "Malaprop"—an idiom that Brown uses not to demean his character but to give him the upper hand in his constant battle to save his own dignity and self-respect, as he gets the better of the marster and the missus each time he joins them in confrontation. Gaines has just gotten a contract to take care of the "property" of neighbor Campbell. Campbell is sending over two of his "boys" who need "tendin to." Gaines tells Cato to take care of it, giving him the procedure to follow in dealing with their ailments sight unseen: "Feel their pulse, look at their tongues, bleed them and give them each a dose of calomel. Tell them to drink no cold water and to take nothing but gruel." And Cato gets his first chance to entertain us. Here's his opening soliloquy:

CATO
I allers knowed I was a doctor, an' now de ole boss has put me at it, I muss change my coat. Ef any niggers comes in, I wants to look suspectable. Dis jacket don't suit a doctor; I'll change it.

He exits and immediately returns with a long coat.

Ah! now I looks like a doctor. Now I can bleed, pull teef, or cut off a leg. Oh! well, well, ef I ain't put de pill stuff and de intment stuff togedder. By golly, dat ole cuss will be mad when he finds it out, won't he? Nebber mind, I'll make it up in pills, and when de flour is on dem, he won't know what's in 'em; and I'll make some new intment. Ah! yonder comes Pete an' Ned; dems de ones massa sed was comin'. I'll see ef I looks right.

He goes to the looking glass and views himself.

I em some punkins, ain't I?

He hears a knock at the door.

Come in!

The point about Cato is that he's up to any occasion. No matter how absurd the situation or how dangerous, no matter how many egregious mistakes he makes, he always lands on his feet. Indeed, his attraction as a character can be measured by how well he rises above the several disasters, many of them self-made, that he encounters. The approach is not too dissimilar from the one Chaplin uses whenever he dismantles someone or something in pursuit of a laugh.

In scene 2, we meet Glen and Melinda. Melinda is the tragic octoroon, a character who had been ensconced in the theatrical lexicon even before *Uncle Tom's Cabin*. Not only is she a light-skinned beauty who is the housemaid of the Gaineses, but Gaines intends to have her flesh to satisfy his flesh, no matter what. Of course, the wife knows that that's what he's after. Glen, who is the slave of Gaines's brother in law, has come to see Melinda, who is his "wife"[18]—they married secretly.

The whole tradition of house slave versus field hand vis-à-vis speech, manners in the literary sense, education, and the rest of it was a lightning rod that created the most intense hatreds among at least three elements of the slave South. The Blacks who had the advantages of living and working in or near the house almost around the clock were even more educated than poor whites. They had to learn how to dress (were required not to appear disheveled and dirty), how to serve a formal meal, how to greet guests and be a part of the conversation when called upon. Their opposite number, the field hands, had none of these advantages because they lacked the opportunity for such advancement by not being exposed to it. The third element were poor whites, who in many cases were as disadvantaged as the field hands—or worse in the sense of not being able to always know where the next meal was coming from.

So Brown, in response to those huge divisions in the society of the South, gives his "house servant" slaves an inflated speech that not only pokes fun at the manners and morals that both master and slave adopted in an immoral society but makes marvelously caricatured characters of his young romantic couple. But he doesn't dehumanize them in the process. Rather, theirs is the discreet attention to niceties that two people who have had the advantages of some breeding to guide them in these matters pay to each other. As the punctuation and the use of outworn words and phrases indicate, there is more than a little bit of camp in this purposefully inflated dialogue. Remember, Brown was learned. None of his prose has the slightest affectation or rant to it:

GLEN
I am glad to see you, Melinda. I've been waiting long, and feared you would not come. Ah! in tears again?

MELINDA
Glen, you are always thinking I am in tears. But what did master say today?

GLEN
He again forbade our union.

MELINDA
Indeed! Can he be so cruel?

GLEN
Yes, he can be just so cruel.

MELINDA
Alas! Alas! how unfeeling and heartless! But did you appeal to his generosity?

Since everything in the work is satire, what better way to satirize the house servant than through language, even though the characters themselves are sincere? White characters, almost regardless of the paucity of educational advantages, are almost routinely presented with a stage speech that is quite competent, except where the Southern drawl is used as a shtick. Brown's use of the exclamation point in these scenes shows that that is what he was attempting. The entire play turns on the humor. He did not leave off using it as his underlying "unity" in writing his hero and heroine; the scene ends with Glen telling Melinda that they have to escape because the good doctor will surely sell her if he finds out that they're married.

In scene 4, Brown gives religion, in the context of Southern slavery, some wonderful body blows. We're back in the Gaines's drawing room. Mrs. Gaines is entertaining the parson, Rev. Pinchen. Hannah, one of the other house slaves, is in attendance. Brother Pinchen is holding forth on the power of God. Hannah makes the mistake of "listening" intently. Mrs. G. spies Hannah "listening" and not only reprimands her for so doing but promises her a beating in the bargain; then, smiling up at the Rev., she asks him to please continue his discourse.

He tells of a dream he had. He was dead and in heaven and so very happy to be there. The first person he runs into is his old parson, Elder Pike, the man who introduced him to the Holy Word. Then he sees Deacon Billings, another elder. Mrs. G. asks him if he saw her first husband. He says he didn't, but he's sure he was there. At which point Hannah pipes up with "Massah Pinchen, did you see my ole man Ben up dar in hebben?" To which Pinchen replies, "No, Hannah, I didn't go 'mongst the niggers." Mrs. G.'s rejoinder to Hannah's temerity is "No, of course Brother Pinchen didn't go among the blacks. What are you asking questions for? Never mind, my lady, I'll whup you well when I'm done here. I'll skin you from head to foot." Then she turns smilingly to Pinchen and purrs, "Do go on with your heavenly conversation, Brother Pinchen; it does my very soul good. This is indeed a precious moment for me. I do love to hear of Christ and Him crucified."

Soon the issue of the scene turns on whether Hannah is qualified for heaven in as much as she stole Mrs. G.'s goose, cooked it, ate it with her man, Sam, and they both had a fine time in the bargain. And even worse, Hannah admits it, fine time and all. Mrs. G.'s question to Pinchen is as follows: "Is Hannah fit to go to the Lord's Supper after stealing the goose?" Pinchen's answer and the ensuing exchange are quite clever. After Pinchen has left, Mrs. G. vents her anger on poor Hannah: "The devil always puts it into your head to disturb me, just when I am trying to serve the Lord. I've no doubt but that I'll miss going to heaven on your account. But I'll whip you well before I leave this world, that I will. Get the cowhide and follow me to the cellar." And the stage directions are: "Exit Mrs. Gaines and Hannah, R."

Act 2 introduces the slave trader, Walker, who is all jollity and business when it comes to buying and selling his "wares." Whoever he runs across is "just the man" he's looking for, be it Gaines, Pinchen, or anyone else allowed to buy and sell "them." As the scene opens, Walker is in good spirits because the "price of niggers is up." Here's his greeting to Pinchen:

WALKER

It is Mr. Pinchen as I live; jest the very man I want to see. Why how do you do? . . . What in the name of Jehu brings you down to Muddy Creek? Any camp revival meetin's, death-bed scenes, or anything else in your line going on down here? How is religion prosperin' now, Mr. Pinchen? I always like to hear about religion.

Pinchen replies by telling him that the "religion business" is in good shape because there's a lot of sin going on that he has to fight. He also tells Walker that as a slave trader, he needs religion more than most. To prove his point, he tells him of another slave trader who used to treat his "Negroes" terribly, but now that that fellow has religion, he buys and sells much more "nicely." Walker's reply is that he knows he'd be happier with religion and the first "spare time" he gets, he's going to try it. He even promises to "scuffle with the Lord" until he gets forgiven, ending with "But it always makes me feel bad to talk about religion, so I'll change the subject." Just then, Gaines walks in, and he has his chance. Says he, "Now, Dr., what about them thar niggers you thought you could sell me?" Gaines says he's willing to sell Hannah and her man, Sam, together, so he won't break them up because they're "married." But Mrs. Gaines comes in right on his heels to put the calabash on that:

MRS. GAINES

Now, gentlemen, that's just the way with my husband. He thinks more about the welfare and comfort of his slaves than he does of himself or his family. I'm sure you need not feel so bad at the thought of separating Sam from Hannah. They've only been married eight months, and their attachment can't be very strong in that short time. [Her reason for not wanting to sell Hannah is because she's "used to (Mrs. G.'s) ways." But Sam, a field hand, is another matter.] But I shall be glad if you sell Sam, for then I'll make Hannah jump the broom stick with Cato, and I'll have them both here under my eye. I never will again let one of my house servants marry a field hand—never! For when night comes on, the servants are off to their quarters, and I have to holler and holler enough to split my throat before I can make them hear. And another thing: I want you to sell Melinda. I don't intend to keep that mulatto wench about the house any longer.

When Gaines refuses to sell Melinda, she accuses him of lustful intentions and says either the wench goes or she does, and she leaves in tears. After she's gone, Gaines and Walker settle on taking a look at Sam and another slave, Big Sally.

The humor of the subsequent scene makes the effect tragic, but that's what good humor does, whether it's serious comedy or not. A similar scene in *Uncle Tom's Cabin* not only is without wit but takes itself seriously in a way that makes it seem as if the slaves are such helpless things that, as bad as the system was, the whites were just being human. Not so here. Brown nails his target—slavery—by making the people who practiced it seem what they were: a generation willing to let greed void any social contract that one human being could have with another in a society, any society, in which the two were merely existing without being official combatants. Here's scene 2 in its entirety:

WALKER
Well, my boy, what's your name?

SAM
Sam, sir, is my name.

WALKER
How old are you, Sam?

SAM
Ef I live to see next corn plantin' time, I'll be 27, or 30, or 35, or 40—I don't know which, sir.

WALKER
Ha, ha, ha. Well, Dr., this is rather a green boy. Well, mer feller, are you sound?

SAM
Yes, sir, I spec I is.

WALKER
Open your mouth and let me see your teeth. I allers judge a nigger's age by his teeth, same as I does a hoss. Ah! pretty good set of grinders. Have you got a good appetite?

SAM
Yes, sir.

WALKER
Can you eat your allowance?

SAM
Yes, sir, when I can get it.

WALKER
Get out on the floor and dance; I want to see if you are supple.

SAM
I don't like to dance; I is got religion.

WALKER
Oh, ho! You've got religion, have you? That's so much the better. I likes to deal in the gospel. I think he'll suit me. Now, mer gal, what's your name?

SALLY

I is Big Sally, sir.

WALKER

How old are you, Sally?

SALLY

I don't know, sir; but I heard once dat I was born at sweet pertater diggin' time.

WALKER

Ha, ha, ha. Don't know how old you are! Do you know who made you?

SALLY

I hev heard who it was in de Bible dat made me, but I dun forget de gentman's name . . .

That's the healthiest way to deal with a holocaust: make fun of it, ridicule its self-righteousness, show how it degrades the human experience. And if that isn't a pretty damn good example of nineteenth-century American theater, then I challenge anyone to find me a better example by an American writer of the midcentury period who had the guts to write about slavery. Walker's "clean" dialogue should prove that Brown was in charge of his language from character to character.

In the next scene, we learn that the doctor has come into great fortune. He will no longer be just a doctor of medicine any longer, for he has just been elected colonel of the militia. He wants Mrs. G. to begin calling him Colonel at once, but she says she couldn't possibly get used to doing that, since she's been calling him Doctor for twenty years. He replies that if she calls him Colonel, he'll give her anything she wants. Whereupon she quickly says,

MRS. GAINES

Well, as I want a new gold watch and bracelets, I'll commence now. Come, Colonel, we'll go to supper.

[Aside] Ah! Now for my new shawl.

Mrs. Lemme was here today, Colonel, and she had on, Colonel, one of the prettiest shawls, Colonel, I think, Colonel, that I ever saw, Colonel, in my life, Colonel. And there is only one, Colonel, in Mr. Watson's store, Colonel; and that, Colonel, will do, Colonel, for a Colonel's wife.

Gaines replies, "Ah! my dear, you never looked so much the lady since I've known you. Go, my darling, get the watch, bracelets and shawl, and tell them to charge them to Colonel Gaines; and when you say 'Colonel' always emphasize the word." They go to dinner and on comes Cato. He runs into Tapioca, who belongs to a Mrs. Jones. He woos her admirably, getting not one but two kisses within the space of half a page of script by telling her how much he loves her and how unworthy of her anyone else is. Gaines returns and overhears Cato bragging about his medical skills at the expense of the doctor. When Gaines makes a sound before identifying himself, Cato thinks he's an intruder and knocks him down. The scene ends with Gaines chasing Cato around the room, promising to whip him.

Act 2 finds Mrs. G. trying to convince Hannah that she wants to marry Cato. But Hannah refuses to be convinced. Scene 2 is in the kitchen, where Hannah is trying to get Cato's cooperation in convincing Mrs. G. that the marriage won't work. Says Cato, "No, Hannah, I ain't a gwine to tell missis no such thing, kase I does want you, and I ain't a gwine to tell a lie for you ner nobody else. . . . I don't see why you need to make so much fuss. I is better lookin' dan Sam . . ." Hannah exits depressed, and Cato sings a song! Mrs. G. comes in and Cato convinces her of his willingness to do anything she tells him to. Hannah comes back in and still refuses, whereupon Mrs. G. takes her downstairs to the cellar, after sending her for the cowhide, and beats her. Another servant, Dolly, begs Cato to say he doesn't want Hannah, but he refuses, arguing that then he'll be the one who'll get the cowhide. And he's not about to take a beating for anyone, concluding with "No, I'll jump de broomstick wid every woman on de place, ef missus wants me to, before I'll be whipped." Hannah and Mrs. G. reenter. She berates Hannah for making her "fatigue" herself so by having to beat her. Hannah ends up "jumping the broomstick" with Cato. The scene ends with Mrs. G. satisfied, offering them whiskey-and-apple toddy to celebrate.

In the meantime, Dr. Gaines, who has promised Mrs. G. that he will sell Melinda, has hidden her away in a cottage in the forest. He's also promised Melinda that he'll not only give her her freedom but let her have the cottage in the bargain, and dress like a lady and be her own mistress (shades of Jefferson and Sally Hemings). After Hannah and Cato have jumped the broomstick, we find Glen wandering around in the forest, trying to find Melinda, but he can't.

The scene switches to the cottage, where the doctor shows up expecting to be loved. Instead, Melinda tells him that she and Glen are married. He tells her he's bought Glen from his owner and will have him crucified for being the cause of his having come ten whole miles for nothing. Before he leaves, he warns her of the dire consequences if he doesn't find her willing to do his bidding when next he comes. He leaves Cato to guard her lest she try to run away. No sooner does Gaines leave than Mrs. G. shows up, saying she suspected what her husband was up to and followed him. Melinda begs her to help her get away. Mrs. G. is willing, but what she has in mind is worse than concubinage. She tells Melinda she has two "choices"—she can either take poison or the knife, both of which she's brought with her. Melinda refuses, and the scene ends with Melinda grabbing a broom to defend herself as Mrs. G. comes at her with the dagger. The stage directions read, "They fight; Melinda sweeps off Mrs. Gaines,—cap, combs and curls. Curtain falls."

Act 4 is in a dungeon. Glen is in chains, and one of the other house slaves, Sampey, tells him where Melinda is and what Mrs. Gaines is up to. In the next scene, Gaines has sent for the overseer, Scragg. He wants him to give Glen a real whipping before he sells him farther South: "Start with 500 lashes. If he's still alive, give him another 200 for good measure." Scragg is filled with enthusiasm for the job because Glen, under his former owner, was allowed to walk around dressed in good clothes and give himself airs, as if he were the equal of a white man. Says Scragg, "I tell you, Dr., I had rather whip that nigger than go to heaven any day—that I had!" But Scragg returns almost immediately in one of Browns several quick exits and entrances. It turns out that Glen gave the beating to Scragg, who's now afraid that he's about to die from his wounds. Glen, he reports, has fled.

Gaines sends for the hounds to track Glen down, but Mrs. G. shows up before he can leave. Having wished that heaven would take her, "For I have had her long enough," the good doctor now puts on a "sober face" as she approaches, "for she looks angry." In tears, Mrs. G. accuses him of never having loved her. And she proves it by pointing to the fact that he has never squeezed her hand whenever he's kissed her, the way a former suitor used to. He tries to pacify her, but she threatens to go to a lawyer to get a divorce, whereupon he immediately recommends the best lawyer in town and offers to pay all expenses. She turns on him and says she'll never leave him and exits. The act ends with Glen finding Melinda and the two of them head for Canada together.

The first scene in act 5 introduces a Mr. White, a Northerner who is passing through the South. The scene is the American Hotel in Missouri. One of the loungers asks him where he's from. He makes the mistake of saying Massachusetts. Everyone in the lobby immediately begins attacking the state. He tries to object, only to be told that it's a free country and a citizen can say what he pleases. White wants to know how it can be a free country if Missouri is a slave state. One of the men replies, "He didn't mean a free country for niggers." White says he's even seen white slaves. The answer he gets to that is "Well, they're white niggers." Whereupon White makes a speech about freedom, which they tell him is treasonous. "This is not a meeting-house," says the bartender. White decides that discretion is the better part of valor and leaves. Gaines, Scragg, and Cato show up looking for Glen and Melinda. Someone suggests that White probably stole them, and everyone leaves looking for him as well. White gets to Ohio before they get to him, glad, he says, to be in a free state again. Cato decides to leave the chase and take leave of Gaines as well.

In the next scene, Cato shows up at the Quaker dining room where Glen and Melinda have also ended up. (This type of coincidence abounds in *Uncle Tom's Cabin*.). They ask him what happened, and he tells them, adding that he borrowed a suit of clothes and decided to "hunt Canada. Ef anybody tries to take me back to ole massa, I'll pull evry toof out of dar heads, dat I will! As soon as I get to Canada, I'll set up a doctor shop, an' won't I be poplar? ... Oh, how I wish I had Hanna wid me! It makes me feel bad when I tink I ain't a gwine to see my wife no more . . . But come chillen . . . Dey say we is most to de British side." When one of the Quakers corroborates this, Cato adds, "Ah, dat's de talk fer dis chile."

In the final scene of the play, at a ferry on the Niagara River, the ferryman has just left his boat and gone to have lunch. White comes in with an umbrella. He sits down and starts to sketch the scene. Several peddlers try to sell him trinkets and knickknacks, but he isn't buying. He then moves to another location, and Gaines and Scragg and an officer of the law come on. The officer suggests that they go farther up the shore, since he doesn't think that Glen and Melinda have crossed yet. Gaines says he hopes not because he wouldn't lose them for $2,000, "especially the gal."

Then Cato comes in after they've left. Says he,

CATO

I is loss fum de cumpny, but dis is de ferry and I spec dey'll soon come. But didn't we have a night in Buffalo? Dem dar Buffalo gals make my heart flutter, dat dey did. But, tanks be to de Lord, I is got religion. I got it las' night in de meetin'. Before I got religion, I was a great sinner; I got drunk, and took de name of de Lord in vain. But now I is a conwerted man; I is bound for hebben'; I feel dat my name is rote in de book of life. But dem niggers in de Vine Street Church las' night shout an' make sich a fuss, dey give me de headache. But, tank de Lawd, I is got religion, an' now I'll be a preacher, and den dey'll call me de Rev. Alexander Washington Napoleon Pompey Caesar. Now I'll preach and pull teef, bofe at de same time. Oh, how I wish I had Hannah wid me!

Then Glen and Melinda come on pursued by Gaines, Scragg, and the officer. They vow to die rather than go back to slavery. Gaines says, "Down with the villain! down with him! but don't hurt the gal!" Before the fight starts, White reenters, sees what's going on, and comes to Glen and Melinda's aid with his umbrella. The ferryman returns from lunch, jumps into his boat, and Glen, Melinda, and Cato get free and jump in after him "and shout loudly for freedom.—Curtain falls. THE END."

AND NOW IT'S BACK TO UNCLE TOM AND HIS CABIN

Harriet Beecher Stowe never wrote a play, of course. Josiah Henson, who had escaped from slavery in 1830, was on his way to Canada when he stopped off in Boston, met Mrs. Stowe, told her what it was like on the old plantation, and then headed to freedom. She put it all down in her novel, which almost didn't get into print because no one thought it would make money; there had been other antislavery novels before it that had failed. Or even worse, it might bring ruin and disgrace on any publisher who put his name to it.

John P. Jewett, who did eventually put his name to it, certainly thought so, but his wife loved it, and the rest is history. Lowell, as in James Russell, was disdainful of it and said so. Mrs. Stowe, as was her right, exercised poetic license and turned a man who had escaped from slavery into the grinning obscenity of her artistic imagination. Henson, unlike the Uncle, was a fighter who was off to a country where slavery was illegal. Not only had he escaped from his slavery, but he founded a settlement and a laborer's school in Canada where other escaped slaves could come and make a life for themselves. And he was literate. He actually wrote his own autobiography (unlike so many other "as told to" autobiographies of the era): *The Life of Josiah Henson, Formerly a Slave, Now an Inhabitant of Canada, as Narrated by Himself*. It was published in Boston in 1849 and sold over six thousand copies. When it was learned that Henson's story was the basis for Stowe's work, the sales ballooned to one hundred thousand copies.

Of the several versions of the play, the one by George Aiken is generally regarded as the best. That version, which was also the basis for the 1933 production in New York at the Alvin Theater by the Players Club, was first produced in Troy, New York, of all places, in 1852. Mrs. Stowe objected to the theater on religious grounds, and since she was unprotected by copyright (it wasn't until 1856 that there was a law), she never realized a penny from the vast sums made not only by producers but by foreign publishers of the book, especially in London. She did see the play at least twice: once early on, when she sneaked into a theater in disguise, and years later, when she went openly with a friend. Her book had been so changed that she was, by her own account, unable to follow the plot. Irrespective of plot and character changes, the play lost none of the power of the novel that had people all over the world weeping. In its heyday, in the decades following the Civil War, the very entrance of an *Uncle Tom* troupe into a town became an American custom as ritualized as the Wild West show, the quarter-horse race, or the Fourth of July picnic. The Black man had been maligned for over three-quarters of a century on the stage of American theater, and now in the year of Our Lord eighteen hundred and fifty-two, in Troy, New York, came a play that said not only that the whole thing was morally wrong but that Blacks had actually been suffering under the peculiar system. To understand how loaded the issue was at the time, imagine a play opening on Broadway calling the Daughters of the American Revolution whores.

Topsy and Uncle Tom were the real thing, so they had to be played in burnt cork. In the 1933 version Otis Skinner, father of Cornelius and a great name in American theater in his own right (he had toured with Edwin Booth and Modjeska, played Armand in Dumas's *Camille*), played the Uncle in blackface. It wasn't the first time he'd done it either. Eliza; her husband, George; and their son, Harry, were all light skinned, so they were played by white actors in "light face" throughout the history of the play. As a matter of fact, these light-skinned parts, so far as is known, were never played by a Black actor or actress except in George

Abbott's musical *Sweet River* (more on that later), at least not before the twenty-first century. Ava Gardner, the real Helen Morgan, Victor Mature, Tony Curtis, Rock Hudson, Jeff Chandler, Ray Danton, and heaven knows who else have all played mulattos, Indians, and Africans at one time or another in film. But a Black actor has never played him or herself in the light roles of this, *The World's Greatest Hit* (Harry Birdoff's name for his history of *Uncle Tom's Cabin*) until 2010. An all-Black made-for-TV film version was made in 1987. As a statistic that should have some value for some social science researcher somewhere.

As an act of exclusion, the play was, in effect, an extension of the minstrel show. And the custom of the cultural in-joke, the entre nous implication of the lampoon continued unabated, even when the joke became a moral preachment. There was a whole new world being created in American theater in the 1850s and '60s, a world that would in time set a standard for the world itself. The blackface minstrel shows became vaudeville, became *Oklahoma!* and *Carousel* and, alas, *Porgy and Bess*. Blacks were there at each crucial step of the way, adding their indispensable genius to the development, without which the thing itself would never have been completely formed. *Uncle Tom's Cabin* did for serious American theater what the minstrel show had done for song and dance. Again, it was the Black experience—in this case in the hands solely of white writers but based on realities that Blacks had lived, had known firsthand—which set the standard for modern theater, for how it is presented not only in America but throughout the world. Another case of blues stolen and run away with. In the 1933 version, the play was originally scheduled for one week, but the reviews were so glowing and the audience response so robust that it was extended three weeks. Eighty-one years later, the Uncle was still bringing them in.

Eliza and Tom are privileged slaves in old Kentucky. She's a house neegrow, and he's given overseer responsibilities. Their master, Shelby, is of the "kind" variety. He's promised Eliza that he will never sell her away from her son, Harry. Eliza and her husband, George, were married by a minister. "Just as if we were white" is one of her lines. George works for a mean master whom we never see. As the play opens, George is telling Eliza that he's going to run away because his master wants him to remarry, to take someone from his own plantation. That way there'll be no need to travel to see his "wife." But Shelby has financial problems and has to do the unthinkable: sell young Harry anyway, along with Uncle Tom. We learn from them how honest and loyal and capable of doing a white man's work Uncle Tom is before the scene is over.

Scene 2 is just that, in the Uncle's cabin. Eliza is going to run away with young Harry. She tells Uncle Tom (this is his first scene) and his wife, Aunt Chloe, what's going on and that she wants him to come with her. He says he can't, not because he couldn't leave his wife, but because he owes it to his master to stay with him in his hour of trouble and to see to it that the plantation doesn't fall apart. Although how he's going to manage that if Shelby sells him, he doesn't say. Nor does anyone else for that matter.

Eliza strikes out on her own and makes it to a tavern on the edge of the Ohio River, but can't cross because the river is frozen. Phineas Fletcher, one of the more successful characters in the play, just happens to be there. He's an ex-sailor who's given up the sea to please his girlfriend, a Quaker. She even makes him give his slaves their freedom without getting a penny for it. He pays for Eliza to rest in a room in the tavern while he waits for the river to thaw so he can cross over and tell his sweetheart that he's willing to become a Quaker too so she'll marry him. After he leaves, Haley, the slave trader who has bought Uncle Tom and little Harry from Shelby (they were sold during the first intermission), arrives hot on Eliza's trail and engages two cohorts to help him catch her. One of them, the lawyer Marks, becomes crucial to the rest of the story. The scene of Eliza crossing the ice with little Harry in her arms and the bloodhounds in hot pursuit was one of the most famous and most eagerly awaited. Here's the scene from the 1933 Players script:

SCENE V

River. The entire depth of stage representing the Ohio River filled with floating ice. R. E. and in front.

Eliza appears with Harry R. E. on a cake of ice and floats slowly across to L. E. Hounds chase after her.

Haley, Marks and Loker (another slave catcher) follow across after the hounds.

Curtain

Meanwhile, back at the ranch, which has been relocated to New Orleans, St. Clair, Tom's new owner, and his daughter, Little Eva, have returned from a trip to Vermont. And George, Eliza's husband, has also run away *and* runs into Phineas on the shores of the Ohio. No sooner does Phineas take him to Eliza than the baddies show up: Marks, Loker, and three other catchers, and the chase is on. That scene is called "A Rocky Pass." Phineas and Eliza and Harry and George all clamber up the "Rock." Marks and Loker enter. While George is making a speech about freedom, Marks tries to kill him. Here's how the scene ends with George, Eliza, and Harry on their knees and Phineas standing over them exulting. Loker has just asked Marks why he took a shot at George if he's trying to capture him:

MARKS: Why not? In Kentucky a dead nigger is worth just as much as a live one!
GEORGE: Now, Phineas, the first man that advances I fire at; you take the second, and so on. It won't do to waste two shots on one man!
PHINEAS: Creation! Chaw me up if there ain't stuff in you!
MARKS. I think I must have hit some on'em! [sic] I heard a squeal!

LOKER: I'm going right up for one. I never been afraid of niggers—yet, and I ain't ago-ing to be now! Come on!

(Music. Loker dashes up the rock. George fires. He staggers for a moment, then springs to the top. Phineas seizes him. A struggle.)

PHINEAS: Friend, thee is not wanted here!

(Throws Loker over the rock.)

(Music. MARKS and party run off R.2.E. George and Eliza kneel in an attitude of thanksgiving with the child between them. Phineas stands over them exulting. Tableau.)

CURTAIN

The white guy does the fighting, and in thanking him, the so-called Black charac-ters do the kneeling.

In the next scene, which takes place in the St. Clair Garden, we find out that Little Eva is going to die soon and go to heaven. She and Tom have a metaphysical conversation in which he describes heaven to her and explains the tangible basis on which its institutions in the clouds stand—faith. He sings her a song. St. Clair comes in, and she begs him to promise to give Tom his freedom. He promises he will. In the next scene, she dies in her bedroom, and St. Clair is going to draw up the papers to give Tom his freedom. Then comes the slave auction scene, and while Skeggs, the auctioneer, is talking to the ubiquitous Marks, we find out that St. Clair was killed trying to stop a barroom brawl before he could free Uncle Tom. Enter Simon Legree, and he buys the Uncle. Then we're in a New Orleans street, and the son of Tom's original owner—young George Shelby, who has grown up in the interim—shows up looking for Tom so he can purchase the good fellow and take him back to Aunt Chloe and the children in Kentucky. And who shows up but Marks. He tells Shelby that Legree has Tom and offers to show him where Legree's place is for a fee.

We're next in Legree's cabin. Uncle Tom is no longer in the splendid livery of St. Clair but in tattered old clothes, and he's got a curl of little Eva's hair wrapped up in a piece of paper, and a silver dollar that the elder George Shelby gave him way back in act 1 when he had to sell him. Now Uncle Tom wonders, out of the blue, how young George is. Then Emmeline, a young slave girl whom Legree also bought along with Tom, is offered by the archvillain the job of concubine. She refuses it. Legree gets angry and tells Tom to beat her with the whip since he, Legree, has decided to make Tom his head "boy." Tom refuses, and two of Legree's other slaves, Sambo and Quimbo (also blackfaced along with Tom, Topsy, and Emmeline), give Tom the beating instead.

In the next scene, Cassy makes her appearance. She's an ex-concubine of Legree's, but she has a soft heart and tries to cheer Tom up with water and words of comfort now that the beating is over. And she's also the possessor of the one great attribute of the Black woman who survived the holocaust when her man—all her men—was hanged or beaten until he too turned into Sambo: she's tougher than Legree, and he knows it. The dialogue between Cassy and Uncle Tom is also metaphysical. In the next scene, we meet Gumption Cute (played by Gene Lockhart at the Alvin in 1933), another version of Marks, who tells the lawyer that Legree killed St. Clair and he saw it. Marks and Cute team up to swindle Legree by holding the threat of reporting him to the police over him.

Back at Legree's, Cassy has run off and taken Emmeline with her. Tom is brought in half dead and blamed for it. And Legree knocks him down with a blow from his whip handle to reinforce the point that he's a Black devil. Then young George Shelby, Marks, and Cute enter. Shelby asks for Tom, and before Legree can stop him, Sambo says, "Dere he is!" and points him out to Shelby, for which Legree chases him. Then Cassy comes in, but Legree doesn't see her. (She's done that trick before.) Marks and Cute accost Legree, who chases Cute, grabs Marks, and is trying to strangle him to death when Cassy stabs him in the back and kills him. There is a blackout and then the spot comes up on Shelby and Tom. Shelby says, "Oh, Uncle Tom, dear Uncle Tom! Don't you know me? I'm your *old little*[!] master George!" (italics mine).

(Lights up on Tom.)

TOM: (opening his eyes). Massa George! Bress de Lawd! Dey ain't forgot me, now I can die an' be happy!

GEORGE: Die! No! Don't talk like that! I'm going to buy you and take you home, back to old Kentucky!

TOM: You're too late, Massa George, de Lawd he's going to take me home!

GEORGE: Oh, Tom, you mustn't die ... You mustn't, oh you poor old fellow!

TOM: Massa George, dat's all pas' an' gone now. I's at de doh, goin' into de glory ... oh, Massa George ... look ... look ... Dere's Massa St. Clair an' li'l Eva ... I's comin', I's comin' ...

(He dies.)

GEORGE: He's gone!

GEORGE: (continues). Dear Old Uncle Tom, your body shall rest beneath the blue grass of your beloved old Kentucky, till the Judgment Day!

CURTAIN

SCENE VII

Apotheosis

Beginning with the George Aiken script that an acting family named Howard did in Troy in 1852, *Uncle Tom's Cabin* lasted into the twenty-first century, with an off-off-Broadway production at the Metropolitan Theater on East Fourth Street in 2010. George Abbott's musical version in 1936, *Sweet River*, was probably the first attempt to make it more contemporary by having Black actors play all the Black parts, and it flopped. Wikipedia doesn't even list it in its article chronicling *all* of Abbott's extensive theatrical activity. Blacks have long since objected to not only the characters and the sentiment but also the purported good intent of both novel and play. Uncle Tom, later just Tom, has become as famous as a term of opprobrium as the original became *because* it was, as Harry Birdoff suggests in *The World's Greatest Hit*. That it was and still is the world's greatest hit, there is no doubt (unless you count Shakespeare).

Cassy kills Legree not only because he used her and deserves to die but because he also intends to continue the tradition with Emmeline. Cassie's involvement with Legree has a personal motivation in dramatic terms (albeit melodramatic) that makes sense. A Black character can become involved with a white one successfully as long as the Black character has a reason that goes beyond giving succor to the other just because he, the Black character, is "good" and out of a sense of "goodness" wants to save the other fellow either from himself or from some outside danger. Black theater of the sixties and beyond has long since ceased to be plagued by such anachronisms of character motivation.

But all the angry plays of the sixties and after can't really expunge the disease of the Uncle Tom virus in theater. Because of the immense guilt that subsists in heavy deposits an inch below the surface of the general consciousness, every Black character is "suspect." If he's normal then he should want revenge. If he doesn't want revenge, then what does he want? If he just wants to be left alone or is only concerned with his own people and problems, then he probably won't have any dramatic interest for a "general" audience. If he can allay the guilt of the "general" by being "good" and proving it by playing the rescuer of the white mask, of he who was the committer of the original American sin, then he can be endured. Then he's welcome not only as character but as part and parcel of the dramatic gestalt.

Not only did Uncle Tom concern himself almost exclusively with the Shelbys, even after they sold him, and with St. Clair as well, but his relationship with Little Eva borders on the obscene. He saves her from the river by diving in after her. They are alone in the garden, talking about that garden in the sky in not one, but two—and in some versions, three—scenes. When she suddenly starts dying, it isn't her father, St. Clair, although he's standing right there, who picks her up and takes her to her room, but Uncle Tom. After the Civil War, when the productions really got absurd, some managers even added an apotheosis scene that showed the two of them in heaven, still communing with each other. Of course, even up there, Uncle Tom is on his knees.

The sexual taboo, which was the strongest of all, was not avoided in the Uncle Tom–Little Eva relationship but transferred to the fantasy realm of the platonic relationship of the "old" slave and the "young" girl. Although, oddly enough, in real life, a husband and wife team actually played the parts (see Birdoff for details).[19] But the sexual taboo encompassed, and still encompasses, the very honor of the race—either race. The Black women who were made into concubines for the pleasure of their white masters used the advantage of that position as best they could to get what little power they could. When Jim Crow became the law of the land, Black men were lynched by the thousands in defense of white womanhood that had been raped, was about to be raped, thought it had been raped, or even lied about being raped and admitted to the lie in court. The white man in the South had no intention of letting the Black man turn the tables of history on him. So Cassie could wield the knife; that was custom. Uncle Tom could not have been a hero, could not have had a relationship with Little Eva or little anybody else, except as eunuch.

But in the nineteenth century, even that wasn't enough. He had to also be forgiving. That he's really Black is indispensable to the play's success, because he is legitimizing the formal, public relationship of Black and white throughout the entire country on a personal level. He, the victim of the crime, is untouched by any personal deformity, for all his trauma. Legree, who had personal problems of a "normal" kind, has been twisted into a foul beast by his experience, which is benign by comparison. Only fantasy could have left the one so whole, so clean, so moral and the other so "normal" in his sadism.

Not that Uncle Tom suffers that much as a slave. Even though the play was hated in the South, and even though Lincoln commented when he met Mrs. Stowe, "So you're the lady who started the Civil War," the fact is that the drama never really attacks slavery as a real evil, only as a sometimes one. For some reason, in the minds of the millions of people who saw it, Legree's beating Uncle Tom proved that slavery was an evil. That simple act, which could have happened, and did happen, before the worst days of the Fugitive Slave Act and long after the Civil War was over, won over millions of hearts and minds to the cause of abolition throughout the world.

The question has to be asked, why did Legree's beating the Uncle become, in the minds of the millions, such a heinous act? The answer is a simple one. Because the Uncle was a good nigger and good niggers have a special place in the hearts and minds of America. The bad nigger, unlike Jesse James, is hated. Jesse was a robber, a killer, and an arrant racist (look it up if you want the details), but like Clyde and Bonnie, he won the admiration—indeed, the love—of America in a besotted romanticizing of the bad guy as hero. It's easy to understand the attraction, but the fact of his sadistic treatment of Blacks in his part of Missouri is brushed over. That happens all the time when poetic license is called upon in pursuit of the bad/good guy hero; the hero who is a foul fellow but we love him just the same.

Forget the bad nigger. Take the case of the ordinary one, or the indifferent one. You kill them or castrate them, and you won't hear a whisper, much less a holler. The Black race can be sympathized with, looked at as decent, when we're "good"—as in acquiescent. When we're "normal" or we've done something that could qualify us to be romanticized a la Jesse James or Clyde and Bonnie, the only sound we hear is "Kill the sucka!" For that level of acceptance in the cultural marketplace of the time, you had to be white. And that's why everyone was so upset that poor ole Uncle Tom got himself a whupping from that bad white man who should have known better. Hell, we need the good niggers to prove America is a democracy.

Uncle's Cabin became so famous that in the backlands of Australia, they thought Shakespeare had written it. But Legree's "sadism" in the world of slavery and in the gospel according to Uncle Tom is a pretty mild affair. Life with Shelby and St. Clair is "good," and the personal ties that developed between master and slave were strong ties that, in the context of the relationship as presented in the play, enriched both sides—so that the public at large could take the right position against the more melodramatic aspects of the evil without sacrificing any of its stereotypical notions of the Black character as cultural animal. Not only are George and Eliza and Harry so light skinned that they can pass for white, but they do pass for white in the emotional response of the audience, because they are white. This is crucial again to the life of the Black character on the American stage. Because George was being looked at as white, whatever sympathy he elicited had no effect on the Black character. Only his moral preachments against slavery were breaking new ground in terms of what was acceptable on a public American stage. But not so much even then because he was, after all, a white man pretending to be Black while making the preachments.

Stark Young, one of the great names in American criticism and a man who had no peer when it came to explaining why a play worked, made the rather startling observation in 1936 in reviewing *Sweet River* for the *New Republic* that there were three reasons the novel worked. One was that "no matter how good the master, circumstances might arise by which the slave would fall into bad hands." The second was the separation of families. The third was that "*through miscegenation a man with the characteristics and nervous system of white men might find himself enslaved*" (italics mine).[20] So even though the play ran for close to a century, helped change the history of the world (certainly the Civil War in America has had a strong impact on world history), it could not and did not change the condition of the Black character in American theater for the better. It only reinforced his "lowly" state (the subtitle title of both the book and the play is *Life among the Lowly*). And any sense of human qualities observed that the drama exhibited emanated from "non-Black" men and women.

But worse than that, even though burnt cork as used in the minstrel show gradually disappeared from the Black musicals, and the chicken-stealing, crap-shooting, gold-toothed smoothies who represented so many "end men" of the minstrel show gradually gave way by the 1890s to more serious fare, not so for ole Uncle Tom. He remained the same demeaned servile whose "dignity" was solely a figment of the other ethnic's imagination. And the longer he lived, the longer the baboon triumphed over the man. In the case of Uncle Tom, he was double baboon because he wasn't even on the stage while the mask, the burnt cork, was doing its dirty work. Whatever "pathos" was brought to the part by Otis Skinner or David Belasco (he played it in cork at the age of twenty at Shiel's Opera House in San Francisco, in 1873) and the rest, was pathos created by a white actor for a Black idea in the mind. Eating the cultural cake and having it too had never worked out better.

Percy Hammond—reigning critic of the *Herald Tribune*, who was killed by a voodoo spell cast over him by the African dancers from Sierra Leone after he, Hammond, panned the "Voodoo" *Macbeth*—loved the Players Club revival of *Uncle Tom's Cabin*. In his opening-night notice, he said that not only did "the old idol glow with a surprising luster" but "Mr. Skinner's characterization of the HOLY slave . . . was a profoundly pathetic study in Negro nobility, unmarred by any extravagance. . . . And Fay Bainter impersonated Topsy as if she had never been in the Cotton Club."[21] I'm not so sure that was a good thing. He also reported to have seen many a "wet eye" at that opening night performance!

And John Mason Brown, writing for the *Saturday Review of Literature* (in his column under the title "Seeing Things Topsy Turvy"), was incensed when Blacks in Bridgeport, Connecticut, were able temporarily to ban a musical version of the play as late as 1945. They probably objected to the burnt cork most of all. Said the estimable Mr. Brown (another first-night critic at the Harlem *Macbeth*), "One would have thought that if any book merited the gratitude of those interested in racial equality, Mrs. Stowe's classic would have been that volume. It may not have been the cause of the Civil War, as Lincoln once said it was. But it was one of its major causes, since it blocked the Fugitive Slave Law. . . . This thing of banning books just because they say what we do not want them to is a dangerous business. Book burning is more to the Nazi taste than our own."[22] Brown, a renowned critic in his day, saw nothing demeaning in the "old Classic." Could not sympathize with the Bridgeport and New Haven Blacks who said, "[The play] refreshed memories that tend to portray only the weaknesses of a racial minority, and holds up to ridicule peoples who in the early days of our country were unfortunately subjected to exposures that today would be considered atrocious."[23] Ignoring that, Brown, in his attempt to compare the Bridgeport protest with book burnings in Germany, forgot that the Connecticut protest was against the play, not the book! No wonder Orson Welles and his Black actors had trouble when they tried to do Shakespeare in normal face in 1936, if that was the opinion of one of the opening-night critics a good nine years later.

The early days were the strictly all-white ones. One white actress ended up playing the role of Topsy 3,500 times. Even Sambo and Quimbo, who beat Uncle

Tom when Legree wasn't doing it, were white actors in blackface. A revolution in custom was being created, and Uncle Tom was creating it. The social habits of the country would never be the same again. Theater had been made respectable. That was a miracle in nineteenth-century Protestant America, and *Uncle Tom's Cabin*, white under the face, was doing it.

Politically, the issue was every bit as hot in the minds of everyone who went to see the play as Lincoln implied it was when he gave Mrs. Stowe credit for causing the war. Barnum used a proslavery version that ignores the auction scene and makes Topsy a fool instead of an imp. Mobs in New York were attacking antislavery meetings just a few years before the play opened. So the conflict around it continued right through the pre-civil War period. Barnum advertised his version as not putting Blacks above whites, as that would be foolish. In Philadelphia, students from below the Mason-Dixon protested that no writer can libel the South; the first performance in the city never got to the last act.

In England, retail stores sold Uncle Tom's pure unadulterated coffee and Uncle Tom china. Infant toys with wooly heads, Topsy dolls, and girl children named Eva were the fashions of the day. The play became so popular that it ran in Drury Lane as early as 1852. This, even though Aldridge couldn't without being described as Wallack's Black servant and the rest of it. On the Continent, the impact was just as strong. *La Case de l'Oncle Tom* opened in 1853 at the Théâtre de l'Ambigu-Comique in Paris. One of its two authors, Dumanoir, was also half of the team that wrote *The Black Doctor* (*Le Docteur noir*) that Aldridge translated in 1847. In their version, they don't even use Simon Legree as a character. They make a quadroon former slave the villain—the master that George is running away from. In Germany, over half a million copies of the novel were sold as *Onkel Tom's Hutte*. Florence Nightingale even found soldiers reading it in battle. That none of this notoriety was doing the Black cause any tangible good beyond the waves of guilt can be seen in incidents such as how Boston's Howard Athenaeum Theater, when it put the play on, didn't allow Blacks in the theater.

Once the war started, the play had an immediate resurgence, with four different companies opening in New York at the same time in 1862. By the end of the sixties, as Joe Laurie Jr. reported in an article for the *American Mercury* in 1945 ("The Theater's All Time Hit"), "There were 200 Tom Shows involving 1200 actors, playing in the United States at one time."[24] "Turkey actors" became a phenomenon of their time, actors who followed the holidays by doing the following: Thanksgiving, *Uncle Tom's Cabin*; Christmas, *Uncle Tom's Cabin*; Washington's birthday, *Uncle Tom's Cabin*; Lincoln's birthday, *UTC*; and the Fourth of July, Uncle Tom and His Cabin. Said Birdoff, "The isolated little towns were out of reach of splendid legitimate theaters, and this one crude play held them spellbound. They found it as wholesome as a New England primer. Its influence became so strong that when the time came for choosing a profession, many youngsters headed for the stage."[25] These makeshift troupes did so much doubling that a song soon emerged about how they solved their casting problems a la African Grove: "Act I,

I was a cake of ice; Act. II, I was another; Act III I was the mob outside And Little Eva's mother."[26]

Then in 1876, an acting family, the Howards, used Black singers to sing plantation songs during the show whenever they could be thrown in, and the minstrel-craze era of the show was launched. The demand for the Black singers became so great within a short time that an ad in 1878 in New York newspapers called for "100 octoroons, 100 quadroons, 100 mulattoes, and 100 decidedly black men, women, and children capable of singing slave choruses." But again, no matter how many Black singers adorned the stage, ridiculing them was a favorite pastime that wouldn't die. Birdoff (his book was published in 1947), when he asked a manager how he cast Black actors for his "Tom" shows, got this "amusing" reply:

> We never have any trouble getting all the colored singers we want. . . . [We] just sent word among them, and we had such a crowd the police had to clear the sidewalk. You never saw anything like it. They can all sing. When the orchestra gets to going they can't help themselves, but either stand perfectly still and bewildered or go to dancing and shouting to the music. I've seen them get down and bump the stage with their heads. We don't try each particular voice. I can tell about what each of them can do by the cut of his jib [appearance].[27]

Henson (the original Uncle Tom, you'll remember) met Queen Victoria in 1877, and the Tom rage got a brand-new boost all over again in England. There were about fifty companies at the start of the 1880s. By 1900, there were five hundred. Of course, things were different in the South. Says Laurie, "Some states in the deep South . . . never gave up their prejudice against Uncle Tom. When a 'Tom Show' company landed in forbidden areas, it was customary for the manager to shift suddenly to a less controversial melodrama. If the Southerners even suspected that there was a 'Tom Show' in their midst, however disguised, they promptly burned it up and stoned the actors out of town."[28]

The "dog" period began around 1881. Instead of having actors stand in the wings and howl at Eliza and Harry, one producer decided to use the real thing. It was an immediate success and the show literally "went to the dogs." The troupes, according to Birdoff, soon resembled circuses, with productions carrying fifty actors, twelve dogs, a mule, an elephant, and alligators. The dogs got so good that in one Minnesota town, a critic observed that they were poorly supported by the actors. But the actual hounds were often too quiescent. On one occasion, Eliza slipped during a performance and the hound, instead of tearing her to shreds came over and licked her on the face.

The shows grew in extravagance to the point where city parks with real lakes were used as the actual set in cities like Boston. They even tried to make an opera out of it. And since it had become, in effect, a musical by then, why not? Later on, someone got the idea of getting a prizefighter to play Uncle Tom. The Black boxer Peter Jackson was made up to be the aging "darkie." After he is sold to Legree, he then steps out of character and boxes three rounds with a white fighter and then goes back to being beaten by Legree. Then someone got the bright idea of casting John L. Sullivan as Legree. He was paid to beat up whatever hapless Blacks could be scrounged for Uncle Tom, which he did with all earnestness, since that was what audiences were paying to see. The doubling craze reached the point where there were two actors for every character in the play, thus making every scene and line and piece of business twice as long.

And what film holds the record for the most versions made in the silent era? You guessed it, *Uncle Tom*. The first screen version was in 1903. Between 1903 and 1927, there were at least nine versions. Sam Lucas appeared in a 1914 version. That was the first film to have a Black leading man. In a 1927 version, Black actor Charles Gilpin was originally cast in the title role, but he was fired after the studio decided his portrayal was too aggressive. Oooops! So they went back to blackface and gave the part to a white actor.

Walt Disney's 1933 *Mickey's Mellerdrammer* took us all the way back to *Lucy Did Lam a Moor* with Mickey Mouse in blackface staging his own production of *Uncle Tom's Cabin*. In 1936, Shirley Temple, Frank Morgan, and Stepin Fetchit starred in Fox's *Dimples*, which makes fun of the opening night of the play. Judy Garland was Topsy (in blackface) in the MGM musical *Everybody Sing* (1938). In 1945, Betty Grable and June Haver played double Topsies in *The Dolly Sisters* (Fox, 1945). In 1945, Universal had Abbott and Costello playing Simon Legree and Eva in *The Naughty Nineties*. Says Laurie, whimsically summing it all up, "There isn't anything like the genuine 'Tom Shows' around now. Nevertheless, I'll bet a good many children, movies or no movies, would like to see the hounds baying after poor Eliza, and Little Eva going up to heaven on a wire, and Simon Legree beating poor old Tom. There's life, I insist, in the Tom Show yet, and I wish somebody would revive it all over again."[29] Dear me.

During that mammoth span of history, from before poor old John Brown even got to Harper's Ferry until Franklin Delano Roosevelt became the president of the United States, the trick had worked ad infinitum, ad nauseam. The sympathy had been elicited for tens of thousands of nights all across the continent. There was no end to the absurdity of these takeoffs. The Victoria Theater (in Harlem) put on *Uncle Thomashevsky's Cabin* in 1915. It became a headliner on the variety circuit, with the originals becoming Little Evavitch, Lawyer Markstein, Simon Levy, Elizy, and Topsyadie. But the trick was never successfully transferred to the modern theatrical experience of Black actors suffering under the Southern lash and audiences finding that that made them cry.

WHITE WRITERS AND BLACK PLAYS

The big story down the road after the euphoria of the Civil War wore off and federal troops left the South in 1877, thus ending Reconstruction and bringing on the long night of legal Jim Crow, was, like the original version of Jim Crow, being created on the stage. After William Wells Brown's pioneering effort, it is to the musical stage that we have to look eventually for the passing of the baton. Legal Jim Crow resulted in the most infamous set of laws ever enacted by a nation in "modern times" to disfranchise one of its ethnic minorities. The Grandfather Clause of Louisiana can be said to be the "grandaddy" of these. It stated with a brilliance of economy that got the job done in masterly fashion (making it a legislative gem in the annals of racism), to wit, "Anyone whose grandfather hadn't voted couldn't vote." This, of course, contravened the due process section of the Fourteenth Amendment, but no one argued the point. Things were so bad by the end of the 1880s that Blacks were moving to Canada even faster than before the war. Douglass died disillusioned, if not broken. W. E. B. Du Bois called a conference in Niagara, New York, in 1903, to find a way to stop the determined extermination of the race. It was the precursor of the NAACP.

So far as the legitimate stage is concerned, all the plays about the Black character in the second half of the century that were being done (which obviously excludes *The Escape*) were by white writers. The most important of these, *The Octoroon* by Dion Boucicault,[30] was even revived as late as 1961 by the APA-Phoenix Theatre in New York, and it got major press coverage as an "American classic" rediscovered. Mrs. Stowe's second novel, *Dred* (not based on Taney's infamous decision in the case of Dred Scott—he's an escaped slave living in the Dismal Swamp), was also dramatized, keeping the same title. There followed in 1857 J. T. Trowbridge's *Neighbor Jackwood*, and two years later, Kate Edwards, a twenty-five-year-old actress (who sometimes used her husband's name, J. C. Swayze) wrote *Osawatomie Brown*. While all three plays have the best of intentions they are, alas, only cringeworthy.

Not until a full fifty years later do we have another significant outing for the "Black" character with Edward Sheldon's *The Nigger*, written in 1909. It's one of the miscegenation plays that were a dominating theme of the early part of the new century. Plays written by Black playwrights in the second half of the nineteenth century were nonexistent except for Brown, unless you count Sejour writing "Black" plays with all white characters that have nothing to do with Black life anywhere, not even in Paris, or Aldridge's adaptation of the inconsequential piece *The Black Doctor*, which he performed a few times but never kept in his repertoire for too long.

The problem for Black theater in the hands of white writers was that the Black character continued to be a half-formed thing. Maybe malformed would be more apt. The mulatto heroine was still alive and well in the 1930s and 1950s in *Show Boat* and other "classics." And she was not alone. The forgiving Black, the Black who spoke unintelligibly for no good reason (as opposed to Cato), the Black who could make no cerebral input into the general store of information (unlike Brown, who did only that) or in any way affect the course of history or the general current of contemporary thought—that Black was alive and well also. The great Black men of the nineteenth century (Douglass, Henry Highland Garnet, and their legion) and the women (Sojourner Truth and Tubman, to name but two) had been in the center of national life. They had helped shape history. They expected to have something to say about the afterlife of the Civil War. They didn't really expect to be shunted aside, to have done what they so heroically did for naught. But for naught it was. The same sense of impotence that gripped them in reality was expressed all too accurately on the stage of American theater, when it was expressed at all. Not that Black men and women weren't rising to the occasion and, indeed, above it in the last third of the century. But there was neither a general desire nor a conscious will, on the part of the public at large or the American playwright, to acknowledge that effort and to make the sacrifice of the war mean something in time of "peace" on a public stage. For in the best sense of the well-worn trope, the Black man in America and the North in general in the 1860s and after, had "won the war only to lose the peace."

Neither Kate Edwards's *Osawatomie Brown* (the John Brown story) nor John T. Trowbridge's *Neighbor Jackwood* (he wrote a lot about the racial problems of the times, and a magazine he once edited folded simply because of *one* article he wrote against the Fugitive Slave Act) had any impact on theater, nor did *Dred*. These were scripts of only passing interest. The Boucicault play, on the other hand, *The Octoroon*, was the biggest success in "Black" theater in the nineteenth century after Uncle Tom. Birdoff mistakenly calls him Bourcicault and then says the name was changed to Boucicault, but his real name was Dionysius Lardner Boursiquot; he only pretended that he was a de Bourcicault, of noble French heritage. He was simply an Irishman with a French name, of ordinary French lineage, which he changed to Boucicault.

Unlike Uncle Tom, *The Octoroon* is not about Blacks at all. It has no major Black characters (which was an objection to the play by Blacks then and now). All the non-octoroonish slave types are minor characters, almost. There is old Pete, who makes Uncle Tom look like Malcolm X's meaner brother. Not only is old Pete happy as all get-out on the old plantation (this time we're in the backwoods of Louisiana), but he's willing to be sold and instructs all the other slaves to go willingly to the auction block too, so as not to upset ole Missus, who's only upset because she has to sell her "family." Ole Pete never talks about freedom or about tabernacles in the sky. He never refuses an order. Of course, no one puts him in the position of having to face a moral dilemma such as Uncle Tom faced when Legree wanted him to beat Emmeline. On this plantation, Terrebone, all is well—or at least it would be if it weren't for the fact that the good family of kind massahs and mistresses (the Peytons) ain't got the money for the mortgage on the farm.

Boucicault tries to present as broad a picture as he can of the attitudes of the slave South and the rather byzantine contradictions that these attitudes forced the society into. In the auction scene, we are presented with a group of substantial citizens—a judge, a merchant, et cetera—who don't even bid against one another but rather obey their slaves when they tell them who to bid for so that mother and child, man and wife can be kept together. The only villain is the dirty Northerner,

McClosky. Not only does he want to get the Terrebone plantation, and will use fair means or foul, but he is so degraded that he refuses to observe the "codes" that the good Southern gentleman have created as their honorable way of doing their slave buying and selling business. But because McCloskey's position in society has its safeguards (unlike the slaves themselves), he is allowed to break the unwritten code, since he has a legal right to do so.

Where the legality is presented as morally unjust, though legally right, is through the condemnation of McCloskey for not understanding the code of the Old South. The actual selling of slaves is not only legally right, though regrettable, but morally only a benign sin, if that. All this was viewed at the time as almost revolutionary (the play opened one year before the Civil War). In 1961, the revival at the Phoenix was looked on by the critics as a legitimate theatrical interpretation of history. Because after all, all Boucicault was doing was being accurate in telling it like it was, as it were. Except, of course, that he wasn't. But whatever the reality of Black life, the only reality that existed on the stage of 1859 was the reality according to Uncle Tom and Boucicault.

Boucicault, like any other writer, had a perfect right to present his version of reality in the same way that he had a right to decide what he was going to write about in the first place. He could have written a more strident, more overt apologia for slavery that not only took away the neegrow's varied and sundried "nobilities" but also condemned abolition. (The issue never comes up.) He might have even been given bad marks for so doing, for having presented a too one-sided view of the situation. But the view he did give us was just as distressingly one-sided, certainly from the Black standpoint, as any such material could produce. The insidious half-truths and pretenses at having a moral code in an immoral situation, which was supposed to have worked for all, was far more destructive to Black character and plot on the stage than a more apparently racist view, such as that found in *The Clansman*, would have been. The fact that all the leading drama critics in New York, in 1961, refused to condemn the play's immorality certainly proves the point.

That Black actors had to demean themselves in 1961 by standing on a public stage and reciting the guttural mumblings of this 1859 relic just to get ahead in the business is and was monstrous. It would have almost been better if the whole thing had been done in blackface. But that would have meant that some ridicule was intended and, as we shall see, all the critics gave the Phoenix production high praise for not only not doing that but, in fact, playing it "straight." Here's some of what went on in a public place in New York in 1961: Paul (the slave boy, old Pete's grandson) is doing a "number" on the noble savage Wahnotee, whose language is not to be believed (Mrs. Peyton is the suffering widow):

MRS. PEYTON: I expect an important letter from Liverpool; away with you, Paul; bring the mail-bags here.

PAUL: I'm 'most afraid to take Wahnotee to the shed, there's rum theere.

WAHNOTEE: Rum!

PAUL: Come, then, but if I catch you drinkin', O, laws a mussey, you'll get snakes! I'll gib it you! now mind. (Exit with Indian)

And later on, Ole Pete runs in, looking for Scudder (the good Yankee overseer) to tell him the worst:

Enter Pete, "puffing."

PETE: Mas'r Scudder! Mas'r Scudder!

SCUDDER: Hillo! what are you blowing about like a steamboat with one wheel for?

PETE: You blow, Mas'r Scudder, when I tole you; dere's a man from Noo Aleens just arriv' at de house, and he's stuck up two papers on de gate: "For sale—dis yer property," and a heap of oder tings—and he seen missus, and arter he shown some papers she bust out crying—I yelled; den de corious of little niggers dey set up, den de hull plantation children—de live stock reared up and created a purpiration of lamentation as did de ole heart good to har.[31]

And more and more and more, all to no purpose except to malign the intelligence of Black actors and to reinforce the Black character as idiot. There is no spoof here. Mr. Boucicault's Blacks think and act this way and this way only.

Zoe, the octoroon, talks like white folks, of course, because that's what she is. Like Stark Young's "nervous system of white men" idea, Zoe is damned because she has one drop of "Black blood" (whatever that means)—which means that she's not Black at all, but white. She's been brought up as white and is almost treated that way, except when the law requires that she be sold. McCloskey, a freeman in a slave state, exercises his right to buy her, which is also looked on as immoral, because he wants her for lustful ends; his act is an evil one not because of the buying but because of those intentions. Zoe has always been played by a white actress: Boucicault's wife in 1859, Juliet Randall in 1961. What this means is that no one is put in the uncomfortable position of having to relate to a Black actress (even one who is almost white, which is, of course, an entirely different thing). The nobleness of Black characters that usually elicits so much sympathy from white critics is a more neegrow thing and not nearly so refined as is this business of the "she's really white" concept of how to use Black characters in general American theater.

In one sense, the tragic mulatto heroine is baboon—babooness, if you will—since she has to deny, or at least denigrate, her Blackness in order to be tragic. This goes beyond the honest dilemma of being sorry that her drop of Black blood, like Camille's profession, prevents her from having the man she loves. If her problem were simply that of having to fight the prejudices of her times, of having to rebel against the forces of her clan or her society, as Juliet does in quest of her Romeo, then the Black objections to Zoe would be much more tolerant than they are. But because she actually subscribes to racism herself, she's really one of "them" using "our" problem for dramatic mileage. Zoe laments her fate but doesn't turn on "her own" (meaning the whites), and she holds them blameless in so far as her predicament is concerned, saying that she'd "rather be black than ungrateful."

Her father (old master) had died leaving his wife (not her mother) with a plantation, a parcel of darkies, a lot of debts, and an almost free octoroon daughter. Missus loves the girl as if she were her own and treats her that way, almost. The heir to the place is a young nephew of old marster, who's just returned from Europe. He loves Zoe. Their being first cousins is never raised as an issue because her familial connection is only "real" in so far as old marster's owning up to it makes him an honest man. But the blood tie as fact itself is not a serious consideration, because like the humanity of the neegrows themselves, it doesn't actually pose the kind of problems that would be posed if either the people involved or the blood connection was white. This makes the whole cultural phenomenon a double whammy: a white actress plays a Black woman and elicits all the sympathy she would if she were playing a white part, but because she is really playing a Black part, the regular taboo of marriage in the family, of incest, doesn't operate here because even though she's really white, in point of fact, she isn't. Get it? The young swain has a duty to the plantation, so he is willing to marry the heiress next door to keep the family together. When Zoe finds out that he's only doing it because he's noble, she gives him up, nobly. McCloskey forces the auction to take place even though there's help for the mortgage on the farm and pays a fortune for Zoe. Of course, he's discovered as the one who not only killed Paul, the slave boy, but hid the letter that would have shown that old missus had enough credit and really didn't have to sell the "family" or anything else for that matter. Both the deceit and his murderous act are exposed, and the "noble" Wahnotee (noble and savage) is given permission by the good Northerner Scudder to execute McCloskey.

Probably the worst of all sins committed by Boucicault against Black artistic self-respect is presenting slavery as just one of those things that you can really sort of get used to, the way you can get used to anything, like a horse instead of a mule or honey instead of molasses. Any little inconvenience in one's life can be adjusted to. So can slavery. And if the peculiar institution is looked at in a certain light, it wasn't really the worst thing in the world. In addition to all this, the whole group of Black characters represents, without exception, the baboon and not the man. Zoe doesn't count in this, of course. Not only is she not really one of them, but she's "Miss Zoe" and they "Miss Zoe" her to death. As a character, she's strictly cardboard, replete with noble gesture. Because she heard the young swain declare to himself that he'd rather see her dead than with McCloskey, she obligingly kills herself.

Boucicault made a lot of money from the play. It also ran well in London, riding on Uncle Tom's coattails for all that was worth. In England, Zoe and the young swain get married. That was considered too "explosive" an ending here. The mere fact that that was the case (so that, depending on where the play was performed, either ending could be used) is proof that the political issue of Black as cultural animal was too hot to handle in 1859. And 102 years later? It was still too hot to handle. Zoe and George (the young swain) didn't get married in 1961 either. William Wells Brown must have shaken his head in despair at the hopelessness of his cause. At the fact that a thing so easy for Boucicault to pull off, the mounting of a play, was for him so completely impossible.

Which brings us to 1961 and the big line up of critics who all assembled on several nights at the Phoenix Theatre, then on Twelfth Street, to see what the artistic director of the company called "an American classic." There was John Chapman writing for the *New York Daily News,* John McClain for the *Journal American,* Howard Taubman for the *New York Times,* Richard Watts Jr. for the *New York Post,* Whitney Bolton for the *New York Morning Telegraph,* Michael Smith for the *Village Voice,* and Walter Kerr for the *Herald Tribune.* In addition to these front-line critics, there were reviews in *Newsday, Women's Wear Daily, Variety,* the *New York World-Telegram and Sun,* and the *Wall Street Journal.* With the exception of Guy Savino writing in the *Newark Evening News,* all of the above-named gentlemen and publications had high praise for the 1961 revival. And they all saw the same play. That is to say that all of them agreed with each other on the general effect of the production and on its merits. If fifty million Frenchmen can't be wrong, then poor Mr. Savino and I are both done in. I didn't see the play performed. But I have talked extensively to many of the people who were on the stage of the Phoenix for the four-week run.

All the critics praised the Phoenix and director Stuart Vaughn for doing the play "straight." That is to say, not condescending to it, ridiculing it, turning it into burlesque or any of those things. Which, said most of them, would have been very easy to do. The Players Club did *Uncle Tom's Cabin* "straight" in 1933 also, and the critics at the time also liked the fact that they did. What was interesting about this "doing it straight" was that many of the reviewers, in actually writing their reviews, resorted to burlesque in their styles. The critic for *Newsday,* George Oppenheimer, admitted that he was, confessing that that was the kind of effect the play had on him. They all also thought that Black actor P. Jay Sidney as Old Pete was marvelous and that the neegrow characters all had "dignity" and that their singing was marvelous too. They gave Boucicault high marks for being able to tell a story (something they lamented the absence of in modern theater), and they found his endless plot manipulations "robust," "full of energy," and "rousing." They pointed every now and then to the creakiness of the language, but in the main, it was in their general and considered opinions good fun that should not be taken too seriously. This even though the production was done "straight" and should be laughed at and gone along with because of its innate goodness and sincerity, and where its age shows, it should be winked at, its straightness notwithstanding.

Now, no one is suggesting that these gentlemen in 1961 or after, or even before, were obliged to take a moral stand, or one in the name of art (although both have been done vis-à-vis Black theater on other occasions), and insist that the whole thing was a travesty that made a virtue out of an evil, that made the Black actors sound like asses. Certainly, the private hell of these performers, of the whole history of what they, their peers, and their ancestors, as actors, have had to endure is and was in no danger whatsoever of ever intruding itself onto the consciousness of these estimable gentlemen either then or now. The result of which is simply that the Black cultural reality again got the shock treatment. That no one except a relatively unknown critic, Guy Savino, writing in a Newark newspaper, told us, any of us, that the *Uncle Tom* evil was being let loose again meant that what was also being let loose was a reaffirmation of the two-hundred-year-old cultural lie. That lie being that Blacks are sad, noble, woeful, can sing, and just in general stuck with the miseries and when they aren't worrying about white folks' problems, they really aren't doing very much of anything else.

If William Wells Brown had been produced, if the minstrel show had not been the vicious lie that it became, if plays about all the things that were had been allowed to make it onto a public stage, then Boucicault wouldn't be half as important as he is. When the only thing that gets done is Boucicault or *Uncle Tom* or their ilk, then it's slander, and the fact that both plays were so popular, made so much money, makes the case that the appetite for Black baboons and baboonesses is insatiable. No wonder Broadway producers don't want to hear anything remotely resembling Black characters inveighing against the annihilation they've been bleeding from these many centuries. But the democracy is alive and well, the republic flourishes, and there is no law that prevents anyone from putting on any kind of play that he or she wishes. So what's all the fuss about? Any commercial producer who thought he had a play that would make money would certainly produce it immediately, no matter how strong a Black statement it made. Right? Wrong! And only a theater innocent would be beguiled by that argument.

The *Village Voice* called *The Octoroon* "rare fun," and Richard Cooke, writing in the *Wall Street Journal*, said, "It recalls a bygone attitude . . . and a relationship between human beings which has vanished forever." Cooke then goes on to say, "The Octoroon is to be laughed at for its blatant sentimentalities, its clichés, its simple minded histrionics. But in laughing at it, one does not necessarily despise it"! (I'm exclaiming), adding, "When the colored people playing the parts of slaves dominate the stage with a single dignity [they] over shadowed the fevered virtues and villainies which came before and after."[32] In many ways Cooke's review is the most revealing. He takes a passing shot at the real problems of the American society that are "brought up" by the play, insisting that they are problems "that have vanished forever" and are as "extinct as the mastodon." He, the mastodon, is supposed to no longer be an evil because he's extinct, but as an evil, he really wasn't that much of one either. As Mr. Cooke says, "When the colored people"— they weren't even "actors"—"playing the parts of slaves dominate the stage with a single dignity," they "overshadowed the . . . virtues and the villainies,"[33] et cetera.

Poor ole Uncle Joe and Aunt Jane wandering around somewhere in the imagination of the American critic, her head wrapped in a white cloth, his brow furrowed and his shoulders stooped, the two of them bemoaning their fate, afraid of "de debil" but "countin' on jeeeeesssusssssssss" to see them through, and singing. But, but, but, through it all, they is noble? and they has "dignuyteeeeee." If that isn't the most arrant condescension, the most obscene snobbery, then nothing is. One can't call it racism, of course, that is not fair, nice, nor provable. As Spencer Tracy says in *Judgment at Nuremberg*, "Where did I get the idea that there were any Nazis in Germany?" There are no racists in America, just people. Well, maybe a Ku Kluxer here and there, but we don't really take those people seriously. Besides, they're dying out anyway. One critic, even though he's writing in a world-famous newspaper, shouldn't matter that much, and he doesn't on one level. But it's symptomatic. It's the same myopia that destroyed Federal Theatre. It's the same myopia that will destroy many another production by and about Blacks in the American cultural context.

Thomas Dash, who reviewed the production for *Women's Wear Daily*, called the villain, McCloskey, in his headline a "Perfidious Caitiff." As a noun, the word is archaic. As an adjective, maybe not. In any event (to use an old drama critic trick), Mr. Dash himself is indeed an anachronism, hoisted on his own caitiffery, as it were. After calling Boucicault the founder of American realism in the theater, he quickly follows by saying that we "must respect his fecundity and his ingenuity," adding that "despite the play's clap-trap it does possess a number of noble sentiments. The paternalistic system on the Louisiana plantation made the Negro slaves tranquil. The decency of the white folk in avoiding the breakup of Negro families is something to be cherished."[34] If that is not blatantly immoral, then I retire. The only thing worth cherishing in that context of rape, genocide, and decadence that released the most evil instincts in ten generations of Deep South whites as slave owners, overseers, and the rest was and is the unconquerable human spirit of the Black man that survived that devastation and is today capable of coexisting with the heirs of that evil simply as fellow Americans.

But Dash's dash to the netherworld in one fell swoop of caitiffed claptrap and fustian (another word he uses) values is probably the biggest problem that Black theater has and will have to face. Stated baldly, it's a question of who takes the blame. Since everyone is guilty for what was done to the Black man, no one is guilty. And if the Black man would only forget that any of it ever happened (or still is happening), then we could be one happy family, turning our backs on the past and letting our dead bury dead issues. The Black man (who couldn't be what he actually was in the nineteenth century) now can't even remember the history so as not to repeat it, because everyone's agreed that for the sake of national harmony, we won't do that either.

Any critic (and I agree with the position) will tell you that you can't dictate what a writer writes. It's too personal a choice to be legislated. The problem with that dictum, however, is that it's another one-way street for us. Black playwrights are told, very effectively and without any need to have recourse to subtle messaging, that they cannot resurrect the guilt that history has left us with. We must none of us point a finger at any one segment of the society. We are what we are as a nation because of the Black experience on our shore from first to last, and there are enough white historians who have made this point for it not to be necessary for me to explain it in any detail, but in theater, the Black experience doesn't exist, only Uncle Joe and Aunt Jane and little Sammy somewhere in the distance eating a hoe cake and dancing. Dash then says that "the nobler sentiments of pre–Civil War days" should not be lampooned or made into burlesque because we're in a time of desegregation, which would make doing so "disastrous." Figure that one out. His final gambit is to leave us with this bit of erroneous history: "The Octoroon was to the theater what Harriet Beecher Stowe's 'Uncle Tom's Cabin' was to the novel."

Frank Aston in the *World-Telegram and Sun* began his review with enthusiasm, saying simply, "It worked." The performance turned the theater into "a charming curiosity shop." Aston enjoyed the "candy-colored skirts and ribbons" that Zoe and the young heiress were dressed in, as well as what he called a "tasteful holocaust." I kid you not! But through it all, he would no more think of "cackling" (his word) "over it anymore than I would over an old-fashioned mother."[35] End of quote. George Oppenheimer called it a "good-bad play," and the "I'd rather be black than ungrateful" line was to him "a lofty sentiment." He saw "assorted Negroes with hearts of gold and voices of silver," ending with a very curious play on the title of the play: "The Octoroon may be only one-eighth colored but it has a far higher percentage of fun and excitement. I never suspected that so bad a play could be so good."[36] Richard Watts Jr. did mention that the Black actors had an "Uncle Tom quality," but he spoiled that by talking about their sympathy. Walter Kerr tried to keep it all at arm's length, almost as if it were too slight to be taken seriously, but he allowed himself such observations as "[It] is irresistibly charming" and "It's all like that . . . innocent and terrible and curiously sincere and I'm sure you'll love its lollypop colors." He found P. Jay Sidney "an ancient retainer with a clear sense of his value on the auction-block," whatever that means. He summed up with "The trick of The Octoroon is that it is sympathetic"—it is, of course, no such thing—"to everybody and everything: slaves, slave-holders, Yankees, Indians, photography, steamboats and young love." And he too will settle for this "bad old [play]. . . . If we can't have good new [ones]."[37]

Only the unsigned review in *Variety* and Guy Savino, writing in the *Newark Evening News*, made observations that touched on the duplicity of the proceedings with a sense that indicated they weren't prepared to join in the fun. *Variety* called it "dubious box-office," adding that "there may be some question as to how suitable it would be for unsophisticated audiences, particularly where some of its questionable assumptions might be taken seriously."[38] Savino went further, calling it an outdated bore, and writing, "If the spectacle presented on the stage of the Phoenix last night were in any way remotely typical of life as it was in Louisiana, then the men who gave their lives in the . . . Civil War were silly." Adding, "Depicted was a plantation on which everything was crinoline and mint juleps and only the mean old conniver with the mortgage was to be feared." And ending with, "In a program note, T. Edward Hambleton, managing director of the theatre, called Boucicault's play, 'an American classic,' adding 'it retains today what made it significant, moving, entertaining and above all, theatrical to its first audience in 1859.' Here is at least one exception. To this viewer *The Octoroon* was a crashing bore and an offensive bore, at that."[39]

1961 was a long time after 1936. Even longer in time in many ways than 1936 was in distance from 1859. We had had the Harlem Renaissance and James Weldon Johnson had written his novel *The Autobiography of an Ex-Colored Man* just to prove that a Black man could write a novel between 1859 and 1936. But 1961! Surely the Black man had entered a new era after World War II. He had in the real world, but not on the bare stage. On that platform, the old grinner, Sambo, was alive and well. He had reached forward in time and triumphed.

"How many ages hence shall this our . . . scene be acted over, in states unborn and accents yet unknown! How many times shall Caesar bleed in sport, that now on Pompey's basis lies along no worthier than the dust!" How many times, indeed.

3 · NEW BEGINNINGS FOR A NEW CENTURY

1890–1920

After the North and the Republican Party won the Civil War, they both tried to nail down the victory with the Thirteenth, Fourteenth, and Fifteenth Amendments. Blacks became a very substantial part of that legislative process throughout the South in the decade from 1865 to 1877. The first laws ever passed in the former slaveholding states to grant divorces and give free public education and free public health services to everyone were passed in statehouses with Black lawmakers leading the way or providing the deciding votes. However, once the Federal troops left the South in 1877 and the Confederacy began to rise again with a two-pronged attack of mob violence and the passing of laws which contravened the Fourteenth and Fifteenth Amendments, neither the Supreme Court nor the presidency (regardless of who was in office) did anything about either. The prevailing mood by the eighties was "heal the wounds," "reunite the nation." And the North was told to let the South handle its neegrow problem, and in turn, the South would ensure that the North's business investments below the Mason-Dixon Line would be protected, and that would mean a profit for all. David De Armond (who was not only a Missouri congressman for eighteen years but a member of the Missouri state senate, the Missouri supreme court commission, and a judge!) said that Black people were "too ignorant to eat, scarcely wise enough to breathe, mere existing human machines."[1] This, in spite of the fact that all the ones who were too ignorant to eat were smart enough to campaign against ex-Confederates and win elections to numerous statehouses and to Congress, both the House and the Senate.

So the Black man had to be as cautious as he had to be clever, for the word was out: it was open season on him, and there wasn't a damned thing he could do about it, even though he had fought and died valiantly in winning the war and preserving the Union. In this atmosphere of uncontrolled violence and lawlessness,

Black entertainers began to crawl out from under the minstrel show proper, having just recently been allowed to crawl into it. But the process was more evolution than revolution. Bert Williams, the greatest Black entertainer of the period between 1890 and the Jazz Age, and one of the immortals of vaudeville, never performed without the burnt cork once he put it on. He and his partner, George Walker, even produced their own shows, eventually netting upward of $40,000 a year (a fortune then, and there were no taxes). One year, they even made more than the president.

But no matter how much money they made, they never showed lovemaking in their acts, even when they played opposite their own wives, because they were afraid of public disapproval. As James Weldon Johnson observes in *Black Manhattan*, "One of the well-known taboos was that there should never be any love making in a Negro play [because of] the stereotype that Negroes cannot be supposed to mate romantically, but do so in some sort of minstrel fashion or in some more primeval manner than white people."[2] Thomas Jefferson had given that sentiment prepresidential status in 1783 in *Notes on the State of Virginia* when he wrote, "[Black people] are more ardent after their females: but love seems with them to be more an eager desire, than a tender, delicate mixture of sentiment and sensation." You don't wanna know what he had to say about why Black people smell bad or who chooses the Black woman as their number-one sex object.[3]

At first, there were the minstrel shows, then the *Tom* shows. Then by the late nineties, there came the *coon* shows. Shows by Blacks as well as whites, about Blacks. True, the sobriquet was a term of opprobrium, but such was the low estate of the coon that coon he had to be and coon he was. The term was considered showbiz parlance for something better than nigger but something not quite as good as colored, which had great respectability at the time, as in the National Association for the Advancement of Colored People. That the era of the minstrel show had come to an end and vaudeville, and then the musical, had replaced it beginning in the 1880s meant that the transformation that was taking place in musical theater was epochal. It was a change that marked, indelibly, the end of the nineteenth century and the beginning of the twentieth.

The shows and the men who created this giant transformation are well documented on the white side. Not so on the Black side. All the books on the origins of American vaudeville and American musical theater that I've come across mention the word "minstrel" as one of the progenitors of vaudeville, along with varied and sundried "others." None of them have an American origin, not even minstrelsy. Blackface minstrelsy is listed as an offshoot in such manner as to completely make inconsequential its mammoth impact. There are numerous excursions into the French and English and Italian origins of vaudeville, even to the point of the etymology of the word itself. How very droll.

There are tons of artists listed who came from Europe and who are credited with having made American vaudeville what it was and what it has become. Lydia

Thompson was one such—an English dancer whose impact was so "huge," according to Robert C. Allen in his book *Horrible Prettiness*, that he constantly refers to the pre-Thompsonian and the post-Thompsonian period. According to Professor Allen, Lydia Thompson is the "figurative mother of Sophie Tucker and Mae West and the grandmother of Bette Midler."[4] Heaven protect us! There isn't the slightest scintilla of an effect from this hugely promoted lady that has had even the most minuscule impact on American vaudeville or American burlesque, which in its earliest forms was skit oriented rather than leg oriented. A brief excerpt from Miss Thompson's "hit" *Ixion*, in which she appears as that dastardly rascal of Greek mythology, will suffice to put to rest the issue of "impact":

JUPITER: Who summons us by journey atmospherical?
Whose bawling has made Juno quite hysterical?
Is this the worm? [Examines Ixion through a telescope]
What means this stupid dolt?
I've half a mind to hurl a thunderbolt.

IXION: Don't be excited, Jupiter, and pray
Apologize for me to Mrs. J;
I feel, before your royal carriage, humble.[5]

In addition to what passed for burlesque in roughneck America circa 1870, there are even some of the big names in acting listed as other examples as progenitors: Edwin Booth (who was, of course, American), Edmund Kean, and Charles Macready (who were both English). But as the Brits would say, their effect was simply a one-off. *No*—it wasn't minstrelsy that was a huge precursor of vaudeville in America. It was *blackface minstrelsy*.

Now, it can be argued that since blackface minstrelsy was coopted by white minstrel men, that gift was more or as much a white one as it was Black. Not so. As I've argued in the previous chapter, it was a Black thing; white performers borrowed and imitated it. But they never had the imagination to turn it into something other than what it was when they stole it. Douglas Gilbert in *American Vaudeville*, in the chapter on "Racial Comics of the Eighties"[6] throws whites in blackface in with all the other racial comics: the Irish, Jewish, German, with no mention of *any* Black performer who in any way had an effect on or was involved with vaudeville whatsoever. But Judy Alter in her slim volume *Vaudeville—the Birth of Show Business*,[7] lists at least 300 Black *headliners* working in vaudeville by 1900 and another 1,500 who were making a living in it as well. That's a huge number when you realize that Blacks couldn't even do blackface before the 1880s.

So where are all these artists in the white annals? And why aren't their contributions elucidated as separate and substantive, especially since it was their music and their imagination that gave vaudeville its life by giving it its American father—the blackface minstrel. They don't exist because the chroniclers of the era don't want them to. Put simply, they're Black; therefore they don't really count. Even Ms. Alter, who giveth, also taketh away. She lists Ira Aldridge, with a picture of him costumed for Shakespeare, as having run a vaudeville house in Philadelphia in 1843! In 1843, he was touring the English provinces and never returned to native land after he left in 1824.

The white producers who owned the major circuits that controlled the business of vaudeville were all racists: Tony Pastor and Benjamin Franklin Keith were the two biggest names. Consequently, Black vaudevillians had to survive through what became known as the "chitlin circuit." Nightclubs, dance halls, church basements, and theaters where they could perform without being arrested or run out of town, where there was a reasonable chance that they would get a hot meal and find a place to sleep for the night. There was a Black-owned vaudeville show that traveled the South from 1900 to 1911. The man who made such a pioneering effort possible was Pat Chapette. His troupe and his show were so popular that a white manager bought it out when he died and continued it until 1950—a full two decades after the official death of vaudeville.

Nathan Hurwitz, in his *A History of the American Musical*, does list Williams and Walker's musicals, offering a nugget that is an excellent representation of Williams's comedic style.[8] But the impact of the Williams and Walker musicals can't be relegated to a passing contribution, because they were more than that. They were the living and breathing exemplars of what was the true American idiom, at a time when the general lament was that the European influence was stifling native creativity.

The inability of white chroniclers of the era to go beyond merely "including" the huge Black activity but actually showing how it helped influence the future of the musical leaves a taste in the mouth of the "inclusion" being simply a nod to the democratic principle that "all men are created," et cetera. Says Hurwitz, "Until the 1914–1919 season American culture tended to be imported or copied from Europe."[9] And specifically, he mentions that "operettas continued to be popular through the twenties" and mentions the two big white names: Rudolph Friml and Sigmund Romberg. But according to Johnson, "In 1906, [Bob] Cole and [Billy] Johnson wrote and appeared in a play called *The Shoefly Regiment* which played . . . on Broadway. In 1908 they came out in another play of their own, *The Red Moon*. Each of these plays was a true operetta with a well-constructed book and a tuneful, well written score. On these two points no Negro musical play has equaled *The Red Moon*. [Cole and Billy Johnson] excelled their great rivals [Williams and Walker] in that . . . their plays . . . were better written and had a younger, sprightlier and prettier chorus."[10]

It's a tale often told of Black culture being lost or ignored and then "rediscovered" a hundred years later, if at all. Scot Joplin is one of the more recent well-known examples, rediscovered after having been "lost" for over three-quarters of a century. The racism of that era is the obvious excuse given for such blatant denial, but now that the climate has improved, the democracy—being a living, vibrant being—corrects itself. To the Black mind, it would be much more living and much more vibrant if it could eventually catch up to the Black achievements at the time of their happening instead of being another case of how justice too long deferred is justice denied. Put another way, the climate is always not "right" for recognition of the next endless step in the Black march forward to full "equality" until a few Black people have been killed or lynched or some new draconian method to shut the door on further "advance" is devised, and we're all shocked that that could happen here in America. At least we used to be.

So there are three issues: the form, be it minstrelsy, vaudeville, or musical comedy, with burlesque thrown in; the music; and the pioneers who created the actual change in the form, in the genre, if you will. That Black vaudeville on its own transformed into the Black musical comedy and entertained white America for close to three decades, there is not the slightest doubt. That Black music—the ragtime, the blues, and jazz—evolved into a syncopated form that made the modern musical possible, there is also not the slightest doubt. Which takes us to the performers, the ones who dominated on Broadway and off during this crucial period beginning in 1890 until, by the end of the twenties, critics began to complain that they were tired of Negro musical comedy. That Black performers contributed to the Americanization of the form, again, there is also not the slightest doubt.

Let's look at the record of these "pioneers" and see what exactly did they give us, following in the footsteps of the unknown ancestors who devised that minstrel tradition way back when down south in Dixie, break the heart of me.

In 1890, a white producer, Sam T. Jack, created *The Creole Show*. In addition to having his actors play without burnt cork, Jack also broke from the minstrel tradition by using a chorus of sixteen beautiful Black girls. It was the first time that Black women had been used in burlesque in place of the traditional all-male chorus. In 1895, John Isham, who sometimes passed for white, produced *The Octoroons*. Isham improved on Jack's model, making the women principals and giving them solos. A year later, he produced *Oriental America*. While the basic model was still the minstrel pattern, Isham ended the show not with burlesque specialties (cakewalks and hoedowns and walk arounds) but with an operatic medley, which consisted of solos and choruses from *Faust, Martha, Rigoletto, Carmen*, and *Il Trovatore*. It was the first Black show to play Broadway proper.

Opening in the same year as *Oriental America* was *Black Patti's Troubadours*. Who was Black Patti, and why was she Black? Her name was Sissieretta Jones, and she was called Black Patti because she had such a remarkable voice that it was deemed that the best compliment that could be paid her was to compare her to the popular opera singer Adelina Patti. She sang for Benjamin Harrison in the White House and was very popular in the South. She had not only talent but bearing and beauty. There were plans to star her at the Met in *Aida* in 1892, but they never materialized. *Troubadours* was not remarkable in its format; it followed the minstrel pattern. Its great attraction was Jones's appearance in the second half, when she sang.[11]

The man hired to write *Troubadours* was Bob Cole, for whom James Weldon Johnson—and indeed, everyone else—has high praise. Cole was twenty-six at the time. Johnson calls him "the most versatile theatrical man the Negro has yet produced."[12] He could sing, dance, play several musical instruments, write a drama or a musical (lyrics and music), stage the play, and act a part. He fell out with the white managers of *Troubadours* during the first year of the run and took all his music and left the show. They sued. In court, he exclaimed, "These men have amassed a fortune from . . . my brain, and now they call me thief; I won't give it up!"[13] Of course, they won.

However, as happens so often, the loss only served to propel him to greater achievement, and in 1898, he produced *A Trip to Coontown*. Forgetting the title, the play was a landmark that racked up the following firsts: It was the first show to break away from the minstrel show format, and the first to be written with continuity of characters developing the plot and story from beginning to end—which made it the first Black musical comedy. In addition, it was the first Black show organized, produced, and managed solely by Black talent. Cole later teamed up with James Weldon Johnson and his brother, J. Rosamond, to write popular songs of the period: "Under the Bamboo Tree" and the Lillian Held hit "The Maiden with the Dreamy Eyes" were two of the more successful ones.

The second show to be produced in 1898 that was significant was *Clorindy, the Origin of the Cakewalk*. Paul Laurence Dunbar, the greatest of the folk poets, wrote the lyrics. Will Marion Cook wrote the music. Cook was another trained musician (he graduated from Oberlin), who studied with Dvorak, Joachim, and others both in Europe and at home. The show was a big hit, in no little measure due to Cook's ability to incorporate Black musical syncopation into the score: "He was the competent composer to take what was then known as ragtime and work it out in a musicianly way. His choruses and finales . . . complete novelties as they were, sung by a lusty chorus, were simply breathtaking. *Broadway had something entirely new*" (italics mine).[14] Remember, this is in 1898.

Says Hurwitz, speaking of the 1914–1915 season, "Musical theatre came most often from Vienna, Paris or London, and most American musicals were adaptations of European pieces or written in the style of European musicals or operettas. In the mid 1910's, however, a unique confluence of events created the perfect environment for the Americanization of the musical theatre."[15] He then says World War I gave America the opportunity to become a power on the world stage, which led, along with our economic clout, to a wave of national pride, which in turn led to Irving Berlin and Jerome Kern. And *that's when the American musical came into its own*. But that dismisses not only Will Marion Cook but Williams and Walker, who had produced four full-fledged musicals on Broadway between 1901–1908, as we shall see.

BLACK PATTI (SISSIERETTA JONES)
THE GREAT SINGER

FIGURE 3.1. Sissieretta Jones, one of the greatest voices of her period, known as the Black Patti after the Italian singer Adelina Patti, at the turn of the century. Schomburg Center for Research in Black Culture, Manuscripts, Archives and Rare Books Division, The New York Public Library Digital Collections.

So by the end of 1908 Black talent had done the following: Abandoned the minstrel pattern that it had originally invented. Made significant steps toward a modern-day musical. Had developed on its own the language for the modern musical by transforming ragtime into syncopation—and this development was *not* taking place obscurely, in some *Blues in the Night* subbasement, but on Broadway for all the world to see and applaud and know about. Given the money these artists were making, there was a lot of applause! But no white critic's or historian's mind could accept that because they were seeing something *new* from Black artists, it could be equal to what white artists were doing. It had to be separate *and* equal newness because, after all, it was *Black newness*.

Hurwitz then makes the case for a dearth of good American musicals from 1900 to 1902, dismissing Williams and Walker, who were selling out in 1901. He quotes from a *New York Times* article that questioned whether musical theater had just been a passing fad—"In the distant future the musical comedy . . . will be found among the 'have beens.' . . . Nearly all agree that this cycle is dead"— and adds his own voice to the need for a change to something that spoke to the American "idiom": "Musical theatre had hit an impasse. . . . National identity had begun to call for voices that spoke a clearly American idiom in America's popular culture."[16] His first candidate for such honors is George M. Cohan, listing the musical that gave Cohan his first Broadway hit, *Little Johnny Jones*, but that was in 1903. Next he mentions Victor Herbert, quoting Herbert's biographer, who said he was "one of the grandfathers of the modern musical theater."[17] He then mentions Williams and Walker, saying they were "the first successful African American team in musical theater,"[18] and that alone is the historical importance of their contribution. But *In Abyssinia* played Broadway in 1903, at the same time that *Little Johnny Jones* did. So whatever it was doing was a lot more than just being an African American contribution to musical theater, and making it separate but equal is not doing it justice.

The other important precursor to Williams and Walker was Ernest Hogan. Hogan starred in the *Clorindy* hit at the Casino Roof in New York, but he's remembered more for having written a song called "All Coons Look Alike to Me" and lived to regret it. Tom Fletcher, in his warmly written autobiography, *100 Years of the Negro in Show Business: The Tom Fletcher Story* (published in 1954), credits Ernest Hogan with fathering jazz, ragtime, and every form of popular music except the blues with this one coon song. While it ruffled a lot of feathers, it also, according to Mr. Hogan, put money into a lot of pockets at a time when business was bad. "Bill Bailey" is an old coon song reworded to remove the offensive term.

The real significance of Fletcher's assertion is, of course, that Black America didn't just give the country and the world jazz, but all the popular music of the twentieth century as well. Yet when the Emmy's are held annually, Black musicians don't get a leg up because Black talent invented and created hip-hop and rap; it's everybody's music. When Black America is singled out, it's for the violence in the ghetto, not the horn of plenty overflowing with flowers, fruit, and corn that have been our artistic gifts, greedily coopted by an unappreciative culture since the first white blackface minstrel man played a "genuine nigger."

The gifts notwithstanding, and even though the various Bob Coles and Will Marion Cooks and the several men named Johnson and the rest were "breaking" this new ground, a lot of what was being praised as "a bold new step forward," circa 1900, was still, by the standards of 118 years later, objectionable, if not degrading. Sterling Brown has observed that "the blackface tradition succeeded in fixing one stereotype deep in the American consciousness: the shiftless, lazy, . . . loud-mouthed . . . Negro . . . over addicted to the eating of watermelon and chicken, the drinking of gin and the shooting of dice."[19] At another point, he quotes this line from Dunbar's *Clorindy* script to show how the stereotype continued to live on, even in the hands of Black writers: "Don't you know dere's no sich word in the dictionnumgary as perskivered . . . I's got de best edjumingation."[20] A detailed reading of the material of the period will yield other such examples.

Nevertheless, in spite of having to swallow their pride in carrying the demeaning label of "coon," these tough, full-fledged professionals were laughing all the way to the bank and creating an urban professionalism that had never existed before in Black theater—a tradition of artists who worked with one another whenever it was possible. Sissieretta Jones had gotten to the point where she lived in a style and manner that indicated she was anything but a coon. Her private train was a thirty-thousand-dollar railroad car fitted out with golden upholstery and hand-carved pianos. Eubie Blake as a youngster ran errands for her company. He recalls that a red carpet was laid on the sidewalk from the stage door to the taxi every time she came and went from the theater.

Loften Mitchell in his *Black Drama* was not particularly impressed with any of this "progress" on the part of his confreres. Says he of Williams and Walker's contribution, and indeed the entire contribution of these musical comedy pioneers, they put such a high price on succeeding on the big stage where white audiences would see them that they sold themselves out cheaply in the end. Because when Broadway theater was tired of them, they were not only thrown over but in fact sent packing in segregation, if not in flagrante, to Harlem, where they were kept in strict confinement for the next seven years. Said he, "Bert Williams, George Walker . . . and others were doomed to disappointment, tragedy, and eventual failure. They hitched their wagons to the wrong star. They set out, not believing they were really human beings. They set out justifying their existence, and their new and revolutionary concepts were geared to getting acceptance by those who laughed at them in the first place and hated them violently."[21]

The facts of the matter are true enough; whether the consequences are is another matter. I doubt if any of these inestimable gentlemen and ladies did not think of themselves as "human beings." That the gods of theater in New York and beyond learned in part what it meant to put on a show that was not blackface minstrelsy (but something called musical comedy, American style) from these very same Black artists whom Mitchell condemns for their achievement because they fell prey to racism in the end seems unimaginable as an indictment coming from so esteemed a critic. It's almost like saying Jackie Robinson and all the great athletes who followed shouldn't have left the Negro leagues to seek integration since Bud Selig outsourced the Black ballplayer in the seventies to the Spanish-speaking Caribbean, and now Black representation has gone from an all-time high that saw the world champion Pittsburgh Pirates of 1971 field a team entirely of Black and Latino players to the present-day representation of no more than one or two players on *some* teams. Cultural isolation would be a death knell for Black America in the present era of the internet, and if Mitchell were alive today, he'd probably have to agree. In addition, to not have the ambition, to say nothing of the courage, to succeed on the big stage because in the end segregation will inevitably rear its ugly head is to create a self-fulfilling prophecy of failure.

One consequence of Mitchell's displeasure, however, is to reinforce how huge was the work of these musical pioneers, how brilliantly they forged ahead and helped found a new theatrical language that the whole world has since enjoyed. Which is not to say that the American musical didn't benefit from European operetta. It did, and George M. Cohan was creating his massive input of strictly American musicals in the midst of the operetta craze. But that still leaves the question of why the Black contributions of the aforementioned artists weren't also helping to "form" the American tradition as opposed to just being "what the Negroes did."

BERT WILLIAMS

Williams was born in the Bahamas to Bahamian parents and grandparents. Where he was born is significant (it's often been attributed erroneously to Antigua), since the fact of his not being a Black American is important in understanding the man himself. He started out in natural face, just strumming a guitar and singing. That proved not to be a very successful act. When he teamed up with Walker, they continued to struggle, searching for the right combination that would click with an audience. When Walker became the dandy who had all the fun at Williams's expense, *they found it.* The comedian who went on to fame and fortune was born when he added the cork. It was not something he assumed would be his iron mask (once put on, never taken off). Like Al Jolson, it transformed him. Behind the mask, he suddenly became, in becoming someone else, very funny. They flipped a coin to settle the billing. Bert won the toss and they remained, thereafter until Walker's death, Williams and Walker.

That the cork was all-important to top white comedians as well as Black ones deserves a passing comment. Jolson and his ilk had a choice. They didn't have to put it on, but the device was as instrumental to their success, once they did put it on, as it was to Williams's. Certainly to Jolson's, for even after he had risen to the top, he clung to it for most of the twenties. Says Alan Churchill in *The Theatrical Twenties*, in a caption of Jolson grinning in blackface, white lips and all, "The great

FIGURE 3.2. Bert Williams without the cork. © The New York Public Library.

Jolie still felt unaccountably shy before audiences and liked to appear in blackface until his epochal movie debut in 1927,"[22] in *The Jazz Singer*, where he still played it half-and-half. Eddie Cantor was another famous corker. It was more than a nod to tradition, more than a continuation of the gimmick to degrade the Black man and get the instant guffaw that warmed up a white audience. It was, incredulous as it seems, a means to access the performer's emotions and make him funny. That was what made it so crucial to Jolson and Cantor and why Bert Williams clung to it to his dying day.

A point needs to be made again about the prevalence of cork as an instrumental part of a show business performer's equipment. We have to remember that the blackface minstrel show was, in a sense, more important to white performers than to Black simply because the blackface minstrel show was the only real game in town for what passed for a musical throughout most of the nineteenth century. America had nothing else in the early days that quite matched it in popularity. American musical theater may have been having fun making Black people look absurd by caricaturing the specifics of their facial characteristics, but they were doing a lot more than that. They were "entertaining" themselves the only way they really knew how, irrespective of whatever else was going on, on the American musical stage, at the time that was home grown. That's why cork was so important to Jolson and Cantor and their ilk; it was quite simply the basis of their theatrical language. Dan Emmett and the other white minstrel troupes weren't touring Europe and making a killing because they were offering an entertainment that would only appeal to Georgia Peckerwoods. If that's all it was, doing it on the Continent wouldn't have been worth the price of the trip over. It was one of the ultimate gifts that we gave, and when the country no longer needed it, it was only remembered as a nigger joke of the past, because we were too embarrassed to admit that it was anything else.

Williams reached the point where he knew what he wanted. Not having been raised in the South, he never wanted to play there again after a disastrous experience. He and Walker were cornered in a town near El Paso by a mob, where they were undressed, forced to put on potato sacks, and then chased because the local gentry disapproved of how well they were dressed. Both men had married by 1900. Walker's wife, Ada Overton, was a dancer and singer and one of the leading ladies of the company. Bert's wife, Lottie, also a trooper, stayed on the boards for seven years, making both Continental tours. By 1900, they had found the right formula for the kind of show that would not only put them in the forefront but also take them out of the business, once and for all, of doing "coon shows."

This show was *The Sons of Ham*. It had two drawbacks as far as Blacks were concerned: Bert was by now fully committed to the burnt cork at a time when many Blacks thought that they were beginning to see the end of it, and the title was also considered a put-down, since Ham was responsible for all those terrible things that happened to all those good people in the Bible and was sent to Africa as punishment. But the show ran for two years. Jesse Shipp, a writer who already had a reputation by then, worked with them on the story, which concerned a case of mistaken identity and a fortune for two lost heirs in, of all places, Denver, Colorado. The team was really on its way now. Bert might have been in cork, but this was no coon show; it was an actual musical all the way. No second-half cakewalk, no breakdown or the like, but a complete story from beginning to end. Of course, most of the time was spent on the gags, which the two of them meticulously developed as the work progressed, but isn't that how the Marx Brothers became famous?

FIGURE 3.3. Bert Williams and George Walker as they appeared offstage in the five years they reigned on Broadway, 1903–1908. Photographs and Prints Division, Schomburg Center for Research in Black Culture, The New York Public Library.

And as soon as *Sons of Ham* was finished, they were ready and waiting with the sequel. It was called *In Dahomey*, and it was Walker's brainchild. He knew that the plantation had been worked to death, and audiences were ready for something else. He decided to reach back into Africa, not only in order to present something new and exotic but as a point of race pride. Said he prior to the show's opening, "Managers gave little credit to the ability of Black people on

Black Dance in Photographs

*images from the mid-nineteenth
century to the present*

Schomburg Center for Research in Black Culture
The New York Public Library
Astor, Lenox & Tilden Foundations

515 Lenox Avenue
New York, NY 10037

April 8—May 28, 1982

George & Ada Walker
Photograph by Hall Studios, New York, 1905

FIGURE 3.4. George and Ada Overton Walker in a romantic moment of Black Dance ca. 1905. Art and Artifacts Division, Schomburg Center for Research in Black Culture, The New York Public Library.

the stage before the native African element was introduced. All that was expected of a colored performer was singing, dancing and a little storytelling, but as for acting, no one credited a Black person with the ability to act."[23] He went even further in a later interview, castigating the slapstick bandana school of acting as a lot of rot that ought to die out, and he hoped to kill it. After seven months on the road, the show opened at the New York Theater at Fifty-Ninth Street and Broadway.

They chose Dahomey as the setting because they had worked briefly with Dahomeans when they were just starting out in San Francisco. What was finally produced, with the help of not only Jesse Shipp but Will Marion Cook and Paul Laurence Dunbar as well, was their biggest hit to date. The plot ended up being another version of *Sons of Ham*. This time, they begin in Boston, where some schemers pretend to want to colonize land in Africa to help poor Blacks. They try to get a wealthy old Black man in Florida to finance the scheme, just so they can abscond with the money. Williams got raves. *Theater* magazine, not given to panegyrics, dubbed him "a vastly funnier man than any white comedian now on the American stage,"[24] though seating in the theater was still segregated.

They toured England in the same year, 1903, and become the toast of the London stage when they were asked to give a command performance at Buckingham Palace. Audiences packed the theater, and dukes and duchesses entertained Williams in their clubs and homes. After they sold out in London, they toured the rest of England and Scotland, doing shows in all the major cities. Williams tells one of the funnier stories that took place when Jesse Shipp mistook the king for the head butler: His Majesty had politely inquired if Shipp found anything wrong with the English way of doing things, and Jesse replied by unleashing such a torrent of complaints that it forced the royal personage to retreat hastily!

After a year away and all that lavish praise and royal treatment, they did not, however, return home to a warm reception. The bookings were good, but the only royal reception that they were invited to was a garden party given by Booker T. Washington. But with the success of *In Dahomey*, there was no more hesitation about where they were going and what they wanted to do. They had both direction and a formula, and the next show would double the magnificence of *In Dahomey*. It was to be totally African, according to Walker's plan. That meant that "live jungle animals would have to be purchased. Williams was willing to go along with the idea for expanding the cast, but he drew the line at hiring tigers and giraffes." They finally compromised on live camels, "but contortionists and acrobats would be costumed to imitate the other animals."[25]

The new show was called *In Abyssinia*, and it opened in 1908 at the Majestic Theater on Columbus Circle and Fifty-Eighth Street—bigger and better main stem. *In Abyssinia* did make money, but as Mitchell reports, it was troublesome to the critics: "They liked it, but they stated bluntly that it was a little 'too arty.' It was too Caucasian, some critics said, too serious. In other words, they wanted a fast-moving 'darky show,' but the work was highly successful, and after its New York run, it toured."[26] In spite of the critics' reservations about *In Abyssinia* being "too arty," the fact of its mere existence meant it was doing the very same thing that Hurwitz praises Cohan, Berlin, and Kern for doing: creating an authentic American voice. *Vanity Fair* said of *In Dahomey*, "[It] sets a pace for white comedians to follow in an entire absence of slapstick comedy and in a strict regard for only niceties in funmaking."[27] So with its departure from the "darky show," *In Abyssinia* may be one of the first musicals to anticipate the shows that became what we now think of as a Broadway musical: those of Rodgers and Hart, Cole Porter, Oscar Hammerstein II.

Williams and Walker's next show (which would be their last), *Bandanna Land*, actually outdid all the previous ones, not only in lavishness of production but also in the importance of the statement it made. *Bandanna Land* satirized the "Negro Scare" racket. In the show, Williams and Walker decide on a quick way to make money. They buy up land in a well-to-do white section and move into one of the houses. They then proceed to raise hell by giving a number of parties. The whites immediately agree to buy back the land at twice the amount they paid. It takes no genius to see what they were doing: putting issues that addressed the real lives that Black people lived before a Broadway audience, not just the grinning and giving everyone a laugh in the context of a race-neutral world that has never existed in this country, not ever.

The two African shows, *In Dahomey* and *In Abyssinia* were, of course, about as African as Tarzan. The homeland motif, for all of George's good intentions, was only window dressing at best, a mere device to give them an excuse to do their thing—what the audience really came to see: Walker making a fool out of woeful Bert in one fast skit after another.

When Jolson opened on Broadway in 1922, in a show called *Bombo*, he went on in blackface because, as I've said, his natural face didn't give him the confidence he needed to be "Joli." When he abandoned it in his films, as Mr. Churchill says, "His roles were serious, his acting wooden."[28] So in order to give himself a character who had an excuse for being in cork, he found a story about a cabin boy (Bombo) in Christopher Columbus's voyage to the New World. He was forty-two

FIGURE 3.5. Hattie McIntosh, George Walker, Ada Overton Walker, Bert Williams, and Lottie Williams performing cakewalk in the Broadway production of *In Dahomey*, ca. 1903–1904. Collections of the New York Public Library.

at the time! Since cabin boys can come in all colors, he's a neegrow one. The story was so thin that some nights, he actually stopped the show in the middle, sent the actors home, and sat on the stage in his white lips and grease and sang to the audience, and he opened at *Jolson's* theater, built and owned by the Shuberts. Why was Jolson such a big hit? One reason: He could sing "Mammy" in blackface and everyone loved it. Don't ask anyone Black if that made him a hit; you might not like the answer.

After Mr. Churchill shows how besotted he is with Joli, he makes short shrift of not only Williams but all the other Black actors and shows that helped make the twenties what it was—Paul Robeson, Charles Gilpin, the musical *Shuffle Along*—relegating them to line items. As for jazz, it's mentioned only as an Irving Berlin contribution to Broadway! He even makes it appear as if Bert didn't produce two shows of his own during the decade. And he goes even further and states that George White created the Charleston and the Black bottom. Says he, "White's great contribution to the Twenties would be the dances Charleston and Black Bottom, both of which he claimed to originate."[29] With that bit of clever disingenuousness, Mr. Churchill puts himself at the top of the list of racist appropriators. It's obvious he knows that George White didn't originate either the Charleston or the Black bottom any more than he invented hoppin' john, which is why he says White "claims" he originated them, but he's not about to give Black Black's due, no matter what. The number of people and songs, all Black, who have been given credit for both dances are too numerous to mention. For the curious, I suggest you simply go online and look it up.

Churchill's book runs over three hundred pages, with half of them given over to pictures. There isn't one picture of a Black artist anywhere in it—with the exception, of course, of a production shot of *Porgy*. But Hollywood did him one better; Universal produced a film in 1930 about jazz, titled *King of Jazz*. Who was this king of Jazz? Paul Whiteman! And what instrument did the king play? The violin! But in the film, all he does is wave a baton! And how do they show the birth of that blues? They make it into a cartoon with the bloated Mr. Whiteman blowing a trumpet while his pants fall down.

With the close of *Bandanna Land*, we come to the end of a short-lived but eventful era. The show had the whole team together for the last time: Ada, Lottie, Will Marion Cook's chorus, Jesse Shipp's books and lyrics, but most of all, for the last time, George and Bert, Williams and Walker. George had gone to the Shuberts by now for backing, so *Bandanna Land* had the prestige, in addition to that of opening in New York in a first-run house, also that of touring in first-class theaters out of New York in the Shubert circuit: the Savoy in Atlantic City and the Belasco in Washington, DC, which were pioneering moves in their own way. It may seem trivial years later to make much of getting into a good regional theater after having opened in four successive hits in New York, with at least three of them in a legitimate Broadway house, but the fact is that as late as 1947, Blacks could not perform on the stage of certain theaters in the nation's capital, and they couldn't get a seat as a paying customer in other states. In still others, they could not be employed in any capacity whatsoever. That Byzantine racism is part of the history that helps account for the who gets credit as "the first nigger to cross the Triboro Bridge in a panel truck" syndrome.

There was no penicillin to cure syphilis in 1908. Top white stars, such as Tony Hart of Harrigan and Hart, were victims of the disease, and so was George Walker. By the beginning of 1909, with *Bandanna Land* still going strong, he was stuttering and stammering onstage, and drifting. His wife had to take over the part. George went home to Lawrence, Kansas, and he was dead within two years, never to go on the boards again. Williams and Walker left a legacy, and one of the most endearing aspects of it was their lasting friendship and their ability to work together successfully. George Walker and Bert Williams were able, down to the very end, not only to trust each other completely but to never have an argument over money. And for the two years that George lay dying, Bert split everything he made fifty-fifty and sent George his share so Walker did not want for anything as the end drew near.

Even more remarkable was the fact that the two men were so very much unalike, and as success came, they lived quite different lifestyles and saw less and less of each other off the stage. But the partnership remained. Bert trusted George completely and simply left all the money matters to him and that was that. And it worked. Bert liked his small, intimate groups of friends, his large collection of books. He captained a softball team on Sundays and took up boxing with Joe Gans as his coach, the onetime lightweight champion, which came in handy when he had to knock a manager, Abe Erlanger, on his proverbial derriere after Erlanger had been too aggressive in "showing" Bert how he wanted a boxing match played in a show Erlanger was producing. George, ever the dresser (and he did for a well-made suit what Josephine Baker did for a smile)—the dandy, if you will—had a long list of liaisons, which included Eva Tanguay the "I Don't Care Girl." He lived in the limelight, basked in it. Was always on the avenue, at Jimmy Marshall's hotel—the famous rendezvous on Fifty-Third Street where the Black showbiz crowd had moved to from Ike Hines's (which Tom Fletcher talks about so affectionately in his book) in the Tenderloin. The Marshall attracted the likes of Lillian Russell and Diamond Jim Brady as well as top Black entertainers, because they knew that if they wanted to meet Williams or Walker or their ilk, they had to go to Black-owned Marshall's to do it.

From the stage of the theater on the night that Bert closed *Bandanna Land*, he read aloud a letter from George, adding that his one wish was to have his partner back. But of course, he never would. Bert depended on George emotionally as well as for his business acumen and in fact was never able to create the magic of their full-fledged musicals without him. Bert's successes after 1909 (he worked for another thirteen years) were to come mostly in the Ziegfeld's *Follies*, in solo performances, and in skits where he teamed up with Leon Errol, Eddie Cantor and W. C. Fields and others, and in the two shows that he produced himself. The combination of the loss of Walker plus the trauma of unconscionable racism that he was faced with once he left the security of being the star of an entire Black company that created its own space as it moved about has been offered by many who were there as the chief cause of his early death at the age of forty-seven. He did have legitimate health problems—poor circulation and pneumonia—but he also contracted serious isolation and severe heartbreak. His wife devoted her life to him for those thirteen years, and he had all the comforts that money could buy, but he was a man without a context by then, and that fact killed him as much or perhaps more than any other.

In 1918, he went to West Baden, Indiana, to be treated at a sanitarium run by a well-known Black masseur named Waddy. Williams was there under a doctor's care for two weeks. Part of the therapy was bicycle riding. He was cycling down a country road on the sanitarium's new bicycle when a local sheriff stopped him and demanded to know where he had stolen the bicycle. Williams, of course, explained himself, but the man refused to believe him and confiscated the bicycle, and Bert had to walk back to the sanitarium like a condemned thief, even if in his heart, he knew he wasn't.

When Actors Equity went on strike in 1919, everyone in the *Follies* supported it after months of discussion. Everyone except Bert Williams. Why? Because no one even told him that they were on strike! He showed up to go on one night and found the theater dark. He didn't know what to make of it. Up on the roof, he found actors sitting around. They told him they were on strike and "hoped he was with them." His reply was that he would've been *if he had known about it.* Then he went home, sat down at a table with nine empty chairs, and held a vote: whether to strike or not. The vote was a tie.

Without George, Bert tried a new show, *Mr. Lode of Koal.* But the magic wasn't there, and it closed in six months. In May of 1910, Williams signed with Ziegfeld. It was in one sense a step up for Black show business. The *Follies* were already a first-class act before 1910 and the *Follies* of 1910 cost $50,000 to produce and had more than sixty chorus girls. Singer Anna Held, Ziegfeld's first wife, gave him the idea for the show, using her experience from the *Follies Bergère* with its tradition of pretty girls scantily clad. Fanny Brice was also in the cast that boasted 125. Williams was an immediate success in this lineup of the best white talent of the day. The year 1911 was an even better one for him. "Woodman, Spare That Tree—the Only One My Wife Can't Climb" was a big hit. As was his poker game pantomime, which became a classic. His sketch with Leon Errol caused the reviewer for the *New York Evening Mail* to cry, "Bert Williams makes the need of a White Hope on the Jardin de Paris stage as imperative as Jack Johnson did in the squared ring."[30]

Bert stayed for 1912 as well but the work wasn't satisfying and the material was inferior to what he had been able to do in the days when he and George worked together, so he took a year off in 1913. When he returned in '14, Ziggy had moved to bigger and better quarters, the New Amsterdam. Bert stayed for four straight years. The material never improved consistently, and his continuing isolation had become quite severe by then. His last *Follies* show was in 1919. He put together his own review, *Broadway Brevities*, in 1920. It did fairly well. The next year he did a comedy called *The Pink Slip* with an all-white cast, and he felt bad that he was too sick to stay in the show because it meant "[his] children," as he called the actors he was employing, would be out of work. He collapsed onstage on Saturday, February 25, 1922. On the fourth of March, also a Saturday, he was dead. As the *New York Age* reported, "From last Sunday morning until Wednesday afternoon, people in every walk of life, irrespective of race, creed or color, paid homage to one who, during his life, helped to drive away dull care and worry with his original, quaint humor. Always clean and at no time suggestive of ridicule."[31]

Much has been written about Williams, both before and after his death, especially about how good he was when he was in the *Follies* as opposed to how good he had been before. Heywood Broun, that inestimable drama critic and one of the denizens of the Algonquin Round Table, had some not-too-flattering observations to make about his *Follies* work. This, in turn, led Ring Lardner, the famed sportswriter, to take up the cudgels in Williams's defense. Said Lardner, "The people who wrote the Williams and Walker show knew how to write for Bert—the Follies people didn't. And he was under the impression, the delusion, that Follies audiences were drawn by scenery and legs and didn't want to laugh. He used to say, 'I'm just out there to give the gals time to change.'"[32] Speaking about his dancing, Mr. Lardner says, "If you'd seen him just dance in the old days, you'd have pronounced him both 'comedian' and 'clown' as well as the champion eccentric 'hoofer' of all time. But to judge Bert by Bert in the Follies! Well sir, you might as well Judge Babe Ruth's pitching on his 1920–21 showing with the Yankees."[33] Lardner even praised him for his singing, calling him a natural musician and masterly singer. And he tops it off by crowning Bert as the greatest comedian he ever saw.

Broun, on the other hand, was not so sure. He had to wrestle with the question of which one was the real Bert Williams in making his final judgment of the man as artist, pre-*Follies* Bert or *Follies* Bert. He had seen Williams in only one pre-*Follies* show, *In Abyssinia*, and said that in that show, Williams had been a different man. In his column "It Seems to Me," he gets to the heart of what it meant for Williams to stay in the cork:

> Bert Williams found prosperity and success in the theatre, but his high talents were largely wasted. . . . Color was a factor, but not the only one, which led to his downfall. . . . Since he was Negro, he must be a funny man. . . . Somehow or other laughing at Bert Williams came to be tied up in people's minds with liberalism, charity and the Thirteenth Amendment. . . . [Williams] did "have a gift" in which he was supreme. . . . No man in the theatre of our day could tell a story as well. . . . Bert Williams never told a story as a comic anecdote. By voice and pantomime, he lifted it to the stature of a true [narrative] built for us by a tall man, his face clownishly blackened with burnt cork, who stood still, in the centre of the stage and used no gesture which traveled more than six inches.[34]

Was Bert Williams not really just a clown, not really a vaudeville comic, but a raconteur so gifted that he could transform storytelling into theater? If so, did he not have it in him to take his talent to the next level and become a serious actor? Fellow actor David Belasco certainly thought he had it. He offered Bert the chance to do a play of their own choosing that Belasco would direct and produce. Why didn't Williams take him up on it? He spent thirteen years in the *Follies* just being funny. But as Ring Lardner points out, he thought he was just there to "give the gals time to change." Which meant that the *Follies* years were wasted years in his mind. Some of what he went through during those nine years, as discussed, might help give us an answer.

Whether it does or not, if we put his inability to take that next step—that transition from storyteller to actor—into the larger context of the deadening racist comments of the critics of *In Abyssinia*, we have a clearer view of the iron wall of oppression that faced him. Critics complained that it was too elaborate, had a grand opera style that fitted neither the education nor temperament of Blacks, and wanted them to go back to the plantation melodies for which they were more suited. Others resented seeing Blacks copying white styles when they could get the real thing from white actors. Some were astonished that there was hardly a trace of "negroism" in the play. One reason for the critics' displeasure was the stark contrast between the royal palaces regally caparisoned that Bert wanders, ragged, in and out of during the show and the general condition that most Black Americans lived in at the time.

Critics of *Mr. Lode of Koal* went even further. He was praised for his "apparent spontaneous," "unpremeditated" humor. Always a sign that they think the Black actor can't think and is only good when he's just being a "nigger." A Chicago critic even said that Bert's hands and feet were really his! Oh, my gosh. A Boston reviewer went him one better: he thought the show's flimsiness and lack of structure were actually attributes because "when we succumb to the surreptitious desire for the broad tang of 'nigger' humor, we want no disturbing atom of intelligence busy-bodying about." So he knew what the critics wanted and what the white audiences wanted and he knew how hard he had worked to survive American racism and become a comic miracle—*in blackface*. Blackface gave him the courage to go out on a stage. Did he dare do it naked, in his own face? Apparently not! Many an actor has wrestled with the problem of self-imposed typecasting that they can't break free from, in reality or onstage—Tyrone in *Long Day's Journey*, both in reality and onstage, being probably the most famous example. It was this sort of exclusion that led W. C. Fields to say, "Bert Williams was the funniest man I ever saw, and the saddest man I ever knew."[35]

He had said often that he wanted to show both the serious side and the comic side of the Black character but, as he pit it, the audience only wanted the comic side. The issue of how and why a man can or can't change who he has become even when fame and power and money give him the unchallenged opportunity to do so can be argued extensively, although I suspect to no avail. Belasco had made his offer to do a serious play with Bert firm by the time Charles Gilpin had opened in Eugene O'Neill's *Emperor Jones*. So Bert could see with his own eyes the new horizons. Gilpin in no small way helped establish the young O'Neill as a bona fide Broadway playwright (O'Neill had gotten his first "White Way" break with *Beyond the Horizon*, but it was *Emperor Jones* that really established him) with his superb performance as Brutus Jones. Williams could also see in *Shuffle Along* where the new musicals were going, and he could certainly sit back and smile, reflecting on how much he had helped. But instead, he was riddled with regret and self-doubt.

Not only could he not take the fateful step and discard the mask and show the world Bert Williams, sans cork; he couldn't even, in cork, be the great man of theater that he was because the world of theater didn't want him to be anything but funny. It didn't want to have to deal with his existence beyond the cork because it didn't want to. But it was all right for Jolson to drop it. In London, before the Buckingham Palace performance was about to take place, a group of white friends from New York had gone over to lend moral support. They cornered him in Piccadilly Circus and told him he couldn't appear before the Royal Family in cork; that they, the king and queen, wouldn't understand it. Whether they were embarrassed for themselves as Americans is not possible to tell from this distance. They obviously felt some discomfort that went beyond just doing good ole Bert a favor. But Bert, for good reasons or bad of his own, didn't, probably couldn't, listen to the advice.

The young man who had taken his banjo and put it under his arm and with no discernibly big talent, either as singer or as a strummer, gone out into the world to become an entertainer finally had to realize that the world didn't want him. The world only wanted, indeed had an insatiable need for, another face hidden within him—another persona, one that he didn't even know existed before his coon shows days and *The Sons of Ham*. When he had to spend the next twenty years perfecting this stranger—until the stranger became his only artistic reality—it meant he had to also deny the man beneath the mask of cork until that man no longer existed. He'd sold himself for fame's fleeting embrace, but it was much more of a martyrdom than a desertion of principle. A distance had been traveled, a burden had been laid down never to be borne again.

After Bert Williams, there were no more "real coons" or black Daddy Rice's suffering under the insistence that that was what the audience would pay for so that was what they had to be given. Cantor held on to it long after Bert's death, and it survived in *Tom* shows but it was the end of an era that began in 1828. Call it an era of 105 years. And when Bert died, it died with him, even though it may have been alive after his death, in somewhat the same way that the nineteenth century sputtered on after 1899. So Bert and blackface went together. A marriage born in heaven and hell had destroyed both Romeo and Juliet. The last scene belongs to his wife.

When he had played Scotland during the European tour, Williams had been admitted into the organization of Masons. Now their blackface costume was a very specific affair. No part of the actual skin of the performer was ever shown. Except for the whites of his eyes, every performer, Black or white, covered all other white-nesses and most blacknesses in the bargain. The suit was usually a black one, with a white shirt and black tie. A so-called golliwog wig was used to cover the natural hair of the actor, Black or white, male or female. The black paint took care of the skin around and on the face, ears, neck, including the eyebrows and except for the lips; the latter were smeared with white greasepaint. There was one thing left: the hands. They were always covered with white gloves. When I was in Lon-don in 1973, I saw a blackface minstrel show, and everything that I have just described was still all intact, right down to the white gloves.

Lottie had always been saddened by the fact that no one ever saw Bert's hands, because as she put it, they were such beautiful hands, gentle and soft and very expressive. The Masons arranged for the funeral, and while the preparations were being made, they dressed him according to their tradition. Lottie rushed over in the midst of this and yelled, "Oh please, don't put those gloves on him. Once—this last time, let his hands be seen."[36] But by an ironic twist of fate, the Masonic Order's ritual for burial *also* calls for the wearing of white gloves! And so even in death, Bert Williams couldn't show the color of his hands.

Between 1918 and 1921, Williams's records were taking up a full page in Columbia's catalog, and they were among the strongest-selling songs of the age. At a time when 10,000 sales was considered a very successful major label release, Wil-liams had four songs that shipped between 180,000 and 250,000 copies in 1920 alone. He was, along with Al Jolson and Nora Bayes, one of the three most highly paid recording artists in the world at the time. So much money and so much fame for being a "blackface" Black man. Robeson and Gilpin, in their Broadway appear-ances, never appeared in any but their own faces, so they never knew the Gorgon that was cork. But Bert knew it.

There are inner demons and outer ones. When they collide, the effect can drown ambition. How often before and since the advent of Bert Williams has the Black artistic reality had to face those twin demons? How many poets have lost their rhyme, how many voices have been silenced by the sad realization that the artist, who can only really live when he lives for who he is, had to die in despair because he knew that in the land of his birth, his real self was illegitimate, illegal, a cultural taboo—not allowed to live, by either outright rejection or severe and violent attack, if he dared to show him in his true existential reality?

4 · THE TWENTIES
Roaring—a Precursor

The twenties was a great decade for theater, and the live performance, the act, the spoken word continued its ascendancy almost to the end of the thirties. Before we get into the excitement, the drama, the legends that all came out of the thrilling pages of the Jazz Age, the Roaring Twenties, the Harlem Renaissance, let's pause for a moment. Let's contemplate the Black man's, and woman's and child's, odyssey to this momentous moment in time, when they would see more musicals of their creation that they starred in, produced, and wrote flourish on the Great White Way, and more Black stars perform brilliantly in leading roles, than they had ever thought possible just a few years before. Indulge me.

We have to begin with the events that led to the creation of the Black Harlem of the twenties, which in turn led to the creation of an abundance of theatrical life in Harlem. Let's start with the riots of 1900 that chased Black Manhattan north of the Park and into unchartered territory—into Harlem, which used to be spelled with two *a*'s and where Oscar Hammerstein I and his ilk rode in splendid horse-drawn carriages up and down Seventh Avenue—built for style with two lanes and a green-lawned island in the middle. Hammerstein's Harlem Opera House, on 125th Street, had an Italian marble balcony and a staircase that truly belonged in an "opera house." The seats were blue, and the boxes were three levels high. This is the unwelcoming environment that Blacks running for their lives from Manhattan south of the Park had to "invade" for survival's sake. It only ended up with their creating a flowering of Black theater the likes of which the city had never seen. Funny. No matter how hard they tried, they couldn't kill the Black spirit, because it just refused to die—like Sisyphus who kept rolling that ole rock up the hill no matter how many times they pushed it back down.

What started the 1900 riot took place on the corner of Eighth Avenue and Forty-First Street, where Arthur Harris left his wife on an August night, momentarily, to buy a cigar. He came back to find her struggling against a white man who had her in an iron grip. Harris took on the man, who struck him over the head with a club. At which point Harris took a pocketknife and stabbed the man. The wound proved fatal and the man turned out to be a policeman in plain clothes, and very popular. So after they buried the policeman and they couldn't find Harris, who'd taken off for self-preservation,

a mob of several thousands raged up and down Eighth Avenue . . . and into the side streets. Negroes were seized wherever they were found and brutally beaten. . . . When Negroes ran to policemen for protection, even begging to be locked up for safety, they were thrown back to the mob. The police themselves beat many Negroes as cruelly as the mob. An intimate friend was one of those who ran to the police for protection; he received such a clubbing at their hands that he had to be taken to the hospital to have his scalp stitched in several places. It was a beating from which he never fully recovered. During the height of the riot the cry went out "get Ernest Hogan and Williams and Walker and Cole and Johnson."[1]

But 1900 was just the beginning of two decades of an orgy of race riots, all started against the Black race, which culminated in the Red Summer of 1919, ending with the Elaine Arkansas Massacre, where over 237 Black people were murdered against only five white people killed. For seven years, from 1910 to 1917, Black Manhattan stayed north of 110th Street once they found a home there, in order to stay alive.

So what was the result of this forced migration north? Quite simply, it was a boon to Black cultural life. All of the brilliant activity in theater that had been created for and served to entertain white Manhattan exclusively was now made abundant in its plentitude for Black New York in Harlem! Not only could "Black" go to the theater without fear of being beaten to death or segregated into the balcony, if he was even seated in the first place, but he was now made welcome, indeed solicited to be an audience for *Black theater*, for *Black people*, by *Black people*. And the flowering was prolific. Says Johnson, "[The Black performer] found himself freed from a great many restraints and taboos that had cramped him for forty years. In all those years he had been constrained to do a good many things that were distasteful because managers felt they were things that would please white folks. Likewise, he was forbidden to do some other things because managers feared they would displease white folks. . . . The taboo against [Black] lovemaking [unless it was] broadly burlesqued . . . had been one of the most strictly observed."[2]

In short order, Black theater—that is, serious, legitimate theater—sprung up out of the pavement of Seventh Avenue and Lenox Avenue, between 132nd Street and 135th Street. Two stock companies led the way, taking their names from the theaters they occupied: the Lafayette Players and the Lincoln. They had a repertory that consisted mainly of downtown successes: *Madame X*, *The Servant in the House*, *On Trial*, *The Love of Choo Chin*, *Within the Law*, *The Count of Monte Cristo*, *Dr. Jekyll and Mr. Hyde*. There was even a creditable production of *Othello*. All this activity required talent, and the names of the "new breed" that not only would become Harlem favorites but would be trained, ready, and able to prove their mettle when the time came to reemerge south of the Park were Anita Bush, Inez Clough, Abbie Mitchell, Evelyn Ellis, Edna Thomas, Charles Gilpin, Frank Wilson, Clarence Muse, and Jack Carter, and that's not a complete list.

But white Manhattan had gotten used to being entertained by Black show business, so when a former member of the Williams and Walker team, J. Lubrie Hill, wrote and produced a musical called *Darktown Follies* in 1913, and it got good citywide press, it suddenly became popular to come "uptown" to see what all the fuss was about. The finale to the first act was a showstopper, with "genuine love-making between a Black tenor and a bronze soubrette," and a new dance craze, Ballin' the Jack, came out of it. Ziegfeld came to see and bought that first act finale in its entirety and put it into his *Follies*; it became one of his biggest hits. By 1917, it was safe to go back below 110th Street again, but not in large numbers. And that brings us full circle. Almost.

All the plays that were being done at the Lafayette and the Lincoln were, of course, white. However, three one-act plays of Black life, written by white writer Ridgely Torrence, were performed with all-Black casts downtown in 1917. Johnson calls their advent "the most important event in the entire history of the Negro in the American theater."[3] My how times change! But before we get to Torrence, there is another white writer and issue of Black theater that we must address: the miscegenation play, which remained popular on and off Broadway right through the thirties. Hughes's *Mulatto*, which had a successful Broadway run, is a notable example; however, the play that we will use for our discussion is *The Nigger* by Edward Sheldon.[4]

Written in the first years of the century, produced on Broadway in 1909, and made into a film in 1915, *The Nigger* is the product of a writer well known in his day. His friends and confidants included such luminaries as John Barrymore, Thornton Wilder, Alexander Woollcott, Anne Morrow Lindbergh, Ruth Gordon, and Helen Hayes. At least eight of his plays were made into films, from the silent era up to his *Dishonored Lady* starring Hedy Lamarr in 1947. Because he was bedridden for most of his life with rheumatoid arthritis, which took away his sight by the time he was thirty, he became a kind of guru to the theatrical community, and his advice and words of wisdom were taken very, very seriously by them all. So much for bona fides.

Phil Morrow, the "Nigger" in question, is the scion of a proud old Southern family and inheritor of substantial wealth who is governor of a Deep South state. He's a racist who wants to uplift the Black population by doing such things as denying them access to liquor (because it leads to riots and rape on their part) and who insists on kicking all of them off the local police force to appease a crowd hell-bent on lynching a Black man who has admitted to raping a white woman. The Black man, it turns out, is Phil's great-aunt's grandson. But he doesn't know this at the time that his vacillation proves to be the cause of the man's being caught and lynched. Sheldon develops Phil as a man of honor, in love with a beautiful young Southern belle, also of "good" family. Southern caste system being what it was and is, this is very important to the story, but Phil's deep-seated racism knows no bounds. When the state's senator tells him that "if ev'ry intelligent niggah had the vote, that means he'd have a right pow'ful lot o' self-respect too," Phil answers, "Lazy black beasts—theah's somethin' wrong with their brains—all they got is a spinal co'd!" And later in the scene he adds, "The niggah's not a man he's an animal—he's an African savage—all teeth and claws—it's monkey blood he's got in him, an' you can't evah change it—no, not in a thousan' yeahs."

So here we are, in the first decade of the twentieth century, when lynching might just as well be the law of the land, since *no one* has ever been convicted or punished for any of the five thousand recorded lynchings that took place between 1865 and 1965 because Congress was never able to pass an anti-lynching law. And Sheldon, in the midst of this reality for Black America, attempts to give us a character who can be changed for the better even though his upbringing throughout his entire life has taught him to accept the open lawlessness that the Black man had to live with: he, the Black man, was unable *in reality* to own property; to vote; to be elected to any significant public office or to hold it; to inherit land, property, or title—and this extended to most of the country. When and wherever Blacks did attain any of these "civil rights," they held them only at the behest of local public opinion. If the will of the people, expressed openly at any time and in any place, was to deny these rights, legally gained through honest hard work, the rights were forthwith denied and the object of this citizen disapproval was often lynched. Phil not only knows all of this but is in full sympathy with its ethos. His only sense of fairness, his only nod to humanity, is in the way he treats his "own" Blacks, the ones who serve him: the old family retainers, like the butler and Mammy, who is his great-aunt, unbeknownst to him. In all other aspects of his life, he is honor personified—that is, in his own "white world."

Sheldon wants us to confront this issue of how a Black man is at the whim of white racism in the most extreme sense imaginable. For once Phil admits to the world that he is Black, in spite of what he looks like, because his great-grandmother was Black, then everything that he has done, everything that he has achieved, all the praise being heaped on him by the senator, by the colonel of the militia for the way he handled the riot that ensued from the lynching, all of it will be wiped away in the twinkling of an eye, and he will be a man without property or title or rank, and he will be bereft of the office of governor. Since Black men were being hauled out of state offices and beaten in the streets once the Union army withdrew from the South in 1877, Sheldon is not fabricating the situation or exaggerating it. (Richard Wright's uncle had a very successful bar in Jackson, Mississippi, in the twenties. A white man wanted it. So what did he do? He killed the uncle and took over the business. Then he warned all members of the uncle's family to clear out of town or they would meet the same fate, which is how Wright and his family ended up in Chicago.) But Sheldon has to give us a reason to identify with his man. Otherwise, we'll just say he deserves what he gets.

That's where his Southern belle comes in. Her mother is more arrant in her racism than Phil, at least in the way she "treats" her Black servants. (Phil's beliefs may be extreme, but his manner is "gentlemanly," and while the daughter, Georgie, is much less severe than her mother, she's still a Southern gal.)

Once Phil has been confronted with the indisputable fact of his lineage, he decides that the only honorable option for him is to make the matter known publicly before his enemy publishes it in his newspaper. Phil could have saved himself by doing the man's bidding and blocking the prohibition law that's been passed by the legislature and is waiting on his signature. (All of the "villain's" money is in bars and distilleries.) Instead, Phil decides to accept who he is. He also decides that his view of the Black race is misbegotten, since he doesn't think of himself as doomed to a benighted state of animalism because of "monkey blood." He also accepts that he can no longer marry his intended. The first time he tells her the truth, she runs from him in horror, not willing to let him even touch her. Then she returns to disavow her romantic apostasy, as it were. That gives him the courage to make the public confession of his "bestial" condition—that her love is strong enough to accept him anyway means more to him than his public office or his name. But she wants him to keep the secret, thus ensuring that they can continue as they were and get married as planned. That he refuses to do, for all the noble reasons. Since he is "one of them," the nobility that has ruled his life to this point must be observed in this final, albeit tragic, instance.

She then takes her devotion even further. She won't let him go, no matter what. Her love for him is all that matters to her, and that love will help him face the dread that waits once the world finds out about his "monkey blood," only he won't let her make the sacrifice. She then tells him they can escape to the North, but he's not running away. She tries everything she can, but he's determined to give her up, whether she will or no. In the end, she makes him promise to keep her love with him. He, of course, agrees willingly. Which leaves her with the thought that they will be together in spirit, and the fact that she will still be with him, giving him the strength of that love, is what must sustain her. Since she can't have the man, she can have the thought that he has her love.

Sheldon does not attempt to take us beyond the door to Phil's public pronouncement. There is a crowd waiting to cheer and honor him, with the dignitaries, the band, the citizens, and the militia all in attendance, and they expect a speech of acceptance of their laudations. Could have been a fun scene.

Sheldon's play is by no means a "lost classic." It's hard to tell how the dialect style he employs throughout would play in the acting; I suspect it would drag the performance down as written. Often the dialogue of the white actors is arcane, even in the reading, so you can imagine what his dialogue for the Black actors is like. And while his hero is embedded with all the "octoroonish" niceties of character, Sheldon has no such literary largesse with which to adorn the Black ones. The great-aunt is as abject as they come. The butler is a cliché, and the young man who gets lynched is referred to as "the African" even after he's identified and given a name. The word *negro* is a [*sic*] throughout. At a time when theater was drowning in the boredom of bourgeois taste, to quote Brooks Atkinson, you'd have thought Sheldon's foray into the unknown would have been a welcome relief, but it only ran for twenty-four performances. Said Atkinson, "Although the Broadway of 1900 and of the first decade of the twentieth century was artistically trivial, it had charm and a kind of disarming simplicity. . . . Broadway attracted large audiences of middle class people who paid $1.50 or $2.00 for the best seats and were in search of amusement, excitement, and romance. They were the despair of serious theater people from abroad, but they were a comfort to American producers."[5]

So another chance to give Sisyphus a break and let him get that rock finally up the hill, once and for all, went begging, and the paying public turned its back on any discussion of race in its pleasure precincts. We can speculate why. Given the climate of the times, it's hardly surprising, but it's also why Black theater was up against monstrous odds in its attempt to be artistically relevant at the same time that it had to be commercially viable in order to simply survive. If it ain't box office, it ain't grits and gravy. At least not the kind that pays the bills.

And that quite simply explains why racism is still with us today in such toxic quantities, and why platitudes about race and about how much "progress" we've made abounds to no purpose. The question is not whether there has been progress. It's not possible in any society for that society to exist without change. That's the definition of a living organism; that's the very essence of its being alive—that it has to and must change to continue to exist and that change will lead to progress as well as regression. The issue is that we've allowed ourselves as a country to believe that the progress we have made is eradicating racism when, in an existential way, we are just kicking the can down a future road.

Irrespective of the shortcomings of Sheldon's play, there's a lot there that's entertaining, that would offer an evening of "excitement" and "romance," even if the romance is tragic. And since Sheldon avoids a miscegenated hereafter for the lovers who must be star-crossed to be box office, you'd think that bow to audience distaste for the mixing of white egg and Black sperm would have given it a chance. But that's how deep the racism runs. Of course, the idea that a white ingenue could mature into a full-blown heroine willing to give herself forever to a man "of color" could have been perceived as in itself revoltingly revolutionary, and would certainly take the "conversation" too far! But Sheldon serves one good purpose. He shows us what we've missed with our apartheid approach to Black theater. Just imagine how much richer our culture would be if we allowed serious Black theater to flourish the way we've allowed the singing and dancing and comedy to flourish. In the arena of sports, neither basketball nor football in its present scintillating, dynamic form would be recognizable if either was bereft of the Black style of playing. Sheldon could have served as a real stepping stone to the future, to the new century. Instead, he's just a footnote to history. Someone

FIGURE 4.1. James Weldon Johnson the Renaissance man: novelist, poet, historian, lawyer, executive secretary of the NAACP, highest-ranking U.S. diplomat in Nicaragua, 1911. Collections of the New York Public Library.

who is only of interest to students of the period and to those of us who write books about it.

We now turn our attention to James Weldon Johnson's "most important event in the entire history of the Negro in the American theater": Ridgely Torrence and his *Three Plays for a Negro Theater*. The three plays—*The Rider of Dreams, Granny Maumee*, and *Simon the Cyrenian*—had all-Black casts that included Black actors playing Pontius Pilate's wife and an Egyptian princess. The opening was well attended by the likes of Billie Burke and other theatrical royalty, along with most of the first-line critics. Alexander Woollcott, George Jean Nathan, and Heywood Broun headed the list. The big Black names were well represented by W. E. B. Du Bois, Johnson, and Lester Walton, one of the most influential men of letters of the period, who deserves more credit than he has ever gotten. The plays were produced by Emilie Hapgood, a well-known theatrical socialite who was at one time president of the Stage Society. She was able not only to open her production at the Garden Theater in the Madison Square Garden complex but to move it to a Shubert theater shortly after. None other than Robert Edmond Jones, one of American theater's great set designers, directed.

Three Plays for a Negro Theater opened on the fifth of April at the Garden Theater and closed on the twenty-fourth at a Shubert theater, the Garrick, for a total of seventeen performances. The reviews, except for Woollcott, were generally enthusiastic. George Jean Nathan even named Inez Clough—who played Pontius Pilate's wife, Procula—and Opal Cooper, who played the male lead in *The Rider of Dreams*, in his list of ten best actors for the season.

Rider of Dreams centers around a guitar-playing dreamer whose down-to-earth, practical wife has saved up enough money to buy a house. He withdraws all of it with the help of a white swindler, who forges the wife's name. They plan to use it in a get-rich scheme. But they drop the money on the ground in their haste not to be seen together. The landlord, a kindly one named Dr. Williams, *finds it*, miraculously, where it was dropped. After the improvident husband has had to confess his dastardliness, and wife and child are now faced with the prospect of being not only unable to buy the house but not even able to pay the rent, the good landlord shows up. He gives them the money because he knows it belongs to them and is willing to let them buy the house as well—but not before he makes Madison, the Rider, promise to mend his ways and accept the virtue of good, honest labor!!! And all's well that ends well.

If it sounds uncomfortably reminiscent of *Raisin in the Sun*, you have not been deceived. Madison is described upon his entrance as a "lazy looking man" who's carrying a guitar he obviously can't afford.[6] That about tells everything there is to tell about him. Torrence's aim here is to make fun of a Black man for not wanting to sweat his manhood away doing menial work in a factory and makes his ambitions seem as banal as possible. Madison wants to have "every toof in my haid covehed wif gol. I'll get youah n an Book s [his son] fix dat way too. I goin to have plenty society grub in me all de time." At the end, all he can do is be the feckless dreamer who wallows in self-pity for not being allowed to live his dreams. His wife explains what his problem is:

LUCY: You wuz doin all right till you got mix up wif dat white man an his tricks. De trouble wuz dat dis dream of youahs wuzn t a good dream.

Stupid Black man, trying to dream a white man's dreams.

Murray, in *A Thousand Clowns*, just wants to dream too. And his nephew, who's barely in his teens, is the adult in the relationship. Murray just won't get a job, but he's the articulate one who wins all the mental jousts and gets a social worker to be enamored of him in the bargain, making her male supervisor look the ass. In the end, he gives in to the world and does go looking for a job; he doesn't end up sitting in solace bemoaning the fact that all he wants to do is dream.

The titular character of *Granny Maumee* is blind. She lost her sight years ago when she tried in vain to save her son from a white mob that burned him alive for a crime he didn't commit. She has never forgiven the men for what they did. She's also intensely proud of her noble African bloodline, which she says is royal, and wants a male heir to carry it on. One of her great-granddaughters has given her such an heir, and when mother and child come to visit, it turns out that the great-great-grandson is mixed race. Granny, not knowing this, grasps him ecstatically in her arms. *And miraculously her sight returns.* She sees her light-skinned great-great-grandson and becomes enraged. She vows to destroy the white father, who is expected that night. To make matters worse, the father is a descendant of one of the men responsible for her son's ghastly murder. She gathers relics from that horrible lynching and the voodoo spell that they evoke, and the smoke that comes from it incapacitates both of her great-granddaughters. But when she hears the father at the door, the ghost of her dead son appears and pleads with her to forgive him. She does and collapses.

The great-granddaughters wake up and, seeing that Granny has died in the convulsion of her forgiveness and her connecting with her lost son, escape from the smoke and the spell. Granny's hatred for the men who killed her son has made her need for revenge so all-consuming that it makes any other emotion irrelevant. If *Granny Maumee* were text for an opera, it might work; *Il Trovatore* has a similar plot with Azueena and her son, whom she throws into the fire instead of the son of her villain. But *Il Trovatore*—and indeed, opera in general—does not depend on the book for its dramatic impact; it depends on the music of Verdi and Mozart and Puccini and the rest. Unfortunately, Torrence has no music to rescue this one-note piece and turn it into anything resembling effective theater.

That Torrence cast all Black actors to play both the Egyptians and the Romans in *Simon the Cyrenian* was certainly a noble effort. Does it make this play more effective? Probably not. And it's not because Black actors can't effectively play non-Black parts; they simply need help from the script. The dialogue that he gives Inez Clough to portray Pontius Pilate's wife might help us understand the problem:

PROCULA: Go! Go, send more messengers. Ah, Hera, help me.

[A MESSENGER runs into the garden from the right and kneels before her, breathless.]

PROCULA: Has Simon the Cyrenian been found?
MESSENGER: The swiftest horseman reached him. He is nearing the city.
PROCULA: Hasten him. Bring him. Your freedom for it.

[The MESSENGER hurries out.]

PROCULA [To ATTENDANTS.] Is there no news yet?
ATTENDANT: One messenger has not returned. He who was sent to the royal woman of Egypt.
PROCULA: Send others after him, take wings.

[DRUSUS enters the garden from the left.]

PROCULA: Drusus! Help me draw him swiftly.
DRUSUS: The wife of Pilate speaks. Whom shall I send to her?
PROCULA: Too late, too late. I speak foolishly. I have already sent.
DRUSUS: You are tormented.
PROCULA: Are mine the only eyes that see the doom unrolling?
DRUSUS: You speak strangely.
PROCULA: The Furies whip me.
DRUSUS: Tell me your secret.
PROCULA: This Jesus the Nazarene.
DRUSUS: You need not fear him. He is in Pilate's hands.
PROCULA: Out of that is my agony. Ah, my dream.

Simon the Cyrenian is a conversation piece. Simon is the African overlord who will lead his people in triumph over Rome. But when he orders Barabbas to gather the soldiers together to free Jesus, Barabbas says he can't because he no longer has the spirit for fighting. And besides, "who can stand against Rome"? Simon takes it upon himself to lead the charge and, sword in hand, rushes forth. Before he can get too far, the voice of God, we suppose, tells him to put the sword down because he "who lives by the sword, dies by it." So Simon drops his sword and goes out and helps Jesus carry the cross. And that's your denouement.

I have given so much space to these plays because they caused such a fuss at the time. Susan Curtis, in her *The First Black Actors on the Great White Way*, managed to write over two hundred pages on the subject. In doing so, she also managed to include Ziegfeld, the Pekin Theater in Chicago, Ada Overton Walker, pacifism, Woodrow Wilson, Louis Armstrong, Edward Albee, Ibsen (erroneously calling him Danish—Norway will have something to say about that),

Synge, Stanislavski, and the White Rats of vaudeville (who tried to get Ziegfeld to drop Bert) in the discussion. She tells us that Torrence, in despair over the short run of his work, which he never saw surface again, gave in to petulance and blamed the actors for its quick demise. Without quoting him, she says, "He believed the actors he selected . . . simply lacked the talent to put the plays over."[7] She goes on to say he believed that "had they been more experienced, better trained, or more familiar with working behind the footlights, they might have been able to breathe life into their roles and help audiences and critics see the artistic merit of these 'unusual'"—my scare quotes—"dramas. . . . The production, he believed, could not overcome their weak performances."[8] Earlier, he had said, "We were confronted with . . . the difficulty of finding actors . . . capable of taking serious parts. There had been no serious racial drama; there were no actors with experience of it. [The ones] who had had professional training had only been in minstrel or 'pic' [pickaninny] shows or they had 'Tommed' [been with an *Uncle Tom's Cabin* troupe]."[9] His first opinion about the quality of Black acting came long after the plays had flopped, the second opinion even before rehearsals started. Between those two bleak assessments, he had a very salutary opinion of said actors, unable to "breathe life into their roles." By the second night, "according to . . . Torrence, after the actors read the first wave of reviews, they gained courage and confidence, their performance, *which had been good from the start*, steadily improved, and the audiences grew a bit each night" (italics mine).[10] So the actors, who had been good from the start when the show opened to good reviews, were suddenly incapable of breathing life into these "unusual dramas" that closed after seventeen performances in not one but two theaters. Sounds like a poor workman quarreling with his tools. What Torrence gained from the sudden appearance on Broadway of plays about Black life—written by a young star of the New Theater Movement, produced by a leading light of the theatrical scene, and directed by an Ivy League tyro on the verge of success—was the novelty of the event. Everyone was aghast! With such bona fides supporting these neegrow plays, the American half of the civilized world had to take them seriously. The novel effect made the reviews good at the outset. But the dramatic value itself didn't find an audience in spite of the earnest enthusiasm of Du Bois, Johnson, and Lester Walton, who were all starved for something that would not have actors in cork, slapsticking, singing and dancing, and eating chicken. So they held their combined breaths and breathed a sigh of relief that could be heard as far south as the Mason-Dixon line. Anything, and I mean anything, that showed Black life outside of the plantation jig and the Sambo grin with no greasepaint would have gotten the same response from these three. That's how starved Black America was in 1917 for Black people to be "normal" on a public stage downtown in front of white folks.

But the bewilderingly ignorant opinions about Black humanity (Black people can't mate romantically, are too ignorant to eat, scarcely wise enough to breathe) found their way into the "discussion" of the Black actor's ability to act—beyond what Torrence himself had to say about *his* actors. Robert Benchley, whom you'll remember is the same Robert Benchley who made a name for himself as the alcoholic *Foreign Correspondent* in Hitchcock's film of the same name and other similar parts, writing for the *New York Tribune*, was invited to a rehearsal of *Three Plays*. Said he of the experience,

> Many of those chosen have had experience in elocution and dramatic reading. The director and the author have not tried to direct in the sense that a company of white actors have to be directed. [They] are trying to give the players as free reign as possible, hoping that they will play the parts as they feel they ought to be played. I saw one lithe youth . . . make an obeisance before the king (who was not there). It was a move which, if it were being rehearsed by an average actor, would have to be done over, at a conservative estimate, twenty-five times, and then probably abandoned as impossible. At the first attempt this colored boy, out of his own intuitive sense of what was right, made as perfect and complete a gesture as could have been drawn with a pair of compasses and with infinitely more animation.[11]

Susan Curtis's comment after quoting Benchley is "Left more or less to their own devices, Benchley implied, African American performers were natural actors." But Benchley also taketh away. Curtis says he "noted that few [of the actors] had been chosen from stock companies, . . . 'for it was found that long association with melodrama and comedy written for white actors had made them less natural in their speech, more stagy in their gestures and not so well adapted to the expression of the pure African or those who have not imitated themselves away from it.'"[12] In Benchley's beleaguered mind, there is a "pure African expression" that can be imitated away from by too much association with material written for white actors. Maybe De Armond was right! The reviewer for the *New York Evening Post* seemed to agree with him, partially; Curtis discussed this view, quoting pieces of the article: "The actors' 'feeling,' 'humor,' 'genuine emotion,' and 'intuition,' which shone through in spite of 'insufficient training and experience' and the 'appearance of woodeness' . . . rested on the assumption that African Americans lacked the intelligence needed to move from thought to action. 'The whole secret of what is known as spontaneity in acting lies in the facility and rapidity with which the mental design is translated into outward expression,' a lesson that amateurs— 'the majority of these actors are yet in that category'—have to learn."[13] So the "natural," "instinctive" African who can jigaboo and jump and jive can't really think and the only way to get him to act naturally is not to try to make him think. Just leave him alone and let him be instinctive. The old racist branding that had kept Black actors in blackface and had persisted whenever Williams and Walker moved away from plantation darkie syndrome was alive and well in the minds of the reviewers of *Three Plays* as well as in the mind of its author. Where the hell did Benchley get the idea that "few of the actors had been chosen from stock companies"? Almost all of them had been chosen from stock companies! Which is Sisyphus's cue to make an entrance.

Susan Curtis, to her credit, puts the kibosh on all this nonsense by listing the wealth of training that these "instinctive" actors had that should have "imitated them away from their pure African expression." Lottie Grady (who played the Egyptian princess Acte), Inez Clough (who played Procula), Blanche Deas (who played the wife in *Rider of Dreams*), Jesse Shipp (who played Barabbas—and had insulted the king of England, you will remember), Alex Rogers (who played Dr. Williams in *Rider*), Opal Cooper (who played the Rider), and Marie Jackson-Stuart (who played Granny Maumee) all had dozens of productions under their belt. They had come from the stock companies in Harlem and had performed most of the Broadway hits in Harlem. They had been trained in prestigious acting companies in New England, London, and Austria and had a plethora of experience outside of them, not doing pickaninny roles or having "Tommed." They had traveled to the Continent and to England to perform and had had long runs on Broadway and throughout the country in musical comedy and legitimate theater as well. How do you get more experienced than that? And how do you still have to prove that there is no mythical "pure expression of the African"? There is trained assimilation of American theater that has been imbued with a special African voice. But it's neither instinctive voodoo nor jungle mumbo jumbo. Poor Sisyphus—for all his effort, he's back down on his proverbial ass. And the Black actor has to start all over again to prove that he can think, walk, and talk at the same time, that he has training, and that he doesn't have to be limited to slapstick. This is not a death sentence that no longer has an impact on what Black actors are allowed to do in the twenty-first century. For all the advances we have made since that time, what are the themes that invariably dominate? Comedy—remember Broun saying that because Williams was Black, he *had* to be funny; remember Johnson saying we were not allowed to portray romantic love. Which one of our present headline stars has been allowed to make love to a woman of another race or even one of the same race? As for serious drama—can we honestly say that the material we've been allowed to present on Broadway or in film comes even close to the heroic drama of what we've done throughout the history of this country? Just look at the heroes of legend and ask why neither Broadway producers nor Hollywood will green-light any of their stories.

Susan Curtis is, for the most part, earnest in her attempt to suggest that a great injustice was done to Black theater when Torrence's effort did not become a brilliant success. She constantly refers to the plays as "triumphant." It was a "triumphant opening." *Granny Maumee* was a "shining success," the work was "epochal," and "the decision was nearly unanimous—*Three Plays for a Negro Theater* was a hit on Broadway."[14] Her enthusiasm was more than shared by Emilie Hapgood, who had such high hopes for *Granny Maumee* that she wanted to show it to Stanislavski! And she saw Sarah Bernhardt doing the part—if Torrence could rewrite it "in Creole dialect more suited to the talents of the great Bernhardt."[15] But Professor Curtis's foray into analyzing the social issues and personal interactions that need to be discussed if we are to have a fuller understanding of the immense impact these plays had is, to be kind, astonishing. She says that when Opal Cooper entered the scene carrying a guitar he "obviously could not [afford,] it became clear very quickly that the play would examine competing American dreams within Black families."[16] Having a husband and wife, I submit, argue over money is not a sociological breakthrough that examines competing American dreams. It is a staple of the genre of theater known as domestic tragedy in almost any country where traditional realism is dominant. So we are to assume that because Black people do it too, then that means it is a phenomenon that has *changed the conversation about race*! That in a nutshell is the problem for Black America. We are always being looked at as some exotic subspecies of the human race in a country we have lived in, I repeat, since before the Mayflower. At another point, she offers up this astonishing conclusion: "African American actors spoke Torrence's lines . . . based on what they thought would make such characters believable, but they did so in costumes and on sets designed by Robert Edmond Jones, a Harvard- and European trained exponent of the New Movement in Theater. To categorize them as either black plays or white plays threatens to minimize the interdependence of both races' contribution to the production."[17] I hardly know what to make of so astounding a statement. If a Black actor wears a costume designed by a white designer, then we can't minimize the *joint* contribution that both have made to a play written by a white writer. I've seen this sort of excruciatingly incoherent gambit into "analysis" in doctoral theses, but never outside of one. Does any of this mean Black theater needs Black writers before it can really flourish? Probably. But we'll never really know until or unless we give Black writers a chance to flourish. It's something akin to Black history. While the major Black historians have had their say and, indeed, their day, we always seem to be happiest when white writers are doing the telling of the Black man's tale, and it's the white writer who gets the attention, the publicity, and consequently, the reputation when he does. It is also the white critic who gets the chance to pass final judgment. As a postscript to the *Three Plays* saga, there was no Pulitzer prize given that year because the committee decided that there wasn't one production in the entire season worthy of that much-heralded award.[18]

Now we're ready for the twenties, for the groundbreaking musicals and for the plays on Broadway by white writers writing about Black life and by Black writers writing about it. And the context in which all this took place, certainly from a Black perspective, was the Harlem Renaissance. Written about copiously, argued about in the extreme, even to the point of questioning that it existed or that, if it did, it wasn't a "renaissance." The most generally agreed on dates for the renaissance are 1920–1935: from around the time of the opening of *Shuffle Along* in 1921 to the riots of 1935. In that last year, the huge Triboro Bridge was being built at Harlem's doorstep, with thousands of its citizens suffering dire depravation from want of food and shelter, six years into the Depression; none of them were hired to work on the project that employed hundreds of workers in high-paying jobs. 1917 is also often given as the beginning date as a consequence of the Torrence plays and Johnson's encomium. In theatrically substantive terms, Torrence is praised because his plays were purported to have for the first time "featured African American actors conveying complex human emotions and yearnings." It may have been the first time for the uninformed, but I dare say the rest of us know better.

By the twenties, Harlem had a vibrant middle class of substantial size and impact. The importance of that can't be overemphasized. The Black men and women in the arts making huge sums of money aside, the Black population in general was still largely agrarian at the end of the nineteenth century, but it was slowly transforming into a huge, legitimate working class as a consequence of the Black migrations from the horrific Ku Klux Klan–inspired violence of the South in the second half of the nineteenth century. Two decades into the next, enough of them had sufficient wealth to constitute a leisure class—that is, one that had the time and money to cultivate the arts and thus constitute the backbone of the cultural and artistic flowering of the twenties and thirties. The renaissance reached into all aspects of Black life, first in Harlem and then, through its influence, around the world, with varying degrees of impact. Harlem became a mecca, one with such vibrancy that its afterglow was still shining, albeit with diminishing light, right through the end of the Second World War—as this writer can attest to, having arrived in Harlem in the late forties, in time to witness its setting sun firsthand.

The ideas and the literary flowering that came from this is too voluminous to go into here. Novels were being published by major publishing houses, magazines started, and dialogues about what it means to be a "Negro" who acknowledges his "African" past abounded. Alaine Locke's *New Negro* led the discussion in this literary and intellectual awakening. Countee Cullen's question in the first line of his poem "Heritage"—"What is Africa to me?"—was emblematic of that soul-searching. But the issue of the renaissance itself and of its importance is not the point, not the reason why it needs to be accepted as historical fact. Its limitations, its conflicts of purpose or direction, its inability to eradicate cultural divisions, to overcome forces and events in the society that still separate and destroy us— none of these are at the center of its yearning to be free. It happened, and in happening, it changed New York and the world in some measure, for better or worse, and that is its major triumph. Its major contribution to history, if you will. It existed. It was. It happened, and it is still happening with us and in us today, because after it died, it left its imprint on our imaginings the way all major historical events do. When the first Black play by a Black writer opened on Broadway, and when Eugene O'Neill gave us the Emperor Jones and the law student in *All God's Chillun Got Wings*, none of these theatrical happenings owed their existence or their impact to Harlem or to the renaissance, per se. And that holds true, to some extent, for some of the Broadway musicals of the twenties and thirties, as well as for *Porgy* and *The Green Pastures*. But Black culture had to have a home, and in ways that are clearly discernible, Harlem, and the renaissance, was the literary "home" for whatever passed for Black-inspired art in America. By extension, that meant that it was the home for Black theater, Black plastic arts, Black painting, in the same way that the Irish character in the Northeast was O'Neill's home, or Dublin the home of Joyce's *Ulysses*.

So we can now turn our attention to the business of the theatrical enterprise proper, picking up from where we left off with Mr. Ridgely Torrence.

Hollywood was little more than a cow pasture in the early twenties, and even though stars like Mary Pickford and Douglas Fairbanks and Valentino were great successes in the golden age of the silent film, their impact on the cultural life of the nation was not the overwhelming one that film is today. To be truly glamorous in the twenties, a young starlet didn't appear in an MGM musical; she appeared in the *Ziegfeld Follies*. There were seventy-six legitimate theaters in the Broadway district in 1920. As many as five plays opened in one night, and there were critics aplenty to cover them all, each one a star in his own right. Robert Benchley was at *Life*, E. W. Osborn at the *Evening World*, Stark Young at the *Times*, George S. Kaufman also at the *Times*, S. Jay Kaufman at the *Mail*, Heywood Broun at the *World*, John Anderson at the *Post*, Alexander Woollcott at the *Evening Sun*, Gabriel W. Gabriel at the *New York Evening Telegram*, George Jean Nathan at the *American Mercury*, Charles Belmont Davis at the *Herald Tribune*, Alan Dale at the *American*, and Percy Hammond also at the *Herald Tribune*.

O'Neill was the most important writer of Black theater at the top of the twenties. In addition to *Emperor Jones*, he had already written a one-acter, *The Dreamy Kid*. His foray into the experimental, which characterized his early period, gave way in the end to traditional structure—O'Neill didn't start out as a traditionalist; he grew into one. To the degree that Black themes represented an excursion into the experimental, O'Neill was in the right place at the right time for his own development. That he found Charles Gilpin alive, well, professionally trained, and more than equal to the task of carrying an entire play by himself on Broadway was, in light of the meager advantages that Black actors had to be serious before 1920, little short of miraculous. As O'Neill was to say later, Gilpin was the only actor who did exactly what he, O'Neill, wanted. Gilpin had (in addition to Williams and Walker) Anita Bush and the Lafayette Stock Company to thank—but also, most of all, himself, for being ready when the golden chance came. He was just forty, and he was, by all accounts, fabulous. The Drama League gave awards for the ten people who did the most to advance the theater in that year of 1920. Gilpin was named as one of that precious circle. However, with the award, there automatically came an invitation to dinner, and when it was realized that Gilpin might show up, the first thought was not to name him at all. Democracy prevailed, and he ended up with both the meal and the medal. But neither Gilpin nor the Black character fared well in terms that were really transformative beyond Gilpin's, and later Robeson's, triumphs.

The Black character had all the mystery, the romance, the compelling attraction of fire and wrath that would have made him a demigod, a Valentino, and he had the built-in conflicts in his general war with society to round out his appeal. But he also had the one "joker in the deck" that made his gifts, his pretentions to art, ludicrous. He had to get approval from the other guy. Without it, he was in limbo, since he was the outsider in the other guy's game. What that man said or did determined his cultural life and death. If a white writer was writing about Blacks, then he was perceiving their reality from a point of view that other whites would find meaningful and valid as an interpretation of the issue. His anger, no matter how strong, would not be a threat, but a warning or simply a statement of art in art. The other issue, of what a Black writer is capable of and what the Black man at large is "thinking" at that particular time and place, what message he is sending out and how far he will go in putting down all that his particular tragedy has created, in the context of what the nation fought and died for—all of this goes into the sum total of a Black writer's statement. It either burdens his creative output beyond support in the commercial arena or takes it out of the running in the first place for being socially unacceptable.

O'Neill, in *The Dreamy Kid*, has his protagonist kill a white man. We don't see the killing, but it happens and is essential to the plot and the story progression. In *All God's Chillun Got Wings* (one wag said if they play Paducah, they'll need them), he goes even further and has a mixed marriage, with the white wife kissing her Black husband's hand while she's kneeling and he's standing. O'Neill had gone right to the heart of the two biggest taboos in the society vis-à-vis Black and white commingling: sex and manhood. Not that the two are by any means mutually exclusive. All the Black men who have ever been killed because they were alleged to have raped a white woman, all the Black men who were killed after the First World War in Chicago, Detroit, and east St. Louis (which were only the tip of the iceberg) when they returned home in uniform because they had had that most dangerous of all experiences—they had killed white men (albeit in a white man's war and with a white man's permission—but killed nevertheless) attested to the fact that a Black man's manhood, including his sexual proclivities, was risky business at best when it attempted to display itself publicly.

What O'Neill didn't do was emancipate the Black character from "dem" and "dese" syndrome, not that two out of three isn't bad. If either *The Dreamy Kid* or *The Emperor Jones* is dated or hold little appeal for Black audiences today, it is largely due to the language. With *The Dreamy Kid*, it's almost an unfaltering excursion into a foreign tongue, although not as bad as Torrence's. The play is a funeral dirge, plotless but quite powerful. The Kid's grandmother is dying, but she wants him with her at the end. In order to stay, he runs the risk of being caught by the police, as they are after him for the killing that took place the night before. His is a life outside of the law. Even though he says the murder was justified, it is not something that he either bemoans or has any regrets about. He's nobody's rolling-eyed Sambo. Where the single-incident structure of Granny's dying serves a one-act piece like *Dreamy Kid*, it does not do as well for a full-length play like *All God's Chillun Got Wings*, in which Jim is the Black man who is trying to pass the bar. He can't because of a mental block that society has created in him that makes it impossible for him to exhibit knowledge that he has, which isn't as absurd as it sounds. He has married a white woman, Ella, who is of poor background and who has extricated herself from being the wronged woman of a prizefighter. Ella goes crazy simply because she has married a Black man. The most dramatic sequences are her rantings, sometimes at Jim (she tries to kill him at one point), but even more so at an African mask that becomes a "character" in the play in much the same way that the old tenement house is attacked in *One Third of a Nation*. She duels with it, stabs it, makes prophecy to it or with it. And it's all damned good theater, although apparently more so in the script than in the playing. (One critic noted that it didn't have as startling an effect as he had expected after reading the play.) But the play turns on this one personal transformation and, as such, is so plotless as to make the entire effort fail. O'Neill is at his best when his story line gives his characters something stronger in the way of plot to stand on. (Although his masterpiece, *Long Day's Journey into Night*, triumphs with very little plot.) In much the same way that this element is missing in *A Moon for the Misbegotten* (Walter Kerr put the quietus on *Moon* in a *New York Times* piece many years ago), it's also missing in *All God's Chillun*. Jim holds little interest by the end and only has a good moment when he shows himself capable of loving his wife no matter what and finally being crushed by the realization that he has married that which hates him in spite of not wanting to hate him. But Jim does speak English, as does his sister, and that was well worth the price of a ticket. Having Paul Robeson stand on a public stage in 1924 and not have to do a molasses-mouth version of "colored speech" was in itself *epochal*! Unfortunately, the *Journal American* didn't think so. When it came to light that actress Mary Blair would kiss Robeson's hand in public, the journal stated, "They should not put on plays which are, or threaten to become enemies of the public peace; they should not dramatize dynamite. . . . We refer to the play in which a white woman marries a black man and at the end of the play, after going crazy, she stoops and kisses the Negro's hand."[19] Mayor Hylan's office wanted to close it but could do no more than not allow integration to take place in the schoolyard. That is, the mayor's office refused to give the customary permission for the child actors to perform in the first scene, one that called for Black and white youngsters playing marbles together on a street corner. As a consequence, the director, James Light, came forward on the second evening and asked the audience if they wanted the performance to take place in any event, with him reading the first scene. The audience said yes. So that's what happened. J. J. Shubert's *Artists and Models*, which was a nudie show pure and simple, had no such problems opening and running in the same year—this even though it was probably in violation of the law.

Percy Hammond, drama critic for the *Tribune*, got into the act of being traumatized by the business of Mary Blair kissing her husband's "sable" hand, which he thought "[suggested] that, in Mr. O'Neill's disconsolate outlook, miscegenation, at least, may contain elements of happiness."[20] If ever there was a decently worded sense of distaste for "miscegenation," that was it. John Corbin, in the

Times, seemed startled that "the racial feelings of the negro [*sic*] is shown as no less strong, no less unreasoning, than that of the whites."[21] Heywood Broun called it, simply, "tiresome," pointing out that after O'Neill sets up the problems of inter-marriage in the first half of the play, he sidesteps them in the second half, and we find Ella already mad. Broun then goes on to say, in response to such as the *Journal American* and the mayor et al., "Any objection to the theme of the play should come logically not from the white but from the colored community. The colored man . . . is a high grade individual . . . the white woman he marries is a character tainted [and] painted as the lowest of the low," ending with, "Caucasian superi-ority does suffer a little, because Paul Robeson is a far finer actor than any white member of the cast. . . . In the uneven career of Eugene O'Neill, I think that '*All God's Chillun*' . . . will rank as one of the down strokes."[22]

The Emperor Jones, again, is an incident play. Everything that the protagonist has done to become the emperor of a fictitious island in the West Indies has already happened before the first scene. He spends the next two hours trying to escape the tom-toms. Of course, no such island could exist, since they had all been colo-nized by the Spanish, English, French, or Dutch at least one hundred years before the Civil War and had a large "native" middle class that was as sophisticated and as cultivated as most people living in the average American city, Black or white. Since it was supposed to refer to Haiti, the idea of "natives in the jungle" is even more preposterous. The Haitians had routed, in turn, the French, the Spanish, and the English in organized combat. Their soldiers didn't do it with spears and tom-toms, unless they were able to work voodoo on the modernly equipped armies of three of the greatest military powers in the world at the time. In the play, the character is only half man. He has strength and intelligence and bravado, and the white trader Smithers (played by Jasper Deeter in the original production) is in awe of him. But his descent into destruction is so simplemindedly Greek-like in its fatalism and so based on "primitive" and "native" superstition that not only the emperor himself but the play as well fall far short of offering the Black character an opportunity to develop into fullness as an interesting, dramatic instrument.

In spite of its defects, the play had a long run and was revived at least six times before the decade ended, and it was O'Neill's first major hit. The most successful productions were the original at the Provincetown Playhouse with Gilpin in 1920 (192 performances) and the revival in 1926 at the Mayfair, which ran 81 times. In 1925, it was paired with *The Dreamy Kid* at the Fifty-Second Street theatre but only ran for 24 performances. Heywood Broun, writing in the *New York World*, called the Provincetown Playhouse production "the most interesting play which has yet come from the most promising playwright in America."[23] When the pro-duction moved to a larger theater, Alan Dale, writing in the *New York American*, wasn't as impressed. Said he, "Much of The Emperor Jones is a monologue for a colored actor known as Charles S. Gilpin"—why "known as" is, of course, any-one's guess—"an actor of intelligence, of limited powers, and of a certain vocal monotony."[24] Broun observed, on the other hand, "The Emperor is played by a

negro [*sic*] actor named Charles S. Gilpin, who gives the most thrilling performance we have seen any place this season."[25]

In the 1924 revival, again at the Provincetown, it was Robeson's turn to show
his stuff. This was just a week before he was to premier in *All God's Chillun* at
the same theater. The *New York Times* took an interesting gambit in an unsigned
article in trying to decide who gets the major credit, the playwright or the actor,
for the success of the *Emperor*. Said the *Times*, "Mr. Robeson's triumph in it last
night, following Charles S. Gilpin's striking performance of the part, cannot but
lead to fleeting suspicions that it is the play rather than the player that so holds the
audience."[26] Which may have been a not-too-subtle way of saying either all Black
actors are good or that when an O'Neill writes a play for a Black actor, it's so good
that any Black actor can make it work, no matter his defects. On the other hand,
it might be an ethnic choosing of sides to suggest that the triumph belonged to
those two superb men in that they took a not-first-rate O'Neill play and made it
a triumph of more than one season and one of the big hits of the first half of the
decade. (Top honors for the period would have to go to John Barrymore for his
1922 *Hamlet* with Blanch Yurka as the mother and Tyrone Power Sr. as Claudius.
It was dubbed the *Hamlet* of the century and was the first production to tap the
Freudian implications of the play.)

In the 1926 revival, the Provincetown producers brought back Gilpin, this time
to the Majestic. *Billboard* said of that revival, "This is one play that is not dulled by
time, but would be insufferably dull without a Gilpin or a Robeson in the leading
role." This, if it is true, would give credit equally to playwright and performer for
the continued success of the *Emperor* in the twenties. *Billboard* went on to say of
Gilpin's acting, "[His] performance as the arrogant, blustering, Emperor Jones
of the first scene, and his cringing, cowardly Brutus Jones of the last scenes, is still
as true and as shining as the silver bullet with which he is killed by the natives."[27]
By November, he had played the role 1,408 times, leading a second reviewer in the
same magazine to laud Gilpin for playing the part that many times without diminishing the dramatic impact of his opening-night performance.

Imagine, therefore, how good Robeson had to be in the same part to match
Gilpin. Not only did he match him, but he outshone him according to the dean
of drama critics of the twenties, the veritable emperor himself, Alexander Wooll-
cott: "One who admired exceedingly the performance that Gilpin gave as Brutus
Jones, now rises in meeting to say that it was not so fine a performance as that
which the stalwart and magnificently equipped Robeson gave last night at the
Provincetown."[28] Columbia University's *Spectator*, in January of 1921, said that
Gilpin was one of the greatest actors of the stage. *Life* magazine added this dictum:
"Mr. Charles Gilpin, who plays the crazed, and frightened emperor, must hence-
forth be counted among the leaders in the American stage, even though he should
never have another opportunity to show what he is capable of doing. Someday,
perhaps, there will be more real parts written for our Negro actors, whose rich res-
onance of voice and native genius for emotional expression, with the least effort,

have long since fitted them for more serious work than rolling dice in a musical comedy, or limping about with lumbago after 'de young mars' Godfrey.'"[29] For *Life* to have gone that far in the twenties was indeed a bold declaration in support of the Fifteenth Amendment and due process, to say nothing of the Declaration of the Rights of Man. Suffice it to say that these two giants vied with one another for top honors as the premier Black actor of the decade for the rest of the twenties. Had they been white, their careers would have gone ever upward. Because they weren't, they had to look to other devices for their survival. There were, of course, many white actors in that period and others who not only had checkered careers but faded into history, never to be heard from again. Not so with the giants. And that's what these two men were: giants.

In spite of all that, O'Neill, the young playwright, did take the Black character very far with these three pieces. In many ways, farther than he has been taken since. Which is a hell of a thing to say, I admit. The expressionist nature of *Emperor Jones* as a play was pivotal to the early O'Neill as a writer. He used it again in *The Hairy Ape*. O'Neill owed the experimental symbolism of that expressionism, as a consequence, as much to the Black soul as he did to European Expressionists, who get all the credit. But O'Neill was not able to make a complete man out of the Black character. Jones was up to any occasion, almost. He could tell Smithers where to get off. He could fool an entire island of "natives," and he could even accept the end of the game, when it came, with a mature fatality, but drums and "haint's" and "visions" turned him into a victim of "primitive" vengeance. In a sense, it's a bit much, even though it can be very dramatic in the playing. *All God's Chillun's* Jim is so imbued with a desire to become a lawyer and with a love for Ella that he is, in effect, just a sop who allows himself to be used as a conduit for racism and who is so removed from his mother and sister that he has destroyed those ties insofar as they can have any real meaning for him. Only the Dreamy Kid has a moral vision to guide him. He knows he's going to get caught if he stays with his grandmother until she dies, but he can't bring himself to leave her. He saves his girlfriend, and he intends to go down fighting in the best tradition of James Cagney and Humphrey Bogart. Consequently, he is at the old lady's bedside, gun ready, when the final curtain comes down. It's similar to the heroic fatalism that makes Hemingway's short story "The Killers" so powerful. Because the original design was what it was, Dreamy, as character, has artistic integrity. But O'Neill, in the other two plays, where he sets out to accomplish so much more, really didn't. He saved his best analysis of real men of full-fledged, completely developed character for his white heroes.

Black playwrights also made a somewhat tepid foray onto the Broadway stage in the second half of the decade. Garland Anderson, a former waiter in a San Francisco hotel, gets first honors for the century with his *Appearances*, which opened in 1926 and played twenty-eight times, and was even revived four years later. Mr. Anderson's gifts were limited indeed, but he did understand one thing: America is a salesman's society. He managed in short order to get Al Jolson interested in his play and to also pay for his, Anderson's, trip from San Francisco to New York to get permission from Al Smith to use his name on an invitation that Anderson sent to hundreds of the well heeled, inviting them to his backers' party at the Waldorf. He also got Calvin Coolidge to agree to attend the opening night performance! Needless to say, he raised the money to put on the play. He was deeply religious and deeply humble, as well as forthright and honest. He billed himself as the Bellhop Playwright, who believed not only in the religion of hard work but also that anyone could do anything he set out to do if he really put his mind to it and the rest of that drivel. It was a perfect lesson for an age that bowed to the god of materialism and justified that worship by blaming the condition of the underprivileged on their own defects of character. His success in getting his play produced was the proof of the pudding. If you could sell your wares, no matter what the merit or value of the product, you could become a success. If you couldn't, then merit notwithstanding, you'd more than likely be a failure. That, more than the famous names, made him an instant hit in America in the middle of the twenties. If he had even hinted at having an innate ability that just wanted opportunity, he would have been dead before he opened. But because he was setting out to do something not because he was suited to it but because he was determined to prove that he could, that made him a good unpretentious guy, a safe one too, in everyone's eyes. That the play itself was pretty awful didn't really matter. It wasn't supposed to *not* be awful. Anderson was singing the gospel of "yes, we can" that ruled the twenties. That same gospel that shattered the foundations of everyone's faith by the end of the decade, when the stock market crash proved that sheer will and determination were not enough no matter how hardworking, unassuming, honest, and white we were as a nation. The title of the play means "you can't judge a book by its cover"! And Anderson ends it with the same spiel he used to promote it. His central character, Carl, says, after he has been found innocent of raping a white woman whom he did not rape, "If a black bell boy with not much schooling could imagine himself a playwright, by believing he could write a play that was interesting and entertaining enough to hold an audience, it would prove to the world beyond a shadow of a doubt that everyman can do what he desires to do, can become anything he desires to become." Why, you ask, is a bellboy making a speech in a play about being a playwright? Simply because he imagined the experience and tells everyone else that they have been characters in *his* play. Got it? It hardly matters. Richard B. Harrison, who later made a name for himself as De Lawd in *The Green Pastures*, read the play aloud at the Waldorf when Anderson raised the money and whatever Anderson's sponsors were looking for, the script must have met their aggregate approval.

So much for *Appearances*. But Anderson did, in fact, do some good. Having Black actors play Black parts was still a breakthrough of sorts, as white actors were routinely taking away their work by doing blackface. (Even Ethel Barrymore got into the blackface act as the eponymous Scarlet Sister Mary.) In addition, both Carl and his sister speak the English language. The woman who Carl was supposed to have raped is exposed as being an adventuress employed by the play's villain. But just to make sure that the mayor's office doesn't close him down for illegal miscegenation, Anderson throws in one more safeguard: the white woman turns out to be Black! So no one could accuse Garland Anderson of advocating even incidental race mixing. It seems that any man can do what he desires to do, can become anything he desires to become, only if he makes sure, in the process, that he does not offend the existing racial code. *Appearances* wasn't actually the first Black play on Broadway, but it was the first full-length Black play. *Chip Woman's Fortune* by Willis Richardson premiered in 1923 at the Frazee Theatre and ran for thirty-one performances; it's a five-character piece in one act and has a marvelous simplicity to it.

It wasn't until the end of the twenties that a Black writer made a significant impression on Broadway with a nonmusical play. Wallace Thurman, whose novel, *Infants of the Spring*, is the work for which he is best remembered, saw his *Harlem* premiere in 1929. "Saw" may be an exaggeration, since Mr. Thurman was not allowed a seat in the orchestra of the theater in which his play was being performed; he was relegated to the side or the balcony, lest any white patron object to his African American presence beside them, fifth row center! This even though he had been published in the *Bookman, New Republic, Independent,* and *Macauley's* and had published two novels. The reviews were mixed, but Thurman only gets half the credit in any event, as he had a white collaborator, William Rapp. Rapp, apparently, was a poor man's George S. Kaufman. He'd get an idea, find someone with talent who could make it work, and "collaborate" on the script. Rapp had all the connections and the reputation for being a "professional" hack. So all the characterizations and all the dialogue belonged to Thurman. Thurman was one of the major figures of the Harlem Renaissance; he tried to capture the entire movement in *Infants of the Spring.* Another novel, also inspired by the period, that is much better (it deals with the light and the dark interplay among Blacks) is *The Blacker the Berry.* Thurman died at a young age. He was a wit and a brilliant man of letters whose talent hadn't quite caught up with him before his premature end—born of a Jewish father and an "Indian" mother, although he looked classically Black. *Harlem* opened at the Apollo on Forty-Second Street (not to be confused with the Apollo in Harlem), the heart of the main stem, in February of 1929 and ran for ninety-four performances. In October, it reopened at the Eltinge but only lasted for sixteen performances. The play—while a big, sprawling melodrama that included rent parties, a murder, a young girl "destroyed," and all the rest—was the first to present big-time theater with the urban Black character in his own milieu. The critics found it all too, too much to deal with. This, even though they were able to dissect its faults with ease. Said Burns Mantle in the *Daily News,* "Better citizen elements among the colored people are quite sure to protest against having the play represent their district and their race in the Broadway area." Then suggested that the acting police commissioner would roll out the paddy wagon if the "orgiastic exhibit revealed as a Saturday evening dance in Harlem, isn't cut."

He went on to say, "These two matters cleaned up, it is possible the drama may run on for a considerable period."[30] Just how he was going to manage cleaning up the first one and still expect a considerable run for the play, I can't imagine, but that dancing in the rent party scene certainly set their combined white hairs on end. Alison Smith in the *World* called the dances "barbaric."[31] Richard Lockridge agreed in the *Sun*: "The boys and girls"—there was a lot of "boys and girls"-ing it— "who dance on the stage of the Apollo are unselfconscious and barbaric." Later he says, "Men and women who dance like that have the strength for violence."[32] Look out! Brooks Atkinson used another word for it, "animalism." Said he, "All the animalism springs so naturally from the race that it loses, artistically, the offensiveness it would have in artificial circumstances." Which is sort of good, if you don't mind the condescension, I guess. Then he adds, "But it is animalism, nevertheless, crude, dark and coarse, with none of the poetic exorcism of . . . *Porgy* and for that matter none of the bizarre pornography of *Lulu Belle*."[33] Which is bad, no matter what you think of the condescension. In a separate follow-up piece, Atkinson went into the business of how *Harlem* had broken ground with its excursion into the urban neegrow theme, et cetera, by seeing the urban negro through a negro's eyes. (In those days, they didn't capitalize *the negro*.) For all that, Thurman thought he had better protect himself against too much abuse and gave a glossary of what his animalistic, barbaric culture was all about. So we find, by looking at the program notes that *a rent party* is a Saturday night orgy, that *sweetback* is a colored gigolo, that the difference between *hincty* and *dicty* is that the first is imperious and the second his highbrow. Explaining numbers (as in gambling on a three-number combination) took up a whole paragraph. Gilbert Gabriel in the *Evening Telegram* just plain didn't like it: "[It's] a gross and common mixture of plain reporting and fancy fiction. Never much more than a carbon copy—black carbon, of course, of *Broadway*,"[34] a play that had run two years earlier. Lockridge was more anthropological: "The play is in a sense a motion picture thrown up on the background of negroes [*more sic*] dancing. They dance lustily, swayingly, shamelessly and reveal the simplicity and deep earthiness of the race's hold on life. . . . [They have] *uncerebral directness*. The new negro has revived the jungle and the old one has merely borrowed morals and a religion" (italics mine).[35] Dear me. No wonder we were being lynched in the twenties if we couldn't even "borrow" religion without consequences. The play also showed the Black family in cultural shock, which was another first and part of what Atkinson was alluding to. Poor Blacks from the South who moved to Harlem looking for the promised land found, of course, racketeers, welfare, fast-talkers of both sexes, and a number of more complicated, more grandiose ways to get swindled. Thurman tried to throw up this entire new lifestyle in getting his dramatic effect. I think he overestimated the white critics. Instead of the effect being how the Southern Black is shocked by the Northern way of life, he, in fact, shocked the supposedly sophisticated critics who weren't ready for his full dose of Blackness. Call it a cultural gap and leave it at that. Any further investigation can only bring offense. But there was no attempt to play to the limitations of the white audience. If anything, the production went entirely in the other direction and gave everyone who hadn't been there a taste of what the real thing north of 110th Street was like. The rent party scenes really blew their minds, but there was something about the whole business that didn't really accommodate. Black shows, whether they are musicals or not, must have that inherent grin that relaxes a white audience so that the laughter and the jollity come only after a certain signal has been given that says it's safe. Thurman's script seemed to be saying, "It's hell here for us, and don't you think otherwise." Even though, as Alison Smith said, "it has the deep, half unconscious thrill of compassion which the Negro actors give to a study of nostalgia, the bewildered, inarticulate homesickness of a little family, lured from their North Carolina cabin into the smoldering jungle of Harlem."[36] Either the compassion was not enough or the jungle was too much. It did not sire a trend and remains, to today, a unique attempt to blend real themes, a fast-paced plot, and lots of crowd-pleasing bits into a total commercial vehicle. Of the huge cast (there were twenty actors), only one was white, and he got his picture in the paper every time, but it was a fitting piece with which to end the decade.

Lulu Belle, its predecessor by four years and coauthored by Sheldon (he of *The Nigger*) and Charles Mac Arthur (subsequently, Helen Hayes's fourth husband) was much more successful. It used white actors in cork for its leads: namely, Lenore Ulric in the title role and none other than Henry Hull, that famous old actor whose face you know even if you can't remember his name, as her Black lover who follows her from San Juan Hill to Harlem, then to Paris, just so he can kill her because she jilted him. I don't care how young he was at the time, skinny Henry Hull in that plains patriarch speech of his trying to be a Black youth wronged (inside the conjugal bed or out) must have been the funniest thing since Chaplin's *Gold Rush*. But since Belasco produced it, and since it was white authored completely, it spoke the right language and ran at the Bishop's (that was Belasco's nom de Lulu) theater for 461 performances. Just goes to show, East is East. *Lulu Belle* is just what her names implies: a Black lady of ill repute who uses her lusty limbs to move ever upward as the plot thickens, being true to nothing and no one in the process. And that's about it. Percy Hammond was simply appalled. Said he,

Piloted by Mr. Belasco, the playgoers last night did some slumming in the black belt. It was a rowdy evening among the wicked colored folk, with frequent exhibitions of the more scandalous depravities. We saw them committing nearly all the popular intemperances from murder to the Charleston, and doing so in the ardent fashion common to the Afro American temperament. . . . Night excursions to the russet borderlands may be one of your smaller vices. It is, they say, a vivacious feature of tourist life in New York to visit the sable [there's that word again —ed.] pleasure grounds and there unpack the white man's burden. In the event that you are interested in the Negro New Yorker in his more animal aspects, *Lulu Belle* will be to you an ochre extravaganza. . . . I thought it was just a sordid, gaudy, episodic, honk-a-tonk, expensive, daring and sensational.[37]

He may have had the right idea about the play, but I fear for the wrong reasons. To run the gamut of popular intemperances, starting with murder and ending up with the Charleston, is pretty nigh unto being confused about what constitutes an intemperance, popular or otherwise. But Mr. Hammond was always careful to turn a phrase neatly in his polite distaste of Black "ethnicities," speaking as he does of the ardent fashion common to the "Afro" American temperament. Since Mr. Hammond was not himself interested in the more animal aspects of the Negro New Yorker, one assumes he could unpack his white man's burden without having ever to carry it with him. But of course, none of this had anything to do with the play or with Black theater. Neither did most of what Percy Hammond had to say in the many years he was the ranking drama critic for New York's number-two newspaper, alas. Woollcott, after passing MacArthur off as a vagrant newspaper man from out Chicago way, goes on to say of the final encounter between Romeo and Juliet,

> There at the end we find her snaky and content, with pearls around her neck . . . there at the end he finds her too, the negro [shall I *sic* once more?] lad to whom she had given the biggest bum's rush in Harlem history—now he had crawled across the world to be with her again and when she spits on him the silken boudoir becomes for a moment a bit of the ancestral jungle. For . . . he kills her with his bare and bitter hands and he is whimpering over her in bewilderment and sorrow as the final curtain falls. For the most part he, Belasco, has turned the Negro parts over to Negro players, and the performance is the better on that account.[38]

Would he had done so completely. To have seen Henry Hull trying to be neegrow while he was the young lover wronged would have almost been worth enduring Percy Hammond with calm. Atkinson probably summed it all up best when he said *Lulu Belle* is splendid showmanship, but it retains few of the elements of drama. But it made more money than *Harlem*.

Evaluating a decade as rich and varied as the twenties is not easy, especially since it was the first one in American theater in which both serious theater and musical theater of strictly American authorship had made significant growth simultaneously. This was true of Black as well as white theater. If any one group can be said to have dominated the theater of the period, it was the Theatre Guild, an organization that produced its first play in 1919 and had racked up a record of over 230 productions in the following fifty years. Lawrence Langner and Theresa Helbrun were the two prime powers of this mammoth organization that not only had several hits running on Broadway at one time over the years but introduced many European classics to America (Strindberg's *The Dance of Death*, Molnar's

Lilliom), and did major O'Neill and Shaw as well, including the world premiere of *St. Joan.*

The big show then, as now, was the Broadway musical. Ziegfeld started it all with his *Follies*, in a sense. Live theater was still the seat of high glamour. The *Follies*, the *Scandals*, the Shubert shows, Theatre Guild—these were the top of the ladder, while silent movies were still trying to find ever more ingenious ways to be dramatic and still not talk. And the decade was, and remains, the most successful one for the Black musical. Of the more than twenty Broadway productions, at least five were written by Blacks. Hughes lists sixteen musicals that opened on Broadway between 1921 and 1929! The two most successful came at the beginning and at the end of the decade. *Shuffle Along* played 484 times at the Sixty-Third Street Theatre (which was then "way uptown"). Lew Leslie's *Black Birds of 1928* ran for 519 performances. In between there was *Liza*, which ran 172 times; *Runnin' Wild*, which did business for 224 days; *Rang Tang* and *Keep Shufflin*, 119 and 104 respectively; and *Hot Chocolates*, which came in third at 228. These are just the leaders. Why were the Black musicals able to have such a big presence then, only to almost fade away into insignificance for the next forty years, you ask? It's a good question. The usual answer, Langston Hughes's, is "They done stole my blues and gone." Tom Fletcher called it ragtime. Eubie Blake, jazz syncopation. Without getting technical, what happened simply was that the rhythms and the pace that Eubie Blake, Noble Sissle, and their legions introduced in these shows made everyone sit up and take notice. Jimmy McHugh, Dorothy Fields, Harold Arlen, and "their" legion got their training firsthand, either in Harlem cabarets or in the front row of Broadway theaters where they went to watch the Black musicals. But "once the white boys learned how to write the jazz syncopation, nobody used us anymore," Eubie Blake was to observe later. The dancing and the sheer intensity that the Black performer brought to the stage (coupled with the music and the great performers themselves), the energy, the seemingly limitless ability for change, variation, nuance—all the things that make artistry art, these couldn't be copied. But enough was so that the Black musical ceased to be a big force after 1929. Not only has *Shuffle Along* been revived several times since but, after its year on Broadway, it toured for two more. So many legends were born with the show that it's a show within a show. First there was the fact that it was written entirely (books, lyrics, music) by Black talent. It was produced by Blacks (although white Al Mayer had to be brought in when it caught on in New York). Josephine Baker was in the chorus and Florence Mills in the lead and Langston Hughes on the sidelines to put it all in proper perspective. Baker was in Paris within four years, creating future shock at the *Follies Begére.*

Florence Mills became an instant star. Said Gilbert Seldes in the *Seven Lively Arts*, "Merely to watch her walk out upon the stage with her long, free stride and her superb, shameless swing, is an aesthetic pleasure; she is a school and exemplar of carriage and deportment; two other actors I have seen so take a stage. . . . Florence Mills is almost the definition of the romantic 'une force qui va,' but she remains an original, with her presence, her instinctive grace, and her baffling, seductive voice."[39] And St. John Ervine said in London, "The success acquired by Miss Florence Mills, the American colored girl, playing in *From Dover to Dixie*, is something unequaled by any American playing here in the past decade."[40] Edith Isaacs added to the encomiums, "Since there was no doubt that she had a delightful presence, a natural charm, projection, grace, and the voice of a bird turned

FIGURE 4.2. Florence Mills in costume for *Blackbirds*, 1926. Collections of the New York Public Library.

woman, what did [she] lack? [She had] an audience's eyes glued to her every moment of her performance. When she sang and danced at the Palace, you would have to go early to find a seat, and in the audience you would see artists with their sketch books, dancers, poets, whom you gradually came to know as among Florence Mills's most admiring fans."[41]

And the Renaissance was launched. The mainline critics didn't quite know what to make of the show. It was so toney, dignified in its liveliness, that none of the old rules applied. It wasn't until *Liza* and *Runnin' Wild* that the likes of Woollcott and Broun and Garland and Gilbert Gabriel and the rest caught up with the new culture. It had come out of Harlem by way of all the towns that these performers hailed from, this completely new type of Black show. Sissle and Blake and Miller and Lyles, acting as their own producers, got an engagement to play at the Howard Theater in Washington, DC. But when the cast assembled at Penn Station, it turned out that there wasn't enough money to pay everyone's train fare. Some of the actors were ready to turn around and go back to Harlem at that point. In the end, they played the DC engagement and from there went on to the Dunbar in Philadelphia.[42] The costumes were dog-eared, and there was hardly enough money to turn on the lights when they got to New York, but they opened and the rest is history. The show was such a hit that the police had to turn West Sixty-Third Street into a one-way street just to handle the traffic. All four men performed in the show as well as having served in all the other capacities: Sissle singing, Blake playing the piano, and Miller and Lyles doing the main comedy. They played in cork. Said Edith Isaacs of their work, "Miller and Lyles were remarkable for the fact that they were two expert comedians neither of whom played the other into the shadow. They had packed them in' in vaudeville and in Harlem long before they came to Broadway. Many teams (Black and white) had only one first-rate act which they used with slight variants for years. Miller and Lyles had any number and improvised freely on all of them."[43] (They also wrote the book for *Runnin' Wild.*) The *Morning Telegraph* review sneered at *Shuffle Along* thus: "Syncopation in its most virile—not to say virulent—form descended upon our fair city last night within a stone's throw of staid Central Park. The actors in the troupe are all of the negro [sic] persuasion."[44] *Time* thought the syncopation was a plus. The *Evening Journal* didn't like it. Burns Mantle did, though his enthusiasm was decidedly tempered. Mixed reviews aside, it was a groundbreaker. Hurwitz, to his credit, lists the precedent-setting firsts that *Shuffle Along* gets credit for:

It broke the color-barrier in the audience. Prior to Shuffle Along, people of color sat in sections to which they were relegated, but on opening night African-American patrons were seated as far down as the fifth row of the orchestra.

Shuffle Along was the first show in which a genuinely sincere love duet, "Love Will Find A Way" was sung by two persons of color. Up until this time the only love songs sung by African Americans were either satirical or parodies.

The Broadway audience got its first experience of African-American people of depth with whom they could empathize.

Shuffle Along launched the careers of a whole generation of great African-American entertainers including: Josephine Baker, Florence Mills, Adelaide Hall and others.[45]

But as Hurwitz points out, the show did not totally avoid the blackface stereotype. And in order not to appear to be too educated and "white," the players in the orchestra pit committed the entire score to memory because, Eubie Blake remembered, "it was expected of us. People didn't believe that black people could read music—they wanted to think that our ability was just natural talent."[46] They were, in fact, highly trained musicians, many of whom had long careers. Both Hughes and Loften Mitchell credit *Shuffle Along* for launching the Harlem Renaissance. Two of the many standout tunes, "Love Will Find a Way" and "I'm Just Wild about Harry," have endured. Truman used the latter for his campaign theme song.

But it wasn't until *Liza* in 1922 and *Runnin' Wild* a year later that the Black musical of the period got the kind of reviews it deserved. The *New York Times* said Miller and Lyles were "funny, deeply funny," and even liked the show better than *Shuffle Along* adding, "There is, to be sure, the traditional superstition scene, but there is not so much as a line about shooting craps, and ham replaces chicken as the most desirable of all dishes."[47] The *Tribune* review, written by MAG, wasn't going along, though. "MAG" (who doesn't appear in the New York Drama Critics' list from the twenties and thirties) could just as easily have been Percy Hammond himself, judging by his "sable" attitude. Said he or she, "There is no particular reason why one should travel all the way up to 62nd Street to get his vaudeville, unless he insists that its protagonists be a little second rate and a trifle diluted with African. While there is a good deal of risible dental display . . . the best negro [could he help but *sic*?] comedian [is not] anywhere near as good as Eddie Canter as an imitator of one." Ending with the complaint that he could hardly tell if the actors were "African fish or caucasian [*sic*] fowl." Give a racist reviewer credit for one thing in the twenties, he put it on the line, he did. Or she. Along with Hammond's constant use of the nineteenth-century nugget "sable," MAG brought back memories of England and the *London Times* review of Aldridge in 1821 with this observation (we're still in the same review): "The audience included the bootblack who glosses at the corner of 116th Street and Broadway."[48] The democracy had not as yet quite been set in place, you see. So even though bootblacks and the like could not in fact be kept out of a public performance, their actual insistence on showing up for all to see was considered to be, well, at least "forward." Said the *Sun*, "*Runnin' Wild* is a re-write of Liza. In the matter of its embellishments it has far outstripped the other two pickaninnies."[49] Wow! Alan Dale was, by contrast, euphoric. Writing in the *American* he said, "Miller and Lyles are quite as good as they were in *Shuffle Along*. The team work is excellent. They are assuredly extraordinarily funny

FIGURE 4.3. Josephine Baker in a publicity shot when she was the Queen of Paris, ca. 1925–1940. Collections of the New York Public Library.

but they never give you an overdose. It is not as noisy as its predecessors. It may even be a trifle classier—if I may use so nauseating an expression, in its peripheral motion it is endless movement. It is the epitome of animation. It might make an oyster get up on its hind legs and do a jig."[50] But *Liza* was the critics' favorite. The *World* said, "[It's] the fastest dancing show ever seen on Broadway. . . . Let some of the dancers on Broadway who think they can really dance to the king's taste"— I don't know where that reference came from, the Revolutionary War had been won 145 years before—"come to the midnight performance of *Liza* next Wednesday and compare their dancing with his."[51] The "his" referred to Johnny Nit, whom Woollcott praised copiously, as he was not wont to do. Writing in the *New York Herald*, here's some of what he had to say about the show:

> When all this boundless zest converged in the magnificent finale of the first act you had dancing that reached the point of ecstasy and achieved simply and happily the effect for which Irving Berlin strove so laboriously in the infernal scene of the *Music Box Revue*. In some ways we have enjoyed no musical show this season so much as *Liza*. With *Liza* there seemed to come back to the stage something of the infinite relish [of the past] thus when [the dancers] went through Dandy last evening, they did it as if they had been born into the world to do just that.[52]

Dandy refers to one of the numbers in the second act. But it was left to Heywood Broun to take it all into the realm of a major chord:

> The first reportorial responsibility of any reviewer who goes to a Negro musical comedy is to say whether it is as good as *Shuffle Along*. *Liza* isn't—and yet in one respect we found it even better. It sets the standard of ensemble dancing a little higher. We don't remember having seen anything in New York to compare with the extraordinary combination of fury and precision which the chorus puts into its work. After *Shuffle Along* we all said "this is all very well, but it isn't primitive." That can't be said about Liza. It seems to be the contribution of a race in which rhythm is a sense as definite as sight or touch or hearing. When thirty or forty performers begin to sway and throb to the music there comes the realization that here is something which nobody else has. We have seen dancing more beautiful, but none which began to be as exciting. After seeing *Liza* we have a vague impression that all other dancers whom we ever saw did nothing but minuets.[53]

Broun was never afraid to say what was on his mind, even if he ran the risk of discrediting his "liberal" reputation or of being misunderstood by his neegrow friends. Not being primitive enough is, of course, exactly why it was appreciated more by the critics after they saw it than it was when they did. They wanted exotica. The jungle in the city. They came with their prefrontals ready to be lobotomized lest they go insane from too much jungle fever. When they didn't get the full thrust exactly as they had imagined it, they were disappointed. The point about *Shuffle Along* is that it was done for Black audiences. The fact that white ones loved it too was gravy. But Sissle, Blake, Miller, and Lyles were professionals, part of the generation that had grown up making a living north of 110th Street in the tradition of post–Williams and Walker. It was a thriving business in a thriving era, north of 110th Street. That the two cultures met south of the Park, was a happy happenstance for all concerned. By the time they saw *Liza* and the rest, these critics could put the Black beat into a context that they had digested. In spite of all that, the fame didn't last. Like Florence Mills, the Black musical died just when it was at its height. She had started in the business at the tender age of six. She was eight when she sang in *Sons of Ham*. She was thirty-one when she died in 1927.

When Connie Immerman (whose Connie's Inn rivaled the Cotton Club) brought *Hot Chocolates* downtown from Harlem in '29 and it closed, so did Black song and dance on Broadway. What an outpouring it had been. The Charleston was introduced in *Runnin' Wild*. Then came the Black bottom, the shim-sham-shimmy, and the Lindy. The songs are still being sung: "I'm Just Wild about Harry," "Love Will Find a Way," "I Don't Want to Set the World on Fire," "Lover Man," "Goodnight Irene," "Ain't Misbehavin'," "Honeysuckle Rose," and on and on. The names of the talent: Maceo Pinkard, Fats Waller, Roger Ramirez (who was Puerto Rican), Andy Razaf, J. P. Johnson and J. C. Johnson (not related to James Weldon or J. Rosamund), Tom Lemonier, Don Heyward, Henry Creamer, and Porter Grainger—but you've never heard of any of them, right? A great deal of the legacy and the legend began in 1918 when the building that was to become the internationally famous Cotton Club was erected at 142nd Street and Lenox Avenue (see Jim Haskins's *Cotton Club*, Random House, 1977). Jack Johnson, Lil Arthur himself, owned it originally and tried to make it into a fancy supper club. The idea was right, but the pigmentation of the owner wasn't. Gangster Owney Madden, an Englishman by birth, took over the operation as an outlet for his bootleg beer. Prohibition, which became law in 1919, made the cabaret business a boom industry. Madden turned Jack Johnson's "Club De Luxe" into a seven-hundred-seat nightclub with a jungle decor. To ensure loyalty, he only hired musicians and workers from Chicago, and the chorus girls were all very light skinned, under twenty-one, and over five feet and six inches tall. The male performers didn't have to be under twenty-one, over five foot six, or light skinned, just talented. Madden's Cotton Club opened in 1923. All the performers were Black; all the production personnel, artistic or otherwise, were white. That remained a Cotton Club rule, almost without exception, for the next seventeen years. By 1930, it had become as familiar as Thanksgiving turkey. Harlem paid a terrible price for its Cotton Club fame, but Harlem did get the fame. The price came in the degradation of having a club in the heart of what had become Black Harlem that Blacks couldn't go to. It wasn't until '27, '28 that light-skinned Blacks or famous Blacks could make it past the giant who stood at the door. Black women in the company of white men were let in routinely, but not Black men, with women white or Black. Smalls Paradise opened in 1925, and it let in Blacks in all shades and sexes and genders and

all three or both. Connie's Inn followed. They remained, along with the Plantation Club, the big four until the Plantation hired Cab Calloway away from the
Cotton Club. Not only did Madden object; he sent in the goons, who destroyed
the place, throwing chairs and tables and even the bar into the street. The owner
suddenly disappeared, Cab returned to the Cotton Club, and then there were
three. And three they would be for the rest of the two decades that Harlem cabaret
nightlife was in its glory. Smalls Paradise was owned by Ed Smalls, who was the
only Black owner of a major club in Harlem then. Smalls gave his club a different
beat. Waiters danced the Charleston and delivered meals on roller skates. Smalls
never closed and offered a breakfast dance with a full floor show that started at six
in the morning. Connie Immerman may have been the sincerest white man to ever
get involved in Harlem nightclub show business. His place had the reputation of
not having a tough policy when it came to Black patronage. Immerman himself
had many real friends among his Harlem acquaintances. When he moved downtown, he tried to open a Black club in the Broadway district, feeling that Blacks
were ready for their own place in the sun. It didn't work; nevertheless, Connie
Immerman, may he rest in peace, tried. The uptown action had so created its own
reality that by the late twenties, performers, dancers, singers, and musicians from
downtown came uptown after their own shows to get in on the real action. Duke
Ellington became the Cotton Club bandleader in 1927. He almost didn't get the
job because of the old Chicago bias. (He'd never been near the Windy City.)
Other Black musicians talked Duke up, even though they weren't allowed in the
place themselves, and wiser heads prevailed. Cab Calloway followed him in 1930.
In 1931, Clarence Robinson, a Black nightclub man, was the first "sable" show-
man to produce a Cotton Club act—that is, choreograph and create it. By 1930
also, the likes of young Adam Clayton Powell Jr. were being allowed in. He fell in
love with Isabel Washington from the chorus. She had starred in Thurman's *Harlem* and became Powell's first wife. George Raft used to hang around the Cotton
Club, and Powell sent him on errands on more than one occasion. Within five
years, Raft was a Hollywood star, and he was doing the sending. The Cotton Club
shows were costing $4,000 per week. There was gold in them thar hills. Mad Dog
Coll was broke and decided that a sure way to make money was to capture not
only Big Frenchy Demange, the visible hood at the Cotton Club (Madden always
kept a low profile), but Connie Immerman's brother, George, as well. He made
Madden and Connie cough up $50,000 between them to get their respective part-
ners back, whole and breathing. They did get their guys back, and Coll was cornered and killed in 1932 in a phone booth in Chelsea. Louis Armstrong's wife,
Daisy Parker, broke the light-skinned taboo in 1932 and Prohibition was repealed
in 1933. Connie closed up shop and went downtown and flopped. Ethel Waters
sang the Arlen number, "Stormy Weather," and started her own legend. And even
though there was a Depression on, the people who had money were still making
the trip north of 110th Street. Lena Horne was in the chorus by 1934, and Jimmy
Lunceford, with his band, sat where Ellington and Calloway had sat before him.

Despite the success, the chorus girls still made twenty-five dollars a week and were still docked for lateness or for missing a rehearsal and still received no meals that they didn't pay for. Said Lena Horne, "All the lucrative end of the business, the owning of songs, copyrights etc. were all controlled by whites." Maceo Pinkard, Andy Razaf, Handy, Eubie Blake—even Flournoy Miller, who had written, directed, and performed on Broadway, and not only in *Shuffle Along*—couldn't get hired at the Cotton Club except as comedians. By 1935, there was a Cotton Club Boys chorus line, but a year later, the club closed up shop and moved to Forty-Eighth Street. The shows were bigger and better and more successful. Bill Robinson became a headliner. Louis Armstrong played, and Peg Leg Bates performed. Sammy Cahn replaced Harold Arlen. And Stepin Fetchit was about the last of the headliners. The Cotton Club closed in 1940, and Lou Walters (Barbara's father) took over the site and opened his Latin Quarter. It had been quite a story. One could say that it mirrored the life of Harlem in its seventeen-year run. But of course, there was much that Harlem had produced in Harlem and beyond that neither was of the Cotton Club's making nor owed the club fealty in any way, even in the club's bailiwick, putting on the big show.

Harlem and the messages it sent out in the decade of *Shuffle Along*, Florence Mills, and the literary flowering north of Central Park weren't always bright and cheery. A man named Marcus Mosiah Garvey—short, squat, all Black, and full featured—had the magic and the charisma to give the children of the dream a new sense of themselves. He raised millions of dollars from poor, hardworking men and women, dressed them up in uniforms, and gave them organizations with fancy names to belong to. He had coming-out parties for the teenage girls so they could be introduced into society. This at a time when a Black girl couldn't get a job on 125th Street as a cleaning woman, when the police routinely beat Blacks in the street, in the station houses, in their own homes, everywhere. And as Adam Clayton Powell Sr. (father of the congressman)—who had brought his flock north of San Juan Hill (the battleground block on Sixty-Third Street, where whites on one side and Blacks on the other waged a domestic Spanish-American War) and established the Abyssinia Baptist Church as one of the richest, largest, and most powerful of Black churches in the country—was to say, "The coming of Marcus Garvey to Harlem in 1916 was more significant to the Negro than the World War. . . . He awakened a race-consciousness that made Harlem felt around the world. I am not writing a brief for Marcus Garvey, but it's recording truth, and perhaps for the first time, to say that he is the only man that ever made Negroes who are not Black ashamed of their color."[54]

The dreams of not only Garvey but Black theater itself were to be deferred. Moss Hart—in his autobiography, *Act One*—tells of playing Smithers to Gilpin's Brutus Jones in the 1926 revival and of how Gilpin began drinking onstage and was fast losing most of his powers because, as Hart tells it, Gilpin finally realized that he would never ever get an opportunity to do anything other than play in seedier and seedier revivals of *The Emperor Jones*. He was to die five years later, never having done anything else. This for the man whom O'Neill had praised

FIGURE 4.4. Exotic dancers from the Cotton Club Parade, featured at the Cotton Club in New York, ca. 1938. Schomburg Center for Research in Black Culture, Photographs and Prints Division, The New York Public Library Digital Collections.

as the most accurately brilliant actor he had ever known! Jean Eagles, a fleeting flame herself, played in *Rain* for four years and seemed, like Gilpin, to be imprisoned in the role. But it was a confinement of her own choosing, and she was making $3,500 a week for serving time. She too got drunk onstage and forgot lines. She even forgot she was onstage at times. (Ask Leslie Howard, who had to play opposite her.) Once, she even forgot to come onstage. But Hollywood gave her

FIGURE 4.5. Noble Sissle and cast members from the musical *Shuffle Along*, 1921. Billy Rose Theatre Division, The New York Public Library Digital Collections.

a $300,000 contract afterward nevertheless. Charles Gilpin died in a cheap hotel with a half-empty bottle by his side for comfort and last rites. Although the Black community gave him proper burial when they found out. If poverty comes, malnutrition and death can't be far behind.

The Black character had come a long way from the coon show by 1930. He had learned to speak English. He had been addressed in contexts and conflicts that made the idea of using blackface absurd. He had come of age, in one sense. Yet the great playwright to do him ultimate justice had not arrived yet. O'Neill had the talent but not the interest, abandoning the Black character early on. But a new dawn was breaking. Not only was there a community where Blacks were fast coming into power (a community that was theirs), but there was also a body of work that depicted the Black man as citizen and as part of the republic of letters as well. Just how far he would be allowed to continue to go in growing into a full-fledged cultural being was still moot. But he was on his way. It only remained for the society

FIGURE 4.6. Georgette Harvey (Maria) and Percy Verwayne (Sporting Life) in the stage production of *Porgy*, 1927. Vandamm Studio.

at large to let him have his head, as it were, for him to actually come to full flower, to completely realize all of his possibilities. For no matter how much he wanted to do on his own, he was still at the mercy of a larger, stronger power. That he had a unique and vital contribution to make to American theater, there was no doubt. Not that American theater wasn't being liberated without him. It was. But theater in any period can never have too much success. And the voice of reaction was as strong in the twenties as it was a decade later when Father Coughlin, the anti-Semitic priest, had a national audience of ten million, and the keepers of the public morals were as much of a hindrance to good theater as racism itself was to the development of Black theater.

Having gotten his foot in the door, the Black character seemed by the end of the decade to have positioned himself perfectly for a long and successful life. It is unfortunate that when there is a general problem in the republic, the advances made by Black America (that decades of hard work and planning have created) can get wiped out in a week or a month. When the crash on Wall Street descended on the nation in full, in the period between 1929 and 1932, it created havoc in Black theater. Not that all the signs had pointed to optimal growth in 1929, but

FIGURE 4.7. Charles Gilpin in the stage production *The Emperor Jones*, 1920. Billy Rose Theatre Division, The New York Public Library Digital Collections.

they had certainly indicated that, taken in conjunction with everything that had happened since 1898, the decade of 1929–1939 would see Black plays by Black playwrights that didn't have to cater to non-Black tastes as egregiously as had *Appearances*, for example. By the time the party was over and the decade of the thirties had ended, there was still confusion about what Black theater meant, what it stood for, what it could achieve. The issue of race—which was addressed so explicitly *in theater* in the first decade of the century, with Sheldon and the miscegenation play, and later, in the twenties, with O'Neill, lasting into the thirties

FIGURE 4.8. Charles Gilpin as the Emperor Jones, 1920.
Billy Rose Theatre Division, The New York Public Library
Digital Collections.

with Hughes and the miscegenation play again (*Brass Ankle*, on Broadway)—had disappeared by the time World War II was over. Race has not made a meaningful return to the Broadway stage since then. Black theater sans race has continued to dominate, but that's a different cup of cappuccino.

Neither Sheldon's confrontation nor his call to honesty was imitated in theater on Broadway because that theater had to find a more ameliorating role for itself. The most socially explosive issue in America then, and now, was how the issue of race was handled. Would it be stated in egregious terms that were unacceptable to the public at large and to the journalists, those who would have to pass judgment on those would-be works, many of whom were little more than hate mongers themselves? Or would there be a gimmick, a way out for the ordinary man in the street so that the individual wouldn't have to feel like the bastard the entire nation had been when he paid his money, bought a ticket, and expected to be entertained?

Harlem, in spite of Percy Hammond and all his legions, had left a legacy when the twenties ended. It left it in the Black character as actor and in song and in dance and in the elemental beat that Black rhythm created, a beat that was subsequently "borrowed"—and borrowed with such conviction that the borrowing put Black artists out of business. What died with the twenties was spirit. A spirit that broke open the shell that mammies and minstrels and coons had been caged in since the first kid Jumped Jim Crow and saw a white man steal it and give him a dollar. The abandon that made the twenties roar also made it joyous, happy, willing to try anything *new*—anything that would exhilarate, inspire. That gave the Black song and dance man and woman, the Black actor, the Black beauties, the Black writers and comedians a chance they had never had before. It gave them the chance to do what their artistic imagination not only told them but demanded that they do. They became themselves in a way they have never been able to be—either before or since. White audiences came to see Black actors in their true inner reality. A reality that no one had ever seen—not even Black actors themselves, since they never had the license to find out what they could do when the restraints against making love and not doing a plantation jig suddenly weren't there anymore. And that's what made the twenties a decade like no other. It came. It happened. And it went, like a thief in the night, taking all of its immense treasure trove of theatrical genius with it. It has never returned because time and circumstance have once again put the Black theatrical persona back in the bottle, if you will. Behind a mask that laughs while it cries.

5 · THE "VOODOO" *MACBETH* AND THE FAMISHED DAWN

Whatever it was that made for the Black vogue of the twenties died with the Depression. No one had to steal anyone else's "blues and gone" in the early thirties, because everyone had them. Poverty had brought the general citizenry to such a low level that it almost destroyed the social barriers that existed between Black and white. And yet Black actors of the WPA played all across the country, as far west as Dallas, side by side with white ones—and in nonsegregated houses. That's as counterintuitive as you can get. But once the war helped Roosevelt and the New Deal solve the Depression and prosperity returned to the land, so did the old barriers, with a vengeance. Hollywood was still up to its tricks of insisting that the seventeen million Black people that existed in America in 1948 didn't exist. An article in the *Amsterdam News* quoted a Hollywood producer as saying that Black characters were "not essential to the structural plot" of a film he was producing about the numbers racket in Harlem.[1] Put that in your bag of racial exclusion tricks under "We see the neegrow but we don't, if you know what I mean." As early as 1946, Ruby Dee, like any Black man or woman, could not set foot in Miami Beach, since she didn't have an identification tag complete with her picture, her name, and the "family" she worked for inscribed on it. Especially since she didn't work for a family. She worked for herself in theater.

But when the crash came in 1929 and the banks closed and stockbrokers jumped out of windows, that was that. Downtown, like a college girl playing at love, returned to the precincts of Park Avenue and left the dark lover to the desolate days of the famished dawn. Again, not premeditated, maybe—who expected the Depression?—but symptomatic nevertheless of the shallowness of the bond, of the dire limitations of the détente. It was, and is, almost as if powerful forces would always destroy any attempt by Black and white to join together permanently. Whether the intent to destroy had always been there or not, its reality seemed always too easily consummated. And when times got hard, as they would get in the thirties, the price Harlem was to pay was a severe one. Van Wyck Brooks

FIGURE 5.1. Crowds outside the Lafayette Theatre in Harlem for opening night of Federal Theatre Project's production of *Macbeth*, April 14, 1936. Schomburg Center for Research in Black Culture, Photographs and Prints Division, The New York Public Library Digital Collections.

has called America a country of first acts, and there is something in the nature of the beast of who we are that we always have to move on. To use up quickly what we have gone to so much trouble to create in the first place. Whether the motion is inherent in the act or whether the genesis of our "usness" has made us perpetual whirligigs, the fact remains that we are a metamorphosis in the act of happening. It's an impulse that didn't die with the nineteenth century and Johnny Appleseed. It's as alive today as it was in the good old covered wagon days, and if the first act never seems to have a sequel, it's only because we grow in fits and starts rather than in logical sequences.

In 1931, with over eight million people out of work, the devastation in the Black communities was twice as bad as it was in any other community. Nationwide, the number would jump to over *twelve million*. Six years later, the Depression so deepened that Roosevelt, in his second inaugural address, would utter the famous words: "I see one-third of a nation ill-housed, ill-clad, ill-nourished." In Detroit, over 40 percent of all the workers were unemployed. In Harlem, fully half the families were out of work and unable to get relief. How they survived is almost too difficult to imagine. In the midst of all this grinding poverty, overt racism was unending in its relentless inequity. In Harlem, no Black man or woman was allowed to work in any department store anywhere north of 110th Street (forget about south) between the rivers. Not in Woolworth's nor in Kress's nor in Blumstein's. On 125th Street, the Fifth Avenue of the area, Blacks couldn't even get seated in the better restaurants. In 1937, the wife of W. C. Handy (the pioneer jazz composer—*St. Louis Blues*, etc.) lay critically ill in an ambulance for over an hour in front of Knickerbocker Hospital, in Harlem, while officials debated whether a Black person should be admitted. Even one as estimable as Mrs. Handy. As if that wasn't as egregious as it gets, in 1934, as reported in the *New York Times*, a twenty-three-year-old man, Albert Jackson, was sentenced to thirty years in jail for stealing thirty-eight cents! His two confederates received from ten to thirty years each for the same crime.[2] So a year later, in 1935, Harlem rioted, ten thousand strong. It was a historical first. It was the first time in America that a race riot in this country had been started by Blacks instead of whites. Word went out that a Puerto Rican youngster had been set upon in a Kress department store and stomped to death because he stole a ten-cent pocketknife. As it turned out, the youngster was safely at home with his mother at the time that thousands had gathered in front of the store on 135th Street, screaming revenge for his brutal murder. Before it was over, there were in fact two dead (both Black), scores of injured policemen, and hundreds of other citizens in the hospital. A new militancy had been set loose in the streets, and Harlem would never be the same again. The Italian-Ethiopian war of 1936 reached all the way to Harlem in this atmosphere of unrest. Mussolini was having a great time killing barefooted Ethiopians, who were fighting his contemporary cannon with nineteenth-century rifles. At PS 75, an Italian and a Black kid squared off to prove which side in Africa was really superior. The press clippings of the time have the Black youngster winning the initial encounter and the white youngster getting help for a return engagement, which in turn not only led to parents from both sides themselves squaring off the next day but forced officials to close the school for two days after that.

On a much more serious note, soapbox oratory on 125th Street and Seventh Avenue (as well as other popular corners in Harlem) became a fixture. The Communist Party took up the Black struggle and ran a Black man, James W. Ford, for vice-president in a national campaign in which the ticket received over one hundred thousand votes. The party also defended the Scottsboro Boys, the last of whom wasn't acquitted until 1978! Briefly: white hoboes were riding the boxcar in 1935 when a group of Black hoboes got on. It wasn't long before the white hoboes tried to throw the Black hoboes off the train. Instead, the Black men did the throwing off. The white ones immediately ran to the authorities and claimed two white women had been raped. (The women, it turned out, were ladies of the night and untouched by Black hands, as one later testified in court.) The authorities stopped the train in Scottsboro, and Alabama condemned all nine of the "Boys" to death. So important was this case that it spawned reams of newsprint, several books, and two plays: *They Shall Not Die* by white writer John Wexley and *Legal Murder* by Black writer Dennis Donoghue. But that wasn't the worst of it. That dubious honor goes to Claude Neal. Blacks were being lynched. We all know that. But it is generally assumed that this was done clandestinely. However, in Greenwood, Florida, an open invitation was sent out across the country to anyone who wanted to come to Florida and watch Claude Neal die. The invitation was carried in newspapers from Louisiana to North Dakota. A radio station in Dothan, Alabama, even broadcast it, and the lynch mob waited a day while a crowd of between three and seven thousand gathered from eleven states to join the fun. The details of Neal's death are too gruesome and bestial to even recount here, but they were a high in sadism, coming as they did not in a time of national war.

All the Jazz Age money had dried up. Slumming at the Cotton Club still remained popular for the first few years, but only for the first few. The Theatre Guild, Ziegfeld, and Al Jolson would all go into eclipse, the first and last to rise again. But there was a new seriousness in the air and in theater. Certainly, the hard times and the near revolution that over twelve years of Harding, Coolidge, and Hoover had wrought had made for sobering thought. Drama of protest became the drama of the day. The Communist Party–influenced Theater Union and the intellectually avant-garde Group Theater, which was not Communist (although there were members of the party in Group Theater), pointed the way with plays that addressed the issues that were considered responsible for putting thirteen million people on relief, when they could get it. "Did the system work?" was the real question everyone was asking in theater and out. Plays about the problems of Black people were not only written in this context but produced for all to see. Where an O'Neill had dealt with issues such as mixed marriages, he had done so at a time when the fabric of theater didn't burden itself with the social implications of an issue in broad, sweeping terms. Not that such plays weren't produced in the twenties. Shaw's *On the Rocks* is at least one example and Elmer Rice's *The Adding Machine* is another. But where they did exist, they posited issues and problems and were content to let the mere exploration be an end in itself. Not so the thirties. In the thirties, theater, like the rest of society, had to find answers as well as ask questions. Or certainly, it had to find them more often than it had in the past. Whether this created a better theater is, of course, arguable. It did, in a sense, create a more intellectually virile one.

Black plays, plays by Blacks and about Blacks, rose to new heights, in large measure because of the times and the crises the times created. White plays like *Green Pastures* continued to make Blacks seem like simpleminded remnants of another era, while others like *Stevedore*, along with *They Shall Not Die* and *Legal Murder*, were taking up the fight for justice. *Stevedore*, which shows the brutality of Southern labor camps, was written by white writers Paul Peters and George Sklar. Black playwrights other than Dennis Donoghue were also being produced on Broadway. Langston Hughes's *Mulatto* opened at the Vanderbilt in 1935 and ran for a record

FIGURE 5.2. Richard B. Harrison, who played De Lawd in *Green Pastures*, 1935. Courtesy James C. Campbell.

373 performances before going on the road. The first Black detective story, *Conjur Man Dies* by Rudolph Fisher, was both published and produced in the thirties. As the first attempt at the classics in over 115 years, not only was the Federal Theatre's *Macbeth* a success when it opened in Harlem in 1936, as we've seen, but it too moved to Broadway and from there on to a national tour of six cities ending at the Texas Exposition in Dallas. All this while people were literally starving, while the

army was ordered out and even shot children in one instance to keep the peace, and while company store bullies were beating up women in the streets and killing them in the dead of night. Why was the army being so draconian? Veterans of the First World War (unlike WWII vets) got no gravy train bill of rights. So their protests led to not only riots that resulted in clashes with the army but an organized march on Washington by what was dubbed the Bonus Army of seventeen

FIGURE 5.3. Harlem Renaissance Five: Langston Hughes, Charles S. Johnson, E. Franklin Frazier, Rudolph Fisher, and Hubert T. Delaney, at a party in Hughes's honor, 1924. Collections of the New York Public Library.

thousand veterans in 1932, who demanded cash payment of the service bonuses promised them by Congress eight years earlier.

Langston Hughes lists the following Broadway plays by Black writers in the thirties: *Louisiana* by Gus Smith (1933), which ran for only 8 performances at the Forty-Eighth Street Theatre. *Run Little Chillun* by Hall Johnson (also in '33)— 130 performances at the Lyric. *Legal Murder* by Donoghue (a handsome young devil according to my mother, who knew him growing up in Brooklyn; 1934)— 7 performances at the President (which became Mamma Leone's). Hughes's own *Mulatto. Conjur Man Dies* by Rudolph Fisher; *Turpentine*, also by Gus Smith as well as Peter Morell; *Haiti* by William DuBois; and *The Case of Philip Lawrence* by George MacEntee were some of the more significant productions of the Harlem unit of the Federal Theatre Project other than the *Macbeth*. They were all done at the Lafayette on Seventh Avenue and 132nd Street. Outside of New York, there was *Androcles and the Lion* (adapted from Shaw) from the Seattle unit; *Black Empire* by Christine Ames and Clarke Painter from Los Angeles; *The Swing Mikado* from Gilbert and Sullivan and *Big White Fog* by Theodore Ward, both from Chicago; and *The Trial of Dr. Beck* by Hughes Allison from Newark. *The Trial of Dr. Beck* moved almost immediately to the Maxine Elliott, where it ran 24 times, thanks to the suggestion of J. J. Shubert. New Jersey wanted a production that came from New Jersey and not New York, and young Black playwright Hughes Allison was found, but before his play could be produced, the democracy had to decide if it could withstand a play by a Black playwright with a mixed cast on a public stage in the sovereign state of New Jersey.

Let's begin at the beginning. *The Green Pastures* opened February 26, 1930, at the Royale and stayed there for two years. Five years later, it was revived at the Forty-Fourth Street Theater and held on for seventy-one more performances, and then again as late as 1951 at the Broadway Theater for forty-four nights. It was also made into a film starring Rex Ingram, Eddie Anderson, Oscar Polk, and Edna Mae Harris. (Wikipedia confuses Rex Ingram with the white director of the same name, not only citing him as playing Adam and De Lawd but showing his picture as well). Like *Porgy and Bess* ("I got plenty of nothin'/ and nothin's plenty for me") and Stepin' Fetchit and a lot of other people and things better left unmentioned it was a favorite with white audiences. And the critics sang its praises to the heavens and beyond. After closing in New York, it toured for three more years. In total, over two million people saw it. Like the *Uncle* before it, it played in so many towns in so many states that *Time* magazine printed a map of its journeys in 1935. *Reader's Digest* did a tongue-in-cheek piece listing all the deaths and loves and youths lost to puberty that the play witnessed during those five years. It was banned in three countries. In London, the censor said no because he called it "blasphemous." A London newspaper printed a copy of the text, which brought outrage from its readers, and the House of Commons debated the censor's ban. According to the article with the copied text, the play depicts a simplistic concept of heaven, where the ignorant Southern Negro goes around mumbling in arcane argot of the antebellum South. Marc Connelly, who wrote it, corroborated the characterization with this: "[These are] untutored black Christians—many of whom cannot even read the book which is the treasure house of their faith."[3]

But Atkinson loved it: "It is a work of ethereal beauty and of compassionate comedy without precedent. When the history of the contemporary theater is written, surely it will stand among the plays that have left the deepest impression upon their times."[4] It has done no such thing, thank De Lawd, but Atkinson was so enamored of it that he was still extolling its virtues five years later. Here's a snippet of what will "have left the deepest impression upon our times":

Mammy Angel is solicitously slapping the back of a girl cherub who has a large fish sandwich in her hand and a bone in her throat.

FIRST COOK: Hurry up, Cajey. Dis yere fat's cryin' fo' mo' feesh.
A VOICE [Off stage.] We comin', fas' we kin. Dey got to be ketched, ain't dey? We cain't say. "C'm'on little fish. C'm'on an' git fried," kin we?
SECOND COOK: De trouble is de mens is all worm fishin'.
FIRST MAN ANGEL: Whut dif'rurrce do it make? Yo' all de time got to make out like somebody's doin' somethin' de wrong way.
SECOND COOK: I s'pose you got de per'fec' way fo' makin' bait.
FIRST MAN ANGEL: I ain't sayin' dat. I is sayin' whut's wrong wid worm fishin'.
SECOND COOK: Whut's wrong wid worm fishin'? Ever'thing, dat's all. Dey's only one good way fo' catfishin', an' dat's minny fishin'. Anybody know dat.
FIRST MAN ANGEL: Well, it jest so happen dat minny fishin' is de doggondest fool way of fishin' dey is. You kin try minny fishn' to de cows come home an' all you catch'll be de backache. De trouble wid you, sister, is you jest got minny fishin' on de brain.
SECOND COOK: Go right on, loud mouf. You tell me de news. My, my! You jest de wisest person in de worl'. First you, den de Lawd God.
STOUT ANGEL [To the CHERUB with a bone in her throat.] I tol' you you was too little fo' cat fish. What you wanter git a bone in yo' froat fo'? [She slaps the CHERUB'S back.][5]

The Englishman William Bolitho, writing in the *World*, was ecstatic about its miracles of creative inspiration:

I think the most wonderful part of it is perhaps that he [Marc Connelly], a white man, a New Yorker, a highly civilized man, should have been able to write and produce it. . . . Not one of themselves has yet been able to achieve this, the inner mysterium of their culture . . . that strange, poor people who make you cry when they sing and laugh when they talk, the American colored people. . . . [Negroes have digested the Old Testament] as if cows might take to a ration of meat and alcohol, as if chickens succeeded in living on tops of trees. . . . It is made to outlast. I would place it . . . beside Uncle Remus.[6]

He's right of course. That's where it deserves to be, right next to Uncle Number Two.

Not only Revelation but the Apocalypse must come. Both were onstage in short order. The year hadn't ended before we had another all-Black play, this time in greasepaint, *Scarlet Sister Mary*. Produced by Lee Shubert at the Ethel Barrymore (which was only two years old at the time) and starring the grand dame herself. She had along with her Estelle Winwood, Marjorie Main, and Ted de Corsia, all in blackface, playing Gullah Negroes. I know, you don't believe it. Neither did I at first. In order to justify their "concept" of an all-white cast doing a play about Blacks who speak such a special dialect that many Black actors can't even do convincingly, Miss Barrymore and Mr. Shubert postulated a theory that would have put Black actors out of business permanently. She intoned that the way to eliminate the race question in casting altogether is for white actors to simply take over the Black parts! He agreed, adding that since white actors had taken over the parts of all the other races, why not the neegrow? For the poor Black actor, who never really had his own character for more than a hot minute to begin with, to suddenly find that the time had come for it to be taken away from him forever, by the very same fellow who had had it pretty much to himself off and on for most of its existence, must have seemed like the final theft in an unending line of thefts, of blues stolen and gone. The critics, god bless 'em, said, "Hey, wait a minute. This is a bit much," and nicely and ever so politely sent Miss B. out of town with her *Scarlet Sister*. Gilbert Seldes, writing in the *Evening Telegraph*, summed it up best when he said, "Miss Barrymore appeared . . . in blackface, smoked a pipe, danced a solo and came out toward the end in virginal white as the forty-year old mother of many. In all honor I do not know what to say of this performance. It was not ludicrous, [but] it seemed to me wholly without illusion."[7] Whitney Bolton, in the *Telegraph*, added for good measure that he could see no reason for a white cast, considering the "enormously poised performance turned in by the Negro actors of *Porgy*, the authentic bits made by the Negro actors in *Lulu Belle*, and finally the mature, ripe work of at least three of the Negro players in *Harlem*."[8] Some even suggested walking across the street and seeing *The Green Pastures* to find out how it's done. *Theater Arts* added, "The barriers between the actress and her goal . . . were not less than appalling."[9] Atkinson, in the *Times*, added his discreet dissent as well: "Most of us will never understand why Ethel Barrymore has chosen to appear in *Scarlet Sister Mary*. . . . As a play it is singularly uninteresting. Acted by a company of white performers in blackface, it merely reminds us that the Negroes are the best actors of plays about Negro life."[10]

But there was one reviewer who surpassed himself for racist arrogance. He was none other than the well-esteemed Mr. Stark Young, who, even though he agreed that Miss Barrymore was not convincing, was himself convinced that no Black actor could have done the part any better. Nor, indeed, that Blacks in general had any business being on a stage in the first place. His review for the *New Republic* ran in the issue of December 10, 1930. In part, he intoned the following:

Often when I see Negro players on the stage and afterward when I hear people saying they are great actors I think . . . that dogs and children should not be allowed on the stage, they destroy the artistic effect. . . . Negroes, we may say in passing, are not great actors. . . . No Negro player at present would be likely to have given a great performance of this character. . . . If the play were given with a Negro cast . . . a genuine black woman, right for the part, Southern, in her own way wonderful enough, could never have been taught either the intricacies of the stage art or the general proportions of the role as it fits into the whole play, even if she could have been persuaded to keep up her attendance at rehearsals, and so, accordingly we should have had . . . a shrill, pale yellow person, doubtless, from Harlem, with a divided quality, half white, half black, a sharp Yankee movement, rouged lips and cheeks, straightened hair, and so on, all of it sheer travesty and sickening rot.[11]

It's difficult to react to racism that stark and that brutal, no pun wanted to intend. To reduce an entire race of people in one paragraph to nothing more than mindless menials is beyond endurance, even as far back as 1930. It is a not-too-unsubstantial measure of the degree to which Black theater was fighting an uphill battle when it came to getting artistic credibility from the arbiters of what was and wasn't credible artistically. In the end, the Shuberts must have realized they went too far. I combed the White Photographic Collection at the Lincoln Center Library for the Performing Arts for pictures of the production in vain. They were too ashamed of what they'd done to do anything else that would add to the disgrace and destroyed the evidence.

As if Ethel Barrymore wasn't enough, along came Walter Hampden—who had played everything from *Cyrano* to Shakespeare to *Arsenic and Old Lace*—to do something called *Achilles Had a Heel* in 1935, in blackface. It was probably a bigger mess than the *Scarlet Sister*. Hampden produced and, like Miss B., saw greatness for himself in the role of a burnt cork elephant keeper. John Anderson's review under the title "Baked Hampden" was the best of the lot. Said he,

I can't think of any actor who looks less like a negro [*sic*], except possibly Eddie Cantor, and Mr. Cantor is only joking. . . . The action takes place in a park zoo where [Hampden] is the keeper of the elephant. He thinks he's better than the keeper of the monkeys. The keeper of the monkeys gets even by hiring an African witch doctor [to] cast a spell on the elephant, who begins to die. He is saved by [Hampden's] Christian prayers and voodoo drumming . . . so the monkey man persuades a girl in the park to try dat ole debbil sex on the elephant. [Not sure how she manages that.] Sure enough [it] works. [Hampden] loses his money in a crap game, the girl jilts him and he is demoted . . . to monkey keeper, while the monkey man gets to keep the elephant. In the last act he sees what a fool he made of himself by associating with monkeys and quits.[12]

Now Walter Hampden, whose bio in *Who Was Who in American Theater* takes up three columns, had every right to make an ass of himself. (You'll remember him as the father in *Sabrina* and the toastmaster in *All about Eve*.) If he could find the money, why not? It's a free country. And after all, the critics did call him on it, so where's the harm? Only in this: Paul Robeson was a better actor than Walter Hampden; Charles Gilpin was better. They not only couldn't get a chance to make an ass of themselves but couldn't get a chance to do anything else once they had their one chance. Certainly not Gilpin.

Which brings us to the other plays on Broadway that concern us, the ones by Black and white writers that dealt with Black themes. We have to begin with the iconic legend Langston Hughes. In addition to running for a year on Broadway, *Mulatto* toured for two more. Which made Hughes the leading Black Broadway playwright prior to Lorraine Hansberry's *A Raisin in the Sun*. Her title, incidentally, comes from a line in a Hughes poem: "What happens to a raisin in the sun, does it just dry up or does it fester and run?" *Mulatto* is a two-act play in three scenes that runs a little over thirty pages. There are three main characters. Colonel Norwood is the plantation massah. He's also a bigoted, unfeeling, self-absorbed narcissist and the father of several miscegenated children by his housekeeper, Cora—the loyal Black woman who lives with and suffers under his hateful tyranny. She is also his servant, caregiver, and the only woman in his life. Finally, there's Ben, the son who looks like him, who is the Mulatto of the play. Two themes dominate: the Deep South racist control over thought, body, and minute actions (such as walking through a front door or not being allowed into a library under any circumstance) that was the day-to-day reality for Black people for most of the twentieth century, long after the Civil War was over; and the contradiction between miscegenation (that horrible word) and the decency of parental feelings for the child of one's own.

Earl Carroll, of the *Vanities*, had made a commercial success out of a sex sensation called *White Cargo* in 1924, which he produced for sixty-seven dollars. (No, that's not a misprint.) He acquired the rights to *Mulatto* and was already in production when Hughes got back from a stint as a merchant seaman. When he finally got to see a rehearsal, he found that his script had been greatly rewritten to exploit the violence and the sadistic elements that flirted vaguely in the background. And a minor character—Sallie, who goes off to college in the original in an early scene—is kept in because she was the only pretty young thing in the cast and also so she could be raped at the end. Maybe Earl Carroll knew what he was doing, since the play as produced was a success. Hughes did force some reinsertions to give back a part of the emphasis that was originally intended, but the final effect was as much Carroll as Hughes in some respects. The great actress Rose McClendon was cast in the leading role of Cora. It was her last triumph before she died a year later. Hughes's original script was not published until thirty years after Earl Caroll's version's Broadway run. It was the only play by the literary

FIGURE 5.4. The Great Rose McClendon, 1927. Vandamm Studio.

genius to be done on Broadway, and it must be said at the outset that Hughes's forte is in poetry and prose.

Norwood is willing to have his daughter by Cora, Sallie, go off and be somebody, like a cook in a big city hotel. When she says she wants to come back and teach school, he tells her no, cotton teaches "these pickaninnies enough." And the son Bert, who looks like him and whom he did allow to become educated as well, has actually come back home and wants to exercise "white man" privileges down in Dixie, break the heart of me.[13]

Not only won't the colonel stand for that, but since he did try to beat the idea out of the boy when he was a kid, he's willing to kill him face to face now that he's a man and too big to whip, just to maintain the racial status quo. Blood be damned. The boy objects. But instead of having him live, Hughes kills him off. The racism is so unrelenting, so all pervasive that all Hughes can do with it is have the son strangle the father to death in response to the father's intransigent hate. Hughes saw no other way that would fit his dramatic purposes, not in the Deep South in the era before (or after) the Second World War. The biggest weakness in the script is its inability to develop Bert into a fully rounded example of Black manhood emancipated, even if only temporarily. Bert robs the lynch mob of a killing by committing suicide, but Hughes has also robbed us of a fully developed Black character grappling with his natural father for their salvation—and maybe even for their souls. Hughes leaves it to Cora in the final monologue to bring the evening to a dramatic climax through the strength of the writing, even though the narrative has already played out to all intents and purposes. Not easy to do. Hughes pulls it off. But he would have been better served if he could have found a way to put some of that dramatic intensity into the earlier proceedings instead of saving it all for the last thing that's spoken; especially since everything else meaningful that takes place has already happened. Makes for a tough slog. But in that monologue at the end, fifty-eight lines long, Rose McClendon must have mesmerized the audience.

Of the other three plays listed by Hughes that ran on Broadway in the twenties and thirties, *Run Little Chillun*, by the famed choir master Hall Johnson and the first after *Appearances*, is an old-fashioned sing-along that touts the spiritual benefits of religion but offers not much comfort for a soul that needs more substantive food to feed itself. However, the singing must have been inspiring, since it had a healthy run of 126 performances. It is, however, this critic's unhappy task to admit that he's unable to judge the quality of the music. I can find no text of *Louisiana* by Gus Smith. *Legal Murder* by Dennis Donoghue offers a different problem: there is no extant copy, but there are reviews.[14] At the time it opened at the President theater, referred to often by the reviewers as a bandbox, its subject, the Scottsboro Boys case, was very much in the news. The preeminent Theatre Guild had another version in production, the one by John Wexley, *They Shall Not Die*, that was scheduled to open the same week, and everyone in town knew it. So much so that some reviewers went so far as to suggest that the Theatre Guild production, sight unseen, would be superior to Dennis Donoghue's effort.

The Wexley play is an exhaustive enterprise, running almost three hours long with a cast of over a hundred counting extras and offstage voices. The white characters run the gamut from *A* to *Z*. The good white ones come from New York and the National Labor Defense, a left-leaning organization that defends workers and minorities. Claude Rains, as the Jewish lawyer hired by them to represent the Boys, has a closing speech two-and-a-half single-spaced pages long. All the Southerners are as blatantly racist as can be imagined except for Lucy Wells, the one "good" Southerner, played by none other than our dear own Ruth Gordon. The Black characters, to quote Shaw, run the gamut from A to B. They are all "poh" in spirit and in how they address all and sundry, except each other; in character, they are practically indistinguishable one from another. The two exceptions are the "mulatto" representative from an NAACP-style group that wants to represent the Boys and an old-time preacher who goes along with him to "preach" the Boys into letting him do it instead of those devil-worshipping "Jews" from New York. The Boys are not spared their lowly designations of "dirty nigger" and "black monkey" at any point, not even from Claude Rains, who in summation says, "I appeal to your reason to give this poor scrap of colored humanity a fair and square deal." Throughout the play, the stage directions are replete with such descriptions of them (even though they all have names) as this "negro" and that "negro." At one point, the sheriff "shakes the unconscious negro" whom he has just beaten into unconsciousness. At the end of the jail cell scene, the directions read, "Medium slow curtain while the negro boys moan and wail." I mentioned how exhaustive the script is. Ruth Gordon's character gets two long scenes back home in Humbolt that go into detail of how she is marked as a "nigger lover" for not being willing to perjure herself to get the Boys convicted. The play even opens with a scene that has not only the sheriff and the local district attorney but a lynch-mob-to-be and all the jailors and deputies and officers of the court and the jail all itching to "lynch them niggers." Nowhere does Wexley's script take us into the homes or the minds of any of the Black characters. They are, in effect, his pawns, put there for the sole purpose of being saved by their white benefactors. To Wexley's credit, he does make the brand of Southern justice, Alabama style, in the thirties a bloodcurdling horror, scary even when read on the printed page. His dialogue, especially in the case of Claude Rains, is credible but serves only one purpose—to prove that the Boys are innocent and are being railroaded unconscionably and illegally. To quote Frederick Douglass, "The man struck is the man to cry out." The real heroism of the Boys has been well documented, as my *The African-American Bookshelf: 50 Must-Reads From Before the Civil War Through Today* points out in "Must Read #32." All of them had managed to conceal a knife in the lining of their pants, and when a deputy began to berate two of them for hiring "Communist Jew Northern lawyers," one of them, Ozie Powell, told him he wouldn't give up the help he had for "no damn southern lawyer." Whereupon the deputy slapped Powell, who "pulled out his knife, yanked [the deputy's] head back and slit his throat. Blood shot everywhere. . . . The sheriff got out and [yelled] 'one of the black bastards cut the deputy. I am going to get rid of all these sons of bitches right now!' He fired into the car and shot Ozie. The bullet went into him above the right ear and came out the corner of the automobile."[15] Wexley doesn't even hint at this heroism.

Now to more of Dennis Donoghue.

Arthur Ruhl, writing in the *New York Herald Tribune*, starts us off with "The shabby little box in West 48th Street now known as the President Theater housed last evening a crude but sometimes entertaining and not unimpressive melodrama based on the Scottsboro case and known as *Legal Murder*."[16] He then goes on to say that whatever eloquence the play has comes from the copied trial scene rather than from anything "contributed by author or actors, although it does seem true that untrained Negro players are never quite so bad as white actors of similar inexperience." The complaint that the trial scene was the most effective because it was "a fairly literal picture" of the actual scene in the courtroom was shared by most of the critics. Although Ruhl does credit Donoghue with an "ingenious" lifting of the scene itself. Ruhl then talks about the fight in the boxcar and the "'framing'" (his scare quotes) of the Boys and of "the noble Mr. Abrahamson from New York fighting hopelessly against an unfair judge and a brutal prosecuting attorney." Why Arthur Ruhl in New York would question whether the Boys (their ages ranged from thirteen to twenty) were actually framed can only be laid to a bias for the lost cause of the Confederacy and calling the Jewish lawyer "noble" is a simple act of condescension. John Chapman in the *Daily News* called it "more a journalistic account than a work of sustained human interest," accusing Donoghue of "[allowing] his anger to cool," and he has a rather curious soubriquet for the women. He calls them "bums." An odd naming for proletarian courtesans. But he ends with "The colored members of the cast do better than their white co-workers."[17] Stephen Rathbun in the *Sun* titles it a propaganda play and proves his indictment with "*Legal Murder* was offered last night as an attempt to arouse sympathy for the Scottsboro defendants. . . . It was frankly a propaganda play." But that's understandable since Mr. Rathbun loved *Green Pastures* and *Porgy*. He then adds his voice to the contention that the last scene is the best because it's simply a copy of the actual courtroom scene, saying of it, "It was an attempt to show that the trial was held before a prejudiced court."[18] That can only mean that in Mr. Rathbun's view, whatever Alabama was doing to the Boys was perfectly legal and circumspect. Condemning nine men to death for allegedly raping two women, one of whom denied the rape, would seem to require a little more sympathy for the condemned instead of an implied defense for the court that condemned them. But history has told us that, like the critic writing for the *Sun*, there are many Southern sympathizers in the North, known to history as "copperheads." The other two reviews that I found were equally contemptuous, one of them noting ominously that (a) there were more Black actors on the stage than white ones and (b) that the author "is colored despite his name." We'll never really know how talented Dennis Donoghue was or how the opening scenes in which he has the "Boys" enjoying themselves with dance and song and "eats" played. All the critics condescended to it egregiously with observations like "They were . . . interspersed with song and dance, crap games and spirituals which were supposed to show the happy, innocent and somewhat ignorant character of the defendants."[19] Lacking a script, we can only hope that whatever this writer's faults, they were not half so bad as his critics made them out to be. And he, at least, was inspired to write about something real and meaningful to the essence of what Black theater is and should be.

But the Black actor would have his turn in large measure thanks to the Depression and FDR's brilliant idea of the government employing out-of-work actors to help get the economy going and the country back on its feet, drip-down economy be damned. The Federal Theatre Project (FTP) of the Works Progress Administration (WPA) came to the Black actor's rescue, as a gift from heaven. FTP employed twelve thousand people a year, eighty percent of whom were actors on relief. In four years, it paid out $42 million in salaries to actors, designers, managers, directors, producers, as well as to stagehands, secretaries, musicians, and other theater personnel, and another more than $4.5 million in theater rentals, scenery, lights, and the rest of it to put the unemployed in the theater back to work. It played to twenty-five million people, one-fifth of the total population of the nation. The total number of Blacks employed, through the four-year span, was 851. The total number of plays produced by the Black units was seventy-five, and the total number of productions was one hundred. All told, there were sixteen Black units, all east of the Mississippi (and that includes Raleigh, North Carolina, and Birmingham, Alabama), except for two in California (Los Angeles and Oakland) and one in Seattle, Washington. Of all the units, the New York unit was the most important. New York was and is the theater capital of the country, and the Black unit (read: "Negro") was the most successful in New York! And its *Macbeth* was its most successful production, says Houseman in his excellent 478-page memoir of his life in the theater, *Run-Through*. Of the serious Black playwrights who were produced on Broadway in the thirties, two, Hall Johnson and Gus Smith, were also produced by the Federal Theatre.

THE BLACK *MACBETH*

We begin with the Harlem Unit itself and with its biggest success, the so-called Voodoo *Macbeth*, *Macbeth* in Harlem. Hallie Flanagan—who was plucked out of Vassar by Harry Hopkins, Roosevelt's man for all occasions—to head the Federal Theatre Project wanted a Black executive head for the unit. She chose the illustrious Rose McClendon, who had starred in *Porgy* and *Mulatto* on Broadway and was esteemed the first lady of Black theater. But Rose McClendon was already too ill to do more than lend her illustrious name to the project. She did, nevertheless, stipulate that it needed a white co-executive head to ensure that it wouldn't get bogged down in unconscionable red tape downtown because of the pitifully low esteem in which the Black man was held at the time. In other words, no one at the downtown office of WPA was going to pay attention to anything a Black man in Harlem had to say. Houseman was chosen because he had worked with Black actors in the Virgil Thompson–Gertrude Stein opera *Four Saints in Three Acts* that ran on Broadway, and he used Thompson to do the music for Macbeth. Thompson insisted on using exclusively Black performers for his opera because, as he said, "They alone possess the dignity and the poise, the lack of self-consciousness that proper interpretation of opera demands. And they are not ashamed of words."[20] Rose McClendon died, sadly, within six months of the project's inception, so Houseman took over dividing the unit into two groups: contemporary and classical. He opened with two contemporary plays: Frank Wilson's *Walk Together Chillun* and Rudolph Fisher's *Conjur Man Dies*. *Chillun'* was used to simply break the ice, as it had serious flaws; Houseman had to take half of the second act out during the fifth week of rehearsal, and the language was antediluvian. *Conjur Man*, on the other hand, was a success, and not because, as *Time* intoned, "Negroes are suitable for mystery stories because they are hard to see in the dark and because white folk, not knowing much about them, believe them primitively prone to violence."[21] Directed by Joseph Losey, it was modern, filled with the type of jokes a Black audience would love and a fast-moving story line. Its success meant Houseman was finally ready to tackle a classic, but in so doing, he was facing the Rubicon. Crossing it meant he had to choose a play that the Black actors could handle. Remember, dese and dems were still very much a part of the order of the day. Regular speech was a pleasant reprieve. But the classics. Verse! Iambic pentameter! Ye gods! But there it was, that forbidding river. So he crossed it. His first move once he got across was a brilliant one. He hired a relatively unknown, twenty-year-old actor who had never directed before to not only direct the classic but choose the play himself! Enter Orson Welles, and the rest is history. The very night that Welles said yes, his wife, Virginia, got the idea that it should be Shakespeare's *Macbeth*, but set in Haiti in the early nineteenth century, with the empire period of Napoleon III as the motif for the costumes and with voodoo priestesses as the Scottish hags. They cast the show together: Jack Carter, Crown in *Porgy*, as Macbeth; Edna Thomas from the Lafayette Players, who also had *The Comedy of Errors*, *Porgy*, *Lulu Belle*, and *Shuffle Along* under her belt, as the Lady; and the fine actor Canada Lee as Banquo. He went on not only to play Bigger Thomas when Welles and Houseman did *Native Son* on Broadway in 1944 but to appear in whiteface with Margaret Webster in *The Duchess of Malfi* in 1941. He's also remembered for his many film roles, notably in Hitchcock's *Lifeboat*, in *Cry the Beloved Country* with Sidney Poitier, and in *Body and Soul*, which starred John Garfield and Lilli Palmer. As soon as word got out that they were planning to do Shakespeare, suspicion was rife that it was a Machiavellian plot to ridicule the race. They needn't have worried; under Welles's relentless energy, the production grew in leaps and bounds. The entire cast, including understudies, reached a total of 137 actors. The huge slabs of scenery and the endless "acres of painted backdrops" ended up pushing *Conjur Man Dies*, which opened a week before, onto the very edge of the stage "to the fury of its director and cast."

The troupe of African drummers and dancers who would replace the witches were from Sierra Leone. They were led by Asadata Dafora. An accomplished choreographer, Dafora had produced and directed and was the lead in a dance drama, *Kykunkor* ("Witch woman") that opened in New York two years earlier. It was well received and got not only good but excellent notices from the likes of Gilbert Seldes, Burns Mantle, and John Martin, critic for the *Times*. Dafora was a classically

trained singer who sang at La Scala in '29. He spoke seven different Western languages and fourteen African ones and fought for the British army in World War I.
It was Dafora who had to create chants for the witches' scenes that would be convincingly voodoo-authentic. His first version wasn't really frightening to Virgil
Thomson, Welles, or Houseman, but when prodded, Dafora did indeed make the
chants frightening, so frightening that they killed Percy Hammond, as we shall
see later.

There was press even before the opening. Bosley Crowther (who had not
ascended to film critic status yet) wanted to know, "Why had they [Houseman
and Welles] mustered the audacity to take the Bard for a ride? What sort of Thane
of Cawdor would find himself in Haiti?" But it was showtime, three days and
counting. A free preview before opening night drew three thousand more people
than the theater could hold. The police had to be brought in to control the crowd.
The WPA office downtown sent word that every first-string critic in town would
be there. One of them, Houseman doesn't identify whom, asked that he and his
wife not be seated, if possible, "next to Negroes."[22] On the fateful day came the
marching bands behind a huge banner that read "Macbeth by William Shakespeare." Two bands joined forces in front of the Lafayette before the show and
played before a throng of ten thousand people. All northbound traffic was stopped
for more than an hour while trucks in the street flared floodlights into the lobby
and cameramen photographed the arrival of the carriage trade—flashing silk hats,
jewels, and ermine—and of celebrities, the likes of Eleanor Roosevelt and then-
mayor Fiorella La Guardia (see chapter 1). The curtain rose on a set that transformed the stage into a jungle habitat that resonated with the sights and sounds
of wild imaginings. The impact was so strong, that within five minutes, "amid the
thunder of drums and the orgiastic howls and squeals of our voodoo celebrants,
we knew that victory was ours."[23] There was so much Birnam Wood on the stage
that it looked like Central Park and Rockland County rolled into one, according
to Houseman. When Macbeth is cornered at last on the highest platform of his
castle, he shoots the messenger who brought him the news of Macduff's approach,
then kicks him, for an eighteen-foot drop, into the courtyard below. And
after they've killed him, Macduff's army sends up a cheer of triumph as his head
comes sailing down from the battlements. And a double cry arose from all the
actors of the classical wing "at the successful outcome of their long and agonizing
ordeal." The applause that followed lasted for fifteen minutes. As to the morning
after, says Houseman, "The notices . . . were a joy to read: [critics] wrote of 'an
Emperor Jones gone beautifully mad,' of 'the dark, sensual rhythms' . . . and of 'a
tragedy of black ambition in a green jungle shot with such lights from heaven and
hell as no other stage has seen.'"[24]

But that, alas, is skillful cherry picking, a practice universally adopted in the
theater. The reviews were universally either bad or a pat on the back by those who
did not want to be destructive of such a well-intentioned effort that held so much
promise for so many of the theatrically disenfranchised. The biggest complaint

was against the way the verse was handled: Shakespeare's devilish iambic pentameter. Houseman defends their interpretation thus: "There were [those] with preconceived notions of poetic delivery and vocal passion, who complained of the very thing that Welles had gone to such pains to accomplish with his Negro cast: the elimination of the glib English Bensonian declamatory tradition of Shakespearean performance and a return to a simpler, more direct and rapid delivery of the dramatic verse."[25] In other words, Welles didn't want them to "sing it," which was fashionable at the time. Gielgud had done the definitive singing Hamlet at the Old Vic in 1934, which critics praised to the heights; in the *New York Times*, Charles Morgan said of it, "I have never before heard the rhythm and verse and the naturalness of speech so gently combined. . . . If I see a better performance before I die, it will be a miracle."[26] Olivier's modern "prose" reading didn't happen until 1948. Houseman was convinced that the critics couldn't accept this natural version from American actors, and Black ones at that. I spoke to him in California in the eighties, before he died, and he explained why the critics were one in not giving the Welles creation of a Black *Macbeth* a good review:

> White critics in America are unsure of themselves whenever they come to a non-British production of an English classic, especially Shakespeare. In 1936 they were afraid that something might be put over on them, so they got insecure and took the easy way out, they decided it wasn't really Shakespeare. Not all of them, mind you. The same thing happened in 1953 with the MGM production of *Julius Caesar*. The London critics gave Marlon Brando first rate reviews, but the American critics were afraid it wasn't really Shakespeare and were generally quite critical. Of course Brando was superb.

Let's take a closer look at those opening night reviews to see if we can conflate the verse and the extravaganza into one cohesive performance, or if alas, they must forevermore be a twain that shall not meet! Said *Variety*, "They have moved the locale of the play to the East Indies [*sic*] in order to make colored performers in the roles acceptable. . . . Having gone so far they should have switched the language to fit. But they didn't. Result is that the Negro players strut about the stage in grandiloquent costumes mouthing antiquated Elizabethan language which, quite obviously, they don't even understand themselves."[27] If it was "antiquated" and "even" they didn't understand it, does that mean no one else understood it either?

Richard Lockridge, in the *New York Sun*, had a very curious opening: "Bands played on Seventh avenue [*sic*] last evening and a great concourse of people of shades appropriate to the neighborhood celebrated outside the Lafayette Theater. Inside . . . the Negro Theater, a WPA unit, put on Macbeth as it probably has never been put on before. . . . The results, while perhaps not precisely Shakespeare, were sufficiently bizarre." Mr. Lockridge, while his heart may have been in the right place couldn't help being surprised that in Harlem he would encounter Black people, "who were appropriate to the neighborhood." His cultural confusions continue: "The program fails to inform me whether it is in the lowlands or the highlands of Scotland that tropical jungles grow, and I can only suppose that Orson Welles, Shakespeare's arranger of the moment, has secretly moved the locale. But the familiar characters are there and, if the lines sound slightly peculiar in the surroundings, they are the old lines." In other words, he was completely lost. Not only didn't he know where he was, but wherever he was, he couldn't understand how he could be in Scotland if he was in a tropical jungle. After describing the opulence of the costumes, he gets to the heart of the matter: "It would be agreeable to add that the principals in the cast acted in a manner in keeping with this challenging, if outlandish, exuberance of décor. Unfortunately, however, almost all of them were, under their finery, simply ineffective actors having the trouble ineffective actors always have with the cadences of Shakespeare." This was his coupe d'ecrit: "[The] general effect was of actors dressed better than they deserved."[28] That's pretty definitive.

Robert Garland, in the *World-Telegram*, is more of the same but to a greater degree. In the paragraph subtitled "Let *Macbeth* Be Forgotten," he writes, "When, hard by the Ubangi Club's overflowing bar, you lay your eye on this sepia Shakespearian project of the Federal Theater you will be wise to forget all past, present and possible performances of the play. It mightn't be a bad idea to forget 'Macbeth' altogether." Makes sense given its proximity to the Ubangi Club's overflowing bar. The name of which was a homage to African ancestry, which shouldn't preclude its total lack of "civilized" validity, but it does make the club more important than the play. Something like saying "hard by the Blarney Stone's overflowing Pub you lay your eyes on a production of Synge at the Irish Rep." After talking about the witches and the decor, he sums up everything but the speech thus: "This part of what may or not be Shakespeare is colorful, exciting and a good show." Then he gets to his final verdict of the speech: "But when it comes to the poetry, the melodrama and what Orson Welles himself has called 'the tears and blood and beer' in which it was written, William Shakespeare's words fail frequently to march like heartbeats or even march at all. Jack Carter as Macbeth and Edna Thomas as his lady know most what they are doing. You should see this Macbeth in Harlem anyway. Some of it is truck, some of it is truckin'. But a lot of it is effervescent and all of it is different. I say try it, by all means."[29] So even for a critic who has gone out of his way to give the effort a good review, the handling of the devilish verse doesn't work. This constant harping on the *one* crucial aspect of the performance puts an awful lot of pressure on Houseman's credibility. At least, it would if the same critics or other confrères of the Fourth Estate hadn't made the same criticism of Brando, who by the way, asked Gielgud to give him a template for the "Friends, Romans" soliloquy, which he rephrased to his own beat.

Percy Hammond did a lot more than just bash FDR for having the audacity to try to solve the Depression with a "boondoggle." He starts off by objecting to the actors being clad not in kilts but "in the gay clothing of the Caribbean." I don't

FIGURE 5.5. Jack Carter as Macbeth at the Lafayette Theatre in Harlem, April 14, 1936.

think I've ever seen the kilt version. He then compliments the race while excoriating it simultaneously: "What surprised me last night . . . was the inability of so melodious a race to sing the music of Shakespeare. The actors sounded the notes with a muffled timidity that was often unintelligible. They seemed to be afraid of the Bard." He then talks about how Jack Carter "BURSTED out in oratory." And "Miss Edna Thomas impersonated Lady Macbeth with a dainty elegance that defied all traditions except those of the WPA." He didn't like them when they "bursted" out or when they had a "dainty elegance." You just can't please some people. He couldn't resist the politics. He gave a long, detailed list of *all* the personnel associated with the production, to wit, "The personnel of the Negro Theater is magnificent in its title and numbers." He then lists every live body associated with the production, from stage manager through to "Superintendant of the Display Department" to ticket takers and ushers; close to fifty by his count, and that didn't even include the huge orchestra that he dismissed as "pathetic." Sounds as if he expected the theater to be run by a handful of teenage volunteers who were in training for an after-school project. No one else complained about either the music or all the bread going into the mouths of so many hardworking actors. He just didn't like his "Negro personnel" that well fed. Or he forgot that in 1936, the Depression was in full swing, which was what the WPA was all about in the first place. He didn't even call them theater professionals, he called

FIGURE 5.6. Edna Thomas as Lady Macbeth at the Lafayette Theatre in Harlem, April 14, 1936. Photographs and Prints Division, Schomburg Center for Research in Black Culture, The New York Public Library.

them "Federal officials" and laid at their door the ultimate shame—that they started the performance an hour late. That was his excuse for getting up in the middle of it and *leaving before Lady Macbeth's sleepwalking scene!*[30] No wonder Asadata Dafora killed him or had him killed!

There are two versions of the story of Hammond and the killing: Orson Welles's and Houseman's. According to Houseman, the only one of the men involved who spoke English was Asadata Dafora, and it was Dafora who read Hammond's review and concluded that it was "evil." Houseman and Welles agreed. "The work of an enemy?" Dafora offered. They agreed to that too. "He is a bad man?" Dafora asked in conclusion. Again, they agreed. He repeated the common agreement to his men, and they all left. The next day, the house manager told Houseman and Welles that during the night there had been "unusual drumming" in the basement "with chants weirder and more horrible than anything that had been heard upon the stage." The afternoon paper announced Hammond's sudden illness.

According to Welles, one other member of the troupe also spoke English. His *nom de la mort* was "Jazzbo," and it was he who declared Hammond a bad man. To which Welles agreed. At which point Jazzbo said Hammond would be dead within twenty-three hours, because he would put the *beri beri* curse on him. Hammond was dead within twenty-three hours; he dropped dead in his apartment the next afternoon—again, according to Welles. In the video in which Welles tells the story, he is not a little condescending in discussing even the idea of putting on the play: "In case you think this is a little too crazy to be believed, let me assure you that there was a Negro *Macbeth*." Adding, "Our purpose was not as capricious or foolish as it sounds."[31] Why putting on a "Negro *Macbeth*" should be either capricious or foolish, I couldn't possibly imagine. Nor can I imagine why a director would work as hard as Houseman insists Welles did on a project he thought "capricious" or "foolish" in the first place. Even if he's imagining what others might think, the suggestion still reeks of supercilious condescension and an affront to Black theatrical aspirations. I'm even suspicious of Welles's "Jazzbo." Houseman never mentions anyone either of the name or the description that Welles gives of him, "a dwarf with gold teeth and a diamond sticking out of each one." That must have been a hell of a sight! Welles, again in the interview, quotes "Jazzbo" thus: "This critic bad mahn." Now that's right out of Tarzan. Welles even indulges in giving the educated Dafora, who spoke twenty-one languages a similar line: "We need live goat for make devil drum." If that's not Tarzan, then it's Tonto, and Houseman's Dafora quote is straight English. Houseman identifies the actual witch doctor as Abdul but says he didn't speak English. So "Jazzbo" was, in all probability, a Wellesian invention, Freudian inspired and intended to adorn an otherwise bald and unconvincing tale, to paraphrase Gilbert of Gilbert and Sullivan. It does boggle the mind that Welles, at the age of twenty, would have thrown himself so heartily into creating such an unusual and epoch-making event only to degrade it years later as just a frolic among the neegrows. Ah Sisyphus! We even have to be wary of our friends.

Neither Hammond's death nor his review was the topper in excoriation. That honor goes to John Mason Brown, the same John Mason Brown who couldn't understand why Black people would object to Uncle Tom. In his second review of the production (he didn't get it all off his chest the first go-round), he begins by saying it's a further consideration of the way in which Welles failed to develop an interesting idea. His point being that because Welles uses a Black witch doctor and an African ritual to replace the white witches and their ritual, it followed that the Macbeth in this version would have to be a rehash of O'Neill's Brutus Jones, who would therefore fall victim to the tom-toms. However, since Welles did not do that, but stuck to Shakespeare's script, he destroyed what seemed like the "diverting stunt [that] it gave every promise of becoming." He further justifies this conclusion by saying this version of the text was "wretchedly cut and stupidly altered." No one else complained about how the text was edited, only about how the lines were read. I'm reminded of an experiment I did long ago of trying to follow Olivier's version of *Hamlet* that he used in '48. I didn't even get past page five! That's how much he cut it up. When I was auditioning an actress years later and we came to Ophelia's monologue "O, what a noble mind is here o'erthrown!" (which I was using in a performance piece I had written), I told her that Olivier cut the entire monologue from the film, which was the high point for any actor playing

Ophelia. She couldn't believe it. Wonder what the estimable Mr. Brown would have thought of that "cut and altered version." Of course, Olivier was an Englishman; Welles, was just, well, Welles. What Brown really wanted Welles to do was turn his production into a *Green Pastures* in the jungle, where the actors dance and sing and run around scaring and killing one another and praying to people, places, and things that white audiences (and critics) think is appropriate for them to pray to or run away from, or sweat and dance and drumbeat to. Here's the heart of that argument:

> It is not the absence of orthodoxy but its presence which one objects to in this Macbeth. If Mr. Welles had done the adapter's job; . . . if he had restated Shakespeare's thoughts in the vivid images that come naturally to men and women who believe in voodoo [that's priceless as well as unimaginably ignorant —ed.]; if he had turned Macbeth into a Black Majesty in Haiti and forgotten about Shakespeare's Scotland, . . . why then his Negro Macbeth would have been something to become excited about. As it is now, it can only be listed as a wasted opportunity—as an interesting idea with which little that is interesting or creative has been done.[32]

Atkinson, under the title "Harlem Boy Goes Wrong," follows the same line. He gave as well intentioned and encouraging a review as he could, but in spite of it, he too, found the actors not up to the task of doing Shakespeare:

> If it is "Macbeth" that the WPA folk are staging in Harlem at the Lafayette Theatre these evenings, we shall have to wear a schoolmaster's frown. If it is a voodoo show suggested by the Macbeth legend, we can toss a sweaty night-cap in the air. . . . Perhaps we should describe it as the witches' scenes from "Macbeth." . . . Ship the witches down into the rank and fever-stricken jungles of Haiti, dress them in fantastic costumes, crowd the stage with mad and gabbling throngs of evil worshipers, beat the voodoo drums, raise the voices until the jungle echoes; stuff a gleaming naked witch doctor into the caldron, hold up Negro masks in the baleful light—and there you have a witches' scene that is logical and stunning and a triumph of theatre art.

Precisely, and to hell with Shakespeare. Just give us more witch doctors in place of Scottish witches. What makes the court semibarbaric is anyone's guess. But let's press on:

> Since the program announces "'Macbeth,' by William Shakespeare," it is fair to point out that the tragedy is written in verse. . . . There is very little of any of that in the current Harlem festival. As Macbeth, Jack Carter is a fine figure of a Negro in tightfitting trousers that do justice to his anatomy. He has no command of poetry or character. As Lady Macbeth, Edna Thomas has stage presence and a way with costumes, and also a considerable awareness of the character she is

playing. Although she speaks the lines conscientiously, she has left the poetry out of them. . . . Although the staging by Orson Welles and John Houseman is uncommonly resourceful in individual scenes, it has missed the sweep and scope of a poetic tragedy. . . . If it is witches you want, Harlem knows how to overwhelm you with their fury and phantom splendor.[33]

Certainly, the extravagant praise he heaps on the power of the acting when they're not doing Shakespeare, and on Welles's imagination in creating such an enthralling evening of theater, is more than generous. But like John Mason Brown, he too can't seem to take seriously the combining of Welles's idea with real Shakespeare. He too drags in Emperor Jones. He too says, or implies strongly, that the idea of a voodoo *Macbeth* is ill conceived if it is wedded with Shakespeare's actual words. He too can't really imagine such a wild coupling as "she should have died hereafter" with "[stuffing] a gleaming naked witch doctor into the caldron" or wild orgiastic dancing among people who believe in voodoo. Although I'm sure the witch doctor wasn't in the altogether naked, or at least I hope he wasn't. So African culture is great theater as long as you don't elevate it to the level of Elizabethan drama. We will see in the next chapter what critics thought of Carter as Mephistopheles in Welles's production of *Faust*. As for Ms. Thomas, *Fortune* said of her, and I repeat, "[She] turned in one of the season's great performances as Lady Macbeth." It is difficult to accuse Brooks Atkinson of harboring any intentional hostility to the actors. He goes out of his way to emphatically praise the "production," more so than any of the other first-night critics, but he is emphatic in disassociating their capacity for being actors capable of tackling Shakespeare on any level from the hijinks of what they do under the spell of Welles's baton. And that's unfortunate. Also, it's hard to believe that so many people in so many different venues in so many different parts of the country sat through this *Emperor Jones* extravaganza and got bored whenever the actors were saying Shakespeare's immortal lines in natural cadence. And that the word of mouth was good enough, in spite of that defect, to fill houses in so many places on so many nights. Something is amiss here. I'd be oh so happy to give Brooks Atkinson the benefit of the doubt. But in all conscience, I simply can't. I rather think that like all the other critics, for him, the whole evening was just too much to take in in one sitting. There was nothing in his experience that prepared him for what Welles had created. He didn't expect it, and when he was confronted with it, he couldn't accept it. The *Emperor Jones* reference is a giveaway. That had to be the dramatic context in which such an undertaking was seen. After all, in 1936, Black Sambo was riding high and handsome on the screen as well as the stage: Eddie Anderson (that fine actor) running faster than a car in the *Topper* series. Mantan Moreland, eyes popping out every time he thought an ordinary skeleton was a ghost, which had him running over Charlie Chan's number-one son to get out the door. And Stepin Fetchit, well, just being Stepin' Fetchit. The name says it all. Of course, all this is subliminal effect but effect nevertheless. The "Voodoo" *Macbeth* had absolutely nothing to do with O'Neill's *Emperor Jones,* and the suggestion that it did as motif or spiritual antecedent or anything of the like is raw stereotyping.

But all was not lost for our poor, beleaguered actors who don't know a damn thing about *character* or *poetry.* Burns Mantle, the reigning critic for the *Daily News* for over twenty years, saw the play both at the Lafayette and downtown at the Adelphi. Here's part of what he had to say about how things were going in the latter venue: "The players led by Jack Carter and Edna Thomas having had several weeks' experience, have acquired poise and an improved diction. . . . The reading is still foreign to Shakespeare. Always will be." He then mentions the "mellifluous" and well-coached performance of Robeson doing *Othello,* adding that "[even so,] there were always the intonations and inflections of the colored man's speech to break the illusion, and the African cast of countenance to give a disturbing touch to the picture in that creation." He then praises the whole production as "an amazing novelty," adding that "it has fascination . . . and a forthrightness in the sincerity of its performances that no other Shakespearean revival has commanded since Burbage was a boy." Of the witches' scenes, he says, "[They] furnish the revival's most exciting and most characteristic feature. They give this 'Macbeth' character as a tragedy of Black ambition in a green jungle shot with such lights from both heaven and hell as no other stage has seen."[34] And he ends by saying it will give the Texans something to talk about for months to come. But confessing that the speech just doesn't ring true coming from a face that's "an African cast of countenance" gives it away. It wasn't the way the verse was spoken so much as it was who was speaking it. Would a white face with a Midwestern twang be less "foreign to Shakespeare?" That notwithstanding, Mantle, to his credit, does give special praise to the Welles "additions" to the text and does not in so doing insist on an artificial separation between it and what the actors do when they are doing the text as it was written, and he doesn't mention *Emperor Jones* or talk about men and women who "naturally . . . believe in voodoo." The Black man's beliefs and superstitions must perforce be used to hold him up to ridicule. Always and forever. Sisyphus is back on his buttocks. None of which suggests that because *Macbeth* was set in Haiti and the witches weren't Scottish ones that the actors had to be a primitive tribe who couldn't possibly comprehend what Shakespeare wrote, much less re-create his genius for a commercial audience. The myths and superstitions of the most advanced cultures, using Western standards, are just as illogical as a belief in voodoo, when held up to the light of unfettered logic, and are seen as anthropological idiosyncrasy and regarded as acceptable historical fact. That Roman Polanski's *Rosemary's Baby* was a critical and commercial success without any hint of ridicule of the powers of darkness proves the point.

Martha Gelhorn, Hemingway's third wife, was a novelist, travel writer, and journalist with a reputation as one of the great war correspondents of the twentieth century. In fact, she had more credibility in that capacity than did her famous husband. She saw the *Macbeth* in Harlem, and Houseman quotes her take on the proceedings:

These Negroes had taken Shakespeare to themselves and that Macbeth would remain in this audience's mind from now on, as a play about people . . . who moved about the stage superbly, wearing costumes that belonged to them and suddenly belonged to the play. Macduff . . . wore a pair of epaulets a foot wide. . . . Macbeth wore a superb military costumes of canary yellow and emerald green. . . . Women came on and off the stage in salmon pink and purple. The impression was of a hot richness that I have almost never seen in the theatre or anywhere else. The lines were spoken without Negro accent, but in those beautiful voices made for singing; and the gestures were lavish, but not amateur or overdone. The audience sat and watched and listened as if this were a murder mystery by Edgar Wallace, only much more exciting.[35]

Well, that's some relief from the pronouncement that they had no idea how to either create character or poetry. And Roi Otley, well-known journalist and the pride of Harlem, also helped salvage the reputation of actors who naturally believe in voodoo and who "strut about the stage in grandiloquent costumes mouthing antiquated Elizabethan language which, quite obviously, they don't even understand themselves." Said Mr. Otley, "The Negro has become weary of carrying the White Man's blackface burden in the theatre. In Macbeth he has been given the opportunity to discard the bandana and burnt-cork casting to play a universal character. . . . From the point of view of the Community, Harlem witnessed, a production in which the Negro was not lampooned or made the brunt of laughter. We attended the Macbeth showing, happy in the thought we wouldn't again be reminded, with all its vicious implications, that we were niggers."[36] They played for ten weeks at the Lafayette "with never an empty seat." Then they moved downtown to the Adelphi on Fifty-Fourth Street and ran for an additional two months even though they were competing with *Tobacco Road, Three Men on a Horse, Mulatto, Dead End, Bury the Dead, On Your Toes,* and *New Faces of 1936.* A Hirschfeld cartoon six columns big, on the front page of the *Times* Sunday drama section, was proof of the stature the Harlem unit had achieved, but according to Houseman, it caused them to lose their *Macbeth.*

Why did Jack Carter walk out of the show during intermission at the Adelphi? Carter was the son of a Florodora girl (who had to be passing to play in a white revue in 1900). He was born in a French château and brought up in the lap of European luxury. He didn't know what it meant to be a "colored" until he returned to America in his teens. The discovery was disastrous. It made a pimp, a killer, and finally, an actor out of him, according to Houseman. His first acting success was as Crown in *Porgy.* On tour, he'd register in a first-class hotel as white, then invite his Black friends up to his room. When they were denied admission, he'd wreck the place. Houseman says he couldn't decide whom he despised more, his mother's side for being the victim or his father's side for being the villain. And he thinks it was the old hatred rearing its ugly head because Carter was playing night after night to a mainly white audience at the Adelphi. He and Edna Thomas were very close. When he couldn't handle the rage inside him except through drink, he began to go on drunk. She was so saddened by what it was doing not only to him but to the performance and to their scenes together that it was affecting her performance as well. He could see he was hurting his dearest friend, but he was unable to do anything about it—except leave the show. That he did on the night Edna Thomas was so upset that she began to cry. He simply went back to the dressing room, changed into his clothes, and walked out of the theater and out of FTP.

Thank goodness there were understudies, and Carter had two of them: Maurice Ellis (Macduff) and the chief stage manager, Tommy Anderson, who knew all the parts as an added cover in case of emergency. When Carter was nowhere to be found after intermission and Anderson couldn't find either Welles or Houseman, he "tore a uniform off the nearest soldier and went on as Macbeth." So after six-foot-four Jack Carter played the first half of the show, five-foot-four Tommy Anderson played the second half. The coda to the story took place in Indianapolis. Maurice Ellis was playing Macbeth there when he got sick. Orson couldn't wait to fill in. He flew to Indianapolis and played the part in blackface for the rest of the week. Hope the grease didn't shine in the light or glow in the dark the way Olivier's did when he played Othello. With the success of *Macbeth* behind him, Houseman realized it was time to leave the Harlem unit. He was told not to waste any time doing it because the honeymoon days were fast coming to an end and drastic cuts were just around the corner. His final farewells were long and emotional and "full of protestations of love." And Welles's goodbyes were equally passionate. Houseman describes what they had been through together as hell, and they had prevailed, but his summing up of the lasting effect that all of that hard work had on the hundreds of actors who showed themselves proud during those tumultuous ten months was a sad one:

> Viewed in the perspective of years, my accomplishments with the Negro Theatre seem far from impressive. Theatrically, their final effects were almost nil: Negro playwriting was not appreciably encouraged by our efforts, and Negro actors (with a few notable exceptions) were held, for another twenty years, within the galling bounds of stereotyped roles. The theatre technicians whom Feder had trained (being excluded from every professional union theatre in America except as cleaners or janitors) went back into other trades. No Negro company came into existence for thirty years after the dissolution of the Federal Theatre and no Negro audience clamored for a continuation of the entertainment they had apparently enjoyed under the auspices of the WPA.[37]

And Hughes has a similar critique of the aftermath of FTP and Black theater: "The Project gave Negroes a chance for the first time to learn something about stage management, lighting and other technical matters . . .—an opportunity the commercial theatre never allowed due to the objection of the white stagehands union and other craft syndicates. Even Negro-owned theatres . . . had to have white stagehands. And in colored movie or vaudeville houses, according to union rules, only white operators could run motion picture projectors or operate spotlights. Negroes could do all these things in the Federal Theatre."[38] Houseman later softened his stand, saying his time on the project had been the busiest, the happiest and the proudest of his life: "Through the rear window of the cab that was carrying me and several large files, to our new domain in the basement of Maxine Elliott's Theatre, I looked back at the worn and dirty face of the Lafayette and saw what I had wrought. And behold, it was good."[39]

Before we get into why he was on his way to the Maxine Elliott, we have to contemplate the terrible waste of our cultural resources and their riches of which killing the Federal Theatre Project was one more example. A waste driven by a conservative agenda that must silence the voices that want to make the country a welcoming reality for the poor, the Black, the needy as well as everyone else. If the power of theater was dynamic enough to sway the hearts and minds of large swaths of the populace, imagine then what a better democracy we would have in the first quarter of the twenty-first century if that free, unfettered theater had been allowed to flourish. We can take that thought further. If Federal Theatre hadn't been killed, it's quite possible we would have been spared the horrors of the McCarthy era. And Buzz Windrip, the demagogue dictator who becomes president in Sinclair Lewis's *It Can't Happen Here* (an FTP production, which opened in twenty-seven theaters across the country on the same night), would not have risen from the ashes to haunt us again, as we seem to fear he is doing now at the end of the second decade of the new century. Having allowed theater to remain solely white in effect, bathetic, and all too often eschewed of any social meaning except what is watered down to not even be worthy of the name, we've given blazing racism the license to have free rein.

The climate in 1939 was somewhat reminiscent of that in the 1950s, when the legendary junior senator from Wisconsin, Mr. McCarthy, was in his prime. His lawyer, Roy Cohn, employed an assistant who, when told by a witness that he (the witness) traced his disobedience back to Thoreau's position as espoused in *Walden,* the assistant replied, "Well, when I get through with you, I'll question this Thoreau fellow." Similarly, Representative Joseph Starnes (Democrat–Alabama) on the Dies Committee, when questioning Hallie Flanagan and citing plays that were in his opinion obvious Communist propaganda (*Coriolanus* was on the list), asked if it were not true that she could only get audiences for Communist plays. She replied, "The plays have ranged from the classics to *Pinocchio.*" Not satisfied with that, Starnes then quoted from an article she had written in which she described Federal Theatre as having a certain "Marlowesque madness." "You are quoting from this Marlowe," observed the representative from Alabama. "Is he a Communist too?"[40] After she lectured him on his ineptness, the committee never called her back. But the prize testimony about the presence of Blacks side by side with whites came from Sally Saunders, a naturalized citizen, who objected to such admixture, either during or after rehearsals, especially when she and they were both in the same show. *Sing for Your Supper* in this case:

MS. SAUNDERS: A colored boy tried to date me. The colored race is savage, still from the jungle.

COUNSEL FOR THE COMMITTEE: We are both Europeans by birth, I believe, and you should believe in what the Pope said recently to Mussolini: there is only one race, the human race.

MS. SAUNDERS: If they are not an inferior race, why did the Creator make them black?

COUNSEL: You surely don't believe in that, do you?

MS. SAUNDERS: Most assuredly.

COUNSEL: I'm sorry you feel that way because a person with your feelings could never live in a country like ours. Why do you suppose this country fought the Civil War in 1861? Doesn't the life of Lincoln mean anything to you?

MS. SAUNDERS: Oh, Lincoln was a fool and I say definitely that if this country will persist in acknowledging the colored race as an equal I shall be willing to give up my American citizenship.[41]

While Ms. Saunders's testimony was eventually repudiated officially, and even though "mongrelization" and "social mixing" as fostered by Federal Theatre were decried, because the unit in Harlem had been one of the most successful, the success of Federal Theatre was to a large degree being equated with the progress of Blacks in it—which meant in the country at large as well. And they were doing straight drama first. All the dancing and the singing took place in a minor key. That killed FTP more than Communism or Southern anti-intellectual, bigoted, hyperbolic ignorance.

When Welles and Houseman left the precincts of Harlem, they ensconced themselves in the Maxine Elliott on Thirty-Ninth Street, with the blessing of Hallie Flanagan and FTP. Houseman had come up with the clever idea to propose a classical unit outside of the Harlem project. He did it before the glow of the *Macbeth*'s success had worn off. So with his winner's reputation, Flanagan gave him the nod. Their first task was to find a name for their new classical unit. They hit upon Project 891 simply because that was the number they were assigned for the unit. They opened with a farce, *Horse Eats Hat*, and followed that with Christopher Marlowe's *Doctor Faustus*. Welles played the title role and Jack Carter played Mephistopheles. Houseman has nothing to say about how either he or Welles repaired their relationship with Carter after he walked out on them except to say that Welles wanted him to play the part in spite of it. There were certainly actors enough, white, who could have successfully essayed the part. Nevertheless, Carter was given the coveted role of the Devil in the Marlowe classic. Not only was he excellent in it, as the reviews attest, but he was at the theater night after night, even when he wasn't called, to do whatever he could to make the project happen. Houseman says of Carter and Welles's scenes,

> Their presence on the stage together was unforgettable: both were around six foot four, both men of abnormal strength capable of sudden, furious violence. Yet their scenes together were played with restraint, verging on tenderness, in which temptation and damnation were treated as acts of love. Welles was brightly garbed, bearded, medieval, ravenous, sweating and human; Carter was in black—a cold, ascetic monk, his face and gleaming bald head moon-white and ageless against the surrounding night. As Orson directed him, he had the beauty, the pride and the sadness of a fallen angel. He watched Faustus sign his deed in blood and later, officiated at his destruction and listened to his last gasping plea for respite.[42]

Atkinson, in his review, mentions the difficulty in putting on Elizabethan theater: "Although 'Dr. Faustus' is a short play, consuming hardly more than an hour in the telling, it is not a simple play to produce. . . . Like most Elizabethan plays it has an irresponsible scenario; it moves rapidly from place to place, vexing the story with a great many short scenes; it includes several incidents of supernaturalism, and of course, it is written in verse." After praising Welles copiously—his conception, direction, and acting—he adds this one-line comment on the rest of the cast: "There are excellent performances in most of the parts, notably Jack Carter's Mephistopheles."[43] So that's all the satisfaction we get as a reprieve for Carter. In the "Voodoo" *Macbeth* he had "no command of poetry or character" when up against Shakespeare's *verse*, but he's most notable in handling Marlowe's. And this is only eight months later. *Faust* opened on January 8, 1937. It's one thing to say that Carter "matured" during those few months, it's another to say that he had no command of poetry or character and suddenly found an ability for both eight months later. If he had been awkward or callow or not up to the mark for Elizabethan theater, all that would have meant was that growth was possible. But to not have any ability whatsoever in those areas, and then suddenly to have it. Naw! I'm not buying.

Project 891 was the last "project" for Houseman and Welles with Federal Theatre. Why they got fired and how they came up with the idea of forming their own acting company are both fascinating stories. Alas, space does not permit my going into the details of either. Suffice to say that after they were kicked out of FTP, their answer was to form a repertory company that would become the Mercury Theatre. More of that later. But what of the other plays put on by FTP, bereft of the magic of Welles's direction or Houseman's producing? *Haiti* and *The Case of Philip Lawrence* were two of the more ambitious projects to come out of the Harlem unit. *Haiti* had a robust run of 180 performances. *Lawrence* wasn't as popular. *The Trial of Dr. Beck* from New Jersey, which had a double run, first in Newark and then in New York, was revived in the '80s. Three out-of-town plays were significant:

Black Empire from Los Angeles, *Natural Man* from Seattle, and *Big White Fog* from Chicago. The plays of the Federal Theatre Project had an advantage over the ones produced independently by commercial producers. FTP had the type of budget that would make any commercial producer drool. The *Macbeth* production was no exception. Plays had casts that were routinely twenty, thirty, forty, and fifty strong, which allowed writers to give free rein to their artistic imaginings. But that didn't always end up having the desired result of good theater. Theodore Browne's *Natural Man*[44] is a case in point. It opened at the Seattle unit in 1937 and was revived at the American Negro Theater in 1941. The legendary John Henry, the steel-driving man, is the *Natural Man*. With such a powerful symbol of Black manhood to tease us, the thought naturally occurs that the hero will be a tower of strength. He's no such thing. He whines in front of the white boss man, spends much of the piece talking about pounding steel, rock, granite, and anything one could imagine into whatever shape he wants to. He's duped by tricksters when he gets too drunk to realize that stolen jewels have been put in his pocket just in time for the police to nab him as the culprit. He goes to a prayer meetin' for solace but doesn't find any. He hoboes only to be laughed at by his fellow boxcar riders. And even when he kills a white guard who beats the dead body of a friend who's on the chain gang with him, his manner is more uncontrollable giant than powerful hero. In the contest between him and a mechanical drill, the drill beats the Natural Man and his hammer. The effect is supposed to be heroic. It isn't. Browne, in an interview with Lorraine Brown archived at George Mason University's FTP project, had this to say about the sort of theater he thought it proper to present: "There are those people, the moderns like Leroy Jones . . . who it has become a sort of fetish . . . to insult people. [They've made] the young college crowd . . . feel as though they were guilty of mistreatment of Negroes and so forth. [*laughs*] Actually, they had nothing to do with it. . . . They have that feeling of guilt and so these people just make it a point of just insulting as much as they can." Then a few questions later: "It's not fair, it really isn't fair to make another group feel uneasy or guilty." And later in the interview: "I try awfully hard to achieve a kind of universality . . . not blaming anyone for the condition that existed. . . . To try to enlist sympathy . . . to appeal to a person's consciousness without exaggerating the material . . . but don't use it as a whipping boy . . . to lash out at somebody."[45] In other words, don't get angry.

Theodore Ward's *Big White Fog*[46] was produced in the Chicago unit in 1938 and in Harlem at the Lincoln Theatre in 1940 under the banner of the newly formed Negro Playwrights Company, of which he was a founding member along with such luminaries as Langston Hughes, Paul Robeson, and Richard Wright. *Fog* killed the Negro Playwright's Company when it died at the Lincoln after only sixty-four performances. As Ward ruefully said, the Harlem community wasn't interested in a problem play. But it was revived in 1995 at the Guthrie. It's a play that has been praised often throughout its history, and rightfully so. Vic Mason is a Garveyite[47] who puts all of his $1,500 into bonds for Garvey's Black Star shipping

FIGURE 5.7. Portrait of Langston Hughes. Collections of the New York Public Library.

line that will build the boat that will take his flock back to Africa. When Garvey is convicted of mail fraud and imprisoned in Atlanta, the movement dies a sudden and gut-wrenching death, and the shares are worthless. And it's the Depression, so Mason's family suffers terribly in those hard times. He's reduced to being a hod carrier who eventually loses everything, even the furniture in his home, half of which is taken away by the bailiffs, with the police as chaperone to ensure the law. (The bailiffs have to be guarded by the police because workers' movements were fighting Depression-era convictions.) His son has to drop out of school to help the family. His older girl becomes a lady of the night to help support the clan and ends up being arrested along with her white john. Vic's wife turns against him in disgust at his refusal to give up on his Black homeland dreams even when the progeniture of the dream is in prison and the family is starving. The two younger children are sick and in need of a doctor. There's hardly enough money for food. His mother-in-law despises him because of his black skin; she sneeringly reminds him of her white blood, which in her eyes makes her superior. Vic's brother, who alternately backs him up and then warns him to be cautious, is a lazy layabout who offers nothing to the proceedings except to get drunk and pronounce the joys of carpe diem. His brother-in-law is a successful businessman who's willing to help financially in exchange for the stocks in Black Star. Vic says no and through it all refuses to give up on Garvey or his dream. What makes Ward's play powerful is the guileless honesty of the man. There's something about the purity of the dreamer that tugs at us when, in the face of all odds and all the tragedy that one life can endure, he still insists on holding on to that dream until in the end it kills him, literally, when he's shot by one of the officers of the law when he tries to stop the bailiff's from leaving him with not even a bed for him and his wife and children to sleep on. Vic's dream and his passion are Theodore Ward's strength and the strength of his play. If he had not thrown so wide a net in making Vic's problems as overwhelming and as unending in their long Greek-like concatenation as they are, he would have been better served. This is particularly true since he's at great length to create all the subplots that his many characters and their many stories force onto the piece. There's a clean, well-defined play in there that is as relevant today as it was when he wrote it. But since the Black theatergoing public of the forties in Harlem wasn't interested in that type of theater, it's problematic if they would be eighty years later, particularly since it is by no means race neutral.

Black Empire[48] by Christine Ames and Clarke Painter is *white travesty*. Done at the Los Angeles unit in 1936, it not only takes a hatchet to the history of the Haitian Revolution but ends up, like most Hollywood movie versions of Black stories, making an obscure young Frenchman, Jacques Le Blanc, who died in reality long before the French had been kicked out, its hero. Henri Christophe is the liberator of Haiti in this version, even though all other sources name Toussaint L'Ouverture as the liberator. Wordsworth even wrote a sonnet in his honor to that effect, for Chrissake. André Rigaud, leader of the light-skinned Haitians who thought they should rule over their darker brothers, was defeated in the field by Toussaint and scurried off to France and the safety of Napoleon long before Christophe declared himself king. In the Ames-Painter version, however, Rigaud is Christophe's chief aide, who's going to use the voodoo to destroy Christophe. Wow! And Jean Jacques Dessalines, who won the final battle against the French, has also been expunged from this *version* of the story. All this would not have been a total loss, however, *if* Christophe had been a character in a well-written drama instead of the one-dimensional sadistic horror that he is here. Obsessed with building his giant fortress, the Citadel, as a last-ditch defense against European invasion, he indulges in such discipline-invoking measures as killing one worker in ten just to make the other nine work faster on that great fort on the hill. When one man is brought before him in the opening scene, he's shot because he was found sleeping during working hours. The next one, whose heresy is that he was found in 3the vicinity of a voodoo temple, is thrown from a cliff down to rocks below so he can contemplate his god on the way down, whom Christophe says should save him. You get the idea. In the end, when the natives have been made restless by the voodoo, Christophe tells the young white hero, Le Blanc, where the money is, as well as the location of the secret door to the coast where ships are waiting to take Christophe's family and Le Blanc's white lover (who was instrumental in getting *Natives* organized enough to storm the castle) to safety. So ole Christophe goes the way of all Black heroic flesh. He shoots himself. And that's your drama, with the young lovers, who had nothing whatsoever to do with either Christophe or Haitian history, going off into the sunset thanks to the gold wrung from the Black bodies of all those voodoo-worshipping "natives."

Haiti isn't about the Haitian Revolution. It's about a mulatto heroine, Odette, and her Haitian father, Jacques, who commits suicide after he's given Christophe the signal to attack. That about sums up this offering from the Lafayette unit that opened in March of 1938. The director was Maurice Clark. He found the material compelling enough to contact the author, William DuBois (not to be confused with W. E. B.), who was a reporter for the *New York Times*. DuBois was a Southerner, and although he was willing to work with Clark to get the script into performance shape, he had one stipulation. No white character could be touched, physically, by a Black one, or vice versa. Clark was smart enough to agree with that and ingenious enough to make it work. Judged by 1938 standards, DuBois's script does seem to hold possibilities, but it's quite simply and blatantly another case of cultural appropriation. In this version of the greatest achievement of the Black man in open conflict with the three most powerful armies of the world at the time (the French, the English, and the Spanish), the Black leader was, again, without question, Toussaint L'Ouverture. Because the French could not defeat him after throwing everything they had at him, they resorted to shooting him in the back—that is, capturing him under a flag of truce. This so incensed his two chief lieutenants, Dessalines and Christophe, that they kicked the French army that Napoleon sent to recapture the island out of Haiti once and for all. It was Dessalines who, in a moment of fury, tore the white out of the French flag, leaving only the red and the blue. But his reign was so brutal that he was assassinated within two years. It was then, and only then, that Christophe established himself as the leader of the northern part of the country, with the mulatto Petion controlling the south. Christophe ruled for eleven years. So any suggestion that Toussaint had become too old to fight and *willingly* allowed himself to be captured and carted off to France is doing more than playing fast and loose with Haitian history. It's a gross distortion. William DuBois has a right to distort history. But his distortions are so extreme that what he's written is tantamount to Shakespeare having Julius Caesar commit suicide and Mark Antony defeating Cassius and the other conspirators and leaving Brutus out of the proceedings. It diminishes Caesar as a heroic character whose ego led him too far. Toussaint was a giant among men. He was compassionate, provided for his former owner and his wife, had the confidence of everyone, Black, mulatto, and white. And he led the charge in battle after battle. His siege of Jacmel has been judged a classic of military strategy by many white historians. But William DuBois is not interested in that type of history, so most of the play is taken up with the general sent to capture Toussaint, Leclerc, and his various subalterns, majors, and captains and the love affair between Odette and one of the French officers, Duval. DuBois has scene after scene with the French officers arguing with one another and intriguing against each other, and he has time to develop both Odette and Leclerc's wife, Pauline, into fully fleshed characters. The only thing he has Toussaint do is tell Christophe how old he is and that he's passing the power of command to him. Christophe is deeply honored and now has Toussaint's permission to destroy the enemy. Which Christophe could not do because Toussaint wouldn't let him! They've come to meet with Leclerc to find out what he wants. Christophe tells Toussaint that Leclerc has come to reconquer the island, and he and Toussaint must return to the hills to fight. Toussaint replies, "(wearily) Must we, Henry? It's a long journey up to those hills."[49] When Christophe gives him his reasons for returning to the hills, Toussaint replies, "I've killed enough."[50] Toussaint never made a sentiment resembling that in any way whatsoever and nothing in the historical evidence suggests that he did. Toussaint is carted off, and the rest of the play concerns the tension between Odette and her father once she finds out that he's the man posing as the servant in the house they're occupying. That makes her decide to stay in Haiti instead of taking to ship with the rest of the fleeing French before Christophe can finish them off. And that's your drama. Maurice Clark can be forgiven for wanting to do the play. And the scenes between Odette and her father, Jacques, played by that fine actor Alvin Childress, are affecting as all father-daughter scenes are capable of being. Clark did the best with what he had available. Rex Ingram as Christophe was accused by some in the cast of "eating up the furniture," which in showbiz parlance means over-acting. Canada Lee took over the part and is reported to have given a more nuanced performance. Of the three giants who made history in making Haiti the only country in history where Black men and women got their freedom and their independence by force of arms, Toussaint L'Ouverture gets practically

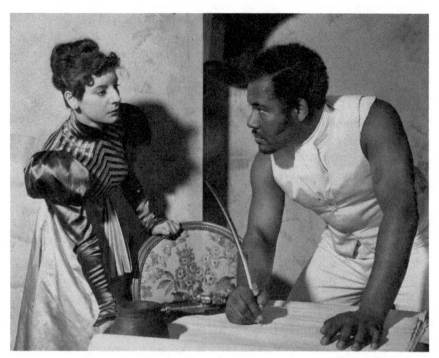

FIGURE 5.8. Rex Ingram and Elena Karam in *Haiti* at the Lafayette Theatre in Harlem, 1938. Works Progress Administration.

no role in the actual achievement and Christophe gets it twice. The only one to make Dessalines the centerpiece of the story is Langston Hughes in his play *Emperor of Haiti.*[51] However, it was never professionally produced so far as I've been able to ascertain, which makes it outside of the purview of this volume, unfortunately, although I wish it were otherwise.

The Case of Philip Lawrence[52] by George MacEntee offers no surcease from pain, unfortunately. It is egregiously bad. Because Philip Lawrence is a college graduate in Harlem in the midst of the Depression and has to work as a redcap, his is a tragic tale. If George MacEntee was able to create a credible character, that idea, by itself, might have worked. But Phil is a sop, depressingly feckless. And he's an innocent. In order to make real money and marry his sweetheart, he takes a job with a gangster. When the gangster kills a white gangster, who's trying to move in on his numbers racket, Phil, who happens to be a witness to the murder, is dazed at the idea that the man is dead, telling his boss, "You killed this guy." The boss frames him for the murder, and he's tried and convicted. During the trial, Phil keeps repeating, "The truth and nothing but the truth"; "Truth . . . truth"; "Tell the truth, so Help [sic] you God." He's dazed and helpless. His sweetheart, his adopted "Mom," the minister, the DA, everyone in the neighborhood, even the gangster's girlfriend, all swear that he is a good boy and couldn't kill anyone. So the law comes to his rescue and tricks the gangster's henchmen and sweetheart into thinking he, the gangster, is dead, and they confess that he did the killing, not Phil. The gangster is presented, and Phil is cleared. Phil's curtain speech is "Thank you Mom and Nancy [his sweetheart]"—the stage directions tell us "he turns to the others."—"Thank you, my friends. You've made me a free man again. Together we'll make this a better world for other Phil Lawrences." Ugh. Can't win 'em all.

The Trial of Dr. Beck[53] is a long-drawn-out spectacle of turgid legalese. A light-skinned doctor thinks that Black people should only procreate with other light-skinned Black people. Why does he think this? Because he wants to expunge the race of its darker-skinned brethren. Why does he want to eradicate the black skin from the Black race? Because black-skinned Black people are the cause of all the problems of Black people. They are intellectually deficient, and they look too different from white people. He bases his theory of intellectual deficiency on a dark-skinned couple who have so many children they don't know how many there are. Their English is as dems and dese as Brother Mose. So why is Dr. Beck in a courtroom on trial for his life? Because he's accused of killing his dark-skinned Black wife, Amanda, who made a fortune in selling hair straighteners to Black people, dark skinned or not. But the doctor never talks! Well, almost never. In 115 pages of text, he has a total of four and a half lines plus one word! In act 1, he says, "That's a damn lie!," in act 2, "If your honor please . . . ," whereupon his lawyer cuts him off. Three pages later, "Miss Hopkins has recovered somewhat now. Would your honor perform the ceremony?" In act 3, "I didn't think you'd be able to come today, Elenore!" And in the penultimate line in the play, he blurts, "Carrie!" He says this last line, according to the directions, "compassionately." Who and what takes up the other 114 and a half pages? The judge gets in some good licks. So do the opposing attorneys and Dr. Beck's affiance, his light skinned love Elenore, whom he marries during the course of the drama, is on the stand a lot, as is his dead wife's sister, Carrie, also dark skinned but bright, as in smart. Pun intended. For the last thirteen pages of the play, Allison drags in a series of witnesses, up to that point unheard from for the most part, who step-by-step expose the killer. There's the photographer who saw the culprit at the airport. The pilot who saw the culprit on the plane. The stewardess who saw the culprit on the plane. The cab driver who picked up the culprit at the airport—his last name is Shaw, and he's at great pains to insist he doesn't want to be confused with that other Shaw: "[I] ain't no sissy like this old long beard dude that's copped my name. I don't write no books like him." So who is the killer? Sister Carrie, of course (apologies to Dreiser). And why did she kill her sister when the two of them had made such a success of their hair-burning business? She confesses the reason: "I wanted him as much as you [meaning Beck's new wife] and Amanda did." Then she turns to Beck. "John . . . a black woman kin love too! A black woman kin love too!" That's when he responds compassionately. And the curtain "speech" is hers. "Goddamn you God! Goddamn you for making me so black!" There's little comfort in the fact that we have both New Jersey and Lee Shubert to thank for this monstrosity being performed in New York. The offensiveness of the idea, the intellectual ineptness of the premise, the actual degrading of the "dark skinned blacks" by giving many of them speech that was routinely ungrammatical all add up to what essentially is a dressed-up superficially "provocative" pretentious bit of detritus. The final proof of which is the very basis on which any courtroom drama must exist if it is to grab us: unless we can root for the main character, hope he doesn't get convicted, find ourselves thinking of ways to get him off, there is no drama. How can you root for a man who has nothing to say? How can you get to know him, to identify with him? And if you can't, then what are you rooting for? A racist idea that occupies the main thesis of the work and that in the end proves what? That dark-skinned Black people are the scourge of the race, since it was a dark-skinned woman who killed her sister because she lusted for her sister's husband? And if that's all we get, then what was the point of Dr. Beck's theory? Did it enlighten us, tell us something new about eugenics? I rest my case.

That covers the FTP plays that can be discussed in this volume. There were others that were quite popular: four Eugene O'Neill one-acts ran for 81 performances; *Androcles and the Lion* from Shaw ran for 104; *The Show Off* by George Kelly (Grace Kelly's uncle) for 73. The Federal Theatre threw a wide net that gave Black actors the kind of opportunity to expand their craft that they have not had since.

When Welles got that amazing contract to direct *Citizen Kane*, which gave him carte blanche over everything, he had no trouble raising money for the last Mercury Theatre production, Richard Wright's *Native Son*. But getting *Native Son* the play written was another matter. By the time they produced it, Mercury Theatre had become a legend in the history of American theater. They assembled an amazing group of actors, headed by Joseph Cotten, Agnes Moorehead, and Canada Lee. They had a brilliant run of successes, which included a modern-dress *Julius Caesar*, Shaw's *Heartbreak House*, and *Chimes at Midnight*. Welles's homage to Falstaff and the Henry plays. *Native Son* was their final collaboration before they left New York for the warmer precincts of California. For the plum role of Bigger Thomas, they chose their Banquo, Canada Lee. Wright had been a member of the Communist Party, but by the time *Native Son* was published, he had become an apostate. In *The God That Failed*, he, André Gide, Arthur Koestler, Ignazione Silone, and Stephen Spender all explained how the party had failed them and why they left. Paul Green had been a "friend" of the neegrow with a reputation as a playwright based on his *In Abraham's Bosom*, a condescending gambit into "Black theater," which had earned him a Pulitzer. So Wright gave him permission to turn his novel *Native Son* into a theater piece. Enter Houseman, who took an option on the book as a consequence of its being a best seller that everyone was reading and because he knew a good thing when he saw one. Houseman says of their collaboration, "Paul Green's attitude . . . was, first and last, insensitive, condescending and intransigent."[54] Green didn't see Bigger's act of violence as the only way a Bigger Thomas could show his defiance against—indeed, his rejection of—the overwhelming dominance that the rigid system of caste and race in which he was surrounded had him shackled in mind, body, and spirit: "Resenting what he called Dick's existentialism, [Green] attempted, till the day of the play's opening—through madness . . . suicide . . . and other . . . sublimating devices—to evade and dilute the dramatic conclusion with which Wright had consciously and deliberately ended a book in which he wanted his readers to face the horrible truth 'without the consolation of tears.'"[55] Some dimension of what Wright was trying to convey can be understood in what he said when Eleanor Roosevelt cried after she read *Native Son*: he thought he had failed. The last thing he wanted from a white audience was the self-serving reaction of pity. The man who's living in hell doesn't want would-be good Samaritans to look down on him in his agony and shake their heads in sympathy for his pain. That just adds to his psychic and physical destruction. Green wanted his Bigger to hallucinate like a deranged down-home preacher calling on heaven and the angels to bring down their wrath and judgment on them awful white sinners. As Houseman explains, Wright wanted to show "Bigger living dangerously, taking his life in his hands, accepting what life had made of him . . . [of the] horror of Negro life in the United States."[56] In Green's rewrite, he has Bigger in his cell shouting, "Ring them bells! Beat the gongs! Put my name on the hot wires of the world—the name of Bigger, Bigger—the man who walked with God—walked this earth like God—was God!" Then Green has him mumbling about the watermelon patch back home while he hears an airplane overhead and begins to yell out, "Fly them planes boys—fly 'em! Riding through—riding through. I'll be with you! I'll—" Then a guard says, "He's going nuts." And Green's Bigger keeps urging them, whoever they are, to "fly them planes smack into the face of the sun!" And they lead him away, with the priest saying, "I am the resurrection and the light."[57] So ends Paul Green's night.

Houseman knew he had a hot property and decided to exercise his producer's rights while he still had the option. He persuaded Wright to rewrite the script. Together, they put Wright's original intention back into the play. Three weeks later, they had a workable script bereft of Paul Green's hallucinations. Houseman gave the script to Welles, and two days later, Welles approved it and they went to work on what would be the final Mercury Theatre production. They cast the likes of Ray Collins, Everette Sloane, Paul Stewart (the last two from *Citizen Kane*) and, from the Lafayette Theatre, Evelyn Ellis, Helen Martin, Rena Mitchell, Bootsie Davis, Wardell Saunders, and Canada Lee. Before they opened, Paul Green showed up. He was appalled that his script hadn't been used and threatened to sue. Houseman told him he didn't have a leg to stand on, since every word in the script they were using came from Wright's book. Orson finished him off with a verbal lambasting, whereupon he got up, left, and Houseman never saw him again. The production was enthusiastically received by almost everyone. That even included some of our old friends, who had gotten religion suddenly—or should I say, eventually. Burns Mantle gave it four stars. The *Daily Worker* loved it: "In comparison, all the productions of the current season seem dim and ancient chromos. The theatre, that slumbering giant, tears off its chains in this production. From the theatrical point of view it is a technical masterpiece. As a political document it lives with the fire of an angry message."[58] Stark Young found Canada Lee's performance to be the best he had ever seen from a *"Negro player"* (italics mine). Well, it was a decade later. Even a Southern leopard can change his spots, I suppose. Not that praising Lee's performance as the best he had ever seen from a neegrow actor was much praise considering what he had said he thought of neegrow actors eleven years earlier. He was ecstatic about Welles, calling him one of the best influences the theater had, adding that his talent was abundant and inspired, "as contrasted with the pussyfooting and the pseudo-intelligence and the feminism that has crept into this theatre of ours."[59] There were pickets on the final night of previews. The Urban League objected to the bad light in which it put the neegrow. The Communist Party was incensed because Wright didn't adhere to party orthodoxy. William Randolph Hearst's *Journal American* detected "propaganda that seems nearer to Moscow than Harlem."[60] Leaving off critiquing the play, they went after Wright for being a former member of the *Daily Worker* and for having approved of the Soviet trials. The only other objections came from lovers of the book who thought, "[The play] is a vivid evening in the theatre, a tragic case of a morally mangled victim of society and circumstance. All the same [it] lacks the novel's . . . charge against the white race for crushing and crippling the Black one."[61] (That was from Louis Kronenberg in *P.M.*) And our old friend John Mason Brown was heard from as well: "In trying to bring *Native Son* to the stage the Mercury has done better than might be expected with the impossible. . . . The production achieves something and [*sic*] the almost unbearable suspense of Wright's novel."[62] Boy was he a master at left-handed compliments even when he was trying to be nice. Said Atkinson in the *Times*, "Mr. Wright and Paul Green have written a powerful drama and Orson Welles has staged it with imagination and force. These are the first things to be said about the overwhelming play that opened at the St. James last evening but they hardly convey the excitement of this first performance of a play that represents experience of life and conviction in thought and a production that represents a dynamic use of the stage." Later on, he calls it "the biggest American drama of the season," adding, "In Canada Lee the authors and producers have an actor for whom they should be devoutly thankful. As Bigger Thomas, he gives a clean, honest, driving performance of remarkable versatility." He then lists Lee's other *accomplishments*—as a prizefighter, violinist, band leader, and host of an establishment called the Chicken Coop in Harlem—and then adding, "As an actor he is superb."[63] No mention of his Banquo. Is it possible that he was talking about some other Canada Lee?

Well, they had done it, Welles and Houseman. They had put a powerful piece of real Black theater on Broadway, and the critical and audience responses were both huge. Sisyphus could rise again from the grave. But as too often happens whenever the Black man shines too brightly on the horizon, the enthusiasm, no matter how strong at the outset, soon wanes, and he is heard from no more—until the next time. Who remembers *Native Son* on Broadway? No one who isn't a student of the history. The hoi polloi, the de facto vote, never gets roused by such Black shenanigans. *We* can't dramatize *our* history: the horror of one hundred years of lynching, the laws that told us what kind of water to drink, where we could eat, where we could worship or sit on a park bench or swim in a public pool. *Native Son* certainly addressed much of that history, and it wasn't howled at. But it died all too quickly and too conveniently. Even though it was doing good business, the producers closed it. Houseman seems to suggest it was because it was an expensive show to run and because of the hot weather. There was no one to protect it, since he and Welles had decamped for Hollywood by then. A shortened version toured several states and it too did good business. But the final ironic dagger in the heart came when Harper & Brothers printed Paul Green's version with the watermelon and the planes flying overhead (their excuse being that it had already gone to press). As a consequence, if an aspiring young writer wanted to read the script that was done on the Broadway stage, he or she couldn't—there isn't an extant copy that I've been able to find. One writer even quoted from Green's version in critiquing the play. Same old sabotage. Welles's staging of those Mercury Theatre plays certainly made his early reputation as a director, one who had few peers. It might even be argued as having laid the foundation for his ability to transfer those talents to film on his first try so seamlessly.

So in our adieu to the thirties, we have to tip our hat to it for its brazenness, for its clarity of purpose, for its daring, its avant-garde bravado to say the unsayable, to think the unthinkable when presenting commercial drama for a paying middle-class audience, the one that Atkinson denigrated in 1904. Black audiences, circa 2020, need more oxygen than Black exploitation films (or their quiescent aftermath) and Raisins in the Sun. We can elect a president, but we can't put on a play, any play, that shows the Black character, man or woman, freed from despair or only angry in some form of feckless, obsequious sweating; or bemused by the problem of his condition in a white man's world; or struggling mightily to find his soul, his identity, himself! We can't be true adults who tackle the problems of our tribe as true adults do and not as postadolescents unsure of what we're about. The grown man doesn't grovel, he doesn't stand confused at the enemy's gate, he doesn't look down at his feet when the occasion calls for putting his foot on the other fellow's neck. The thirties could do that to the best of its abilities because it was a time when, as a nation, we had lost our moorings, so all bets were off and we could think the unthinkable, say the unsayable. Call Alabama racist for wanting to hang nine Black men for supposedly "raping" two ladies of the night. Even Alabama couldn't hang them just for beating up the white boys and throwing *them* off the train. So when we try to present a drama that dares to attempt that type of "controversial" eloquence, we can do no better than what the racist Stark Young (never thought I would quote him not in rancor) called "the pussyfooting and the pseudo-intelligence . . . that has crept into this theatre of ours." Are we saying to ourselves, and to anyone who's listening, that the stronger we become as a nation the weaker we become in moral fortitude, in integrity? Is the price we

FIGURE 5.9. Gladys Boucree, Mabel Carter, and Frankie Frambro, the Three Little Maids from the Federal Theatre Project production of *The Swing Mikado* (Chicago unit), 1938. Billy Rose Theatre Division, The New York Public Library Digital Collections.

have to pay for being the greatest economic, military, and cultural power on the globe that we cannot admit to our own depravities of yesteryear? Can't expunge our sadisms of an earlier era, can't find the moral stamina to use our constitution to free men from oppression instead of using it in strict constructionist dogma to saddle us with what was written in 1787 as a basis for the realities of today, so that the enlightenment of our beginnings can be spun to justify the degrading needs of our present? This is not a plea for political dogma of one form or faction. Let the politics and the social unrest and the economic inequality be or not be as it may. That is not within the purview of this volume. But what can and what should happen on a public stage—even, or especially, on Broadway—is. Are we saying that our theater cannot be more than the pleasure dome of bourgeois entitlement? Even the middle class needs to see itself in dramatic relief *some* of the time. Our realities as Americans go so far beyond deodorized dialogue or Hollywood endings or the ever-so-obvious false dilemmas of families who are in conflict because they can't still live in the glass bubble of the fifties, when being white was all that mattered and any problem that anyone else had was of no interest in whatever national conversation was in vogue at the time. We have evolved; our theater has not. It's become more technically adroit, more adept at spinning false narratives of "equality" based on combinations of race and gender that *seem* to be a step forward but are only a clever way of keeping us comfortable while giving a benign wink to real issues in vacuous, unimportant ways. But not the thirties. The thirties told it like it was. Then the war came, and we became the world's savior from Hitler and European fascism. With that going for us, who could talk about "Yankee Doodle" without throwing his hat in the air and shouting "hooray"? Nobody.

6 · PAUL ROBESON
AND THE FIFTIES

And now on to the new decade and the apocalyptic event of a World War, and to the Black actor who dominated that chapter in our story.

War can do strange things to a nation. We suddenly find that we are not only one but indivisible. In October of 1943, the war was hardly decided, but the Allies had invaded Sicily in July, and in many ways, that marked the beginning of the end for Germany's dominance on the European continent. It had been five years since Joe Louis defeated Schmeling, the German champion who had knocked Louis out in their first bout. When Louis knocked him out in the first round of the second bout, it took Schmeling a long time to get up. Score one for our side. And it had been seven years since Jesse Owens sent Hitler stomping out of his own Olympics by winning four gold medals and proving that no matter how superior Aryans were, they couldn't run faster than the American. At least not the Black one. But a Black man acting on Broadway *opposite a white woman* in a Shakespearean classic? Never. Aldridge did *Othello* on an English stage, but that was in the nineteenth century, and Robeson did it, again in England, with Peggy Ashcroft as Desdemona. But that was in 1930. Not that there wasn't hostility even then. Miss Ashcroft got death threats but was herself unperturbed. As she said, she saw nothing wrong in kissing a "colored" actor on the stage. She not only was quite willing to kiss Mr. Robeson but had met with him and his wife and had nothing but the highest regard for both. So there! (Miss Ashcroft had good reason not to object to kissing Robeson onstage—or off, for that matter—as we shall see.) But in the land of the free and the home of the brave? Nah! However, with neegrows contributing mightily to the war effort, even dying side by side with white men as "brothers" in arms, an English woman, Margaret Webster, decided in 1943 that the time was propitious to test the waters for an integrated, "miscegenated" version of the Bard in the Republic for which it stands. England had rescued Black artistic ambitions that had come a cropper in the land of their birth as far back as the eighteenth century. Aldridge, of course, is the standout, but both Robeson in

FIGURE 6.1. Canada Lee (Banquo in *Macbeth*, Bigger Thomas in *Native Son*) in publicity photograph, ca. 1935–1940. Collections of the New York Public Library.

1930 and Phillis Wheatley in 1773 had to go to England to be free, he to play the Moor and she to get her poetry published, because the enlightened men of the literary establishment in Boston refused to publish her even when her verse was as abject a denial of Black equality as could be imagined. Not only did Miss Wheatley consider white culture to be a salvation for her heathen Black brethren, but she had mixed feelings about slavery itself, even though she had been brought to these shores as a slave. She praised King George for repealing the Stamp Act (the one that started the revolution), and her poetry was in turn praised by Washington. When there was doubt that a young woman only recently emancipated could master the English language so amazingly well as to write credible verse in iambic tetrameter and iambic pentameter, and both in the same poem, she was hauled into court to prove that a victim of voodoo could have the "nervous system" of a white man—or in this case, woman. Leading colonists, such as John Hancock, and both the governor and lieutenant governor of Massachusetts did the examining and declared her to have actually written the poems. Boston still

You saw her on Broadway
in "Anna Lucasta"
You saw her on the screen
in many Hollywood hits
Now hear her as she
interviews celebrities and
brings you the best in
musical entertainment

.... Every morning is
"Ladies Day" with
Hilda Simms
8:30 to 9:00 A.M.
Monday through Saturday on

WOV
1280 on your dial

FIGURE 6.2. The luminous Hilda Simms, who starred on Broadway in *Anna Lucasta* for over two and a half years, in an advertisement for a radio show, ca. 1954. Schomburg Center for Research in Black Culture, Photographs and Prints Division, The New York Public Library Digital Collections.

wouldn't publish. So a year later, she sailed for England and that's how the miracle came about.

Margaret Webster probably didn't know Phillis Wheatley's story, but she knew she had her work cut out for her if she wanted to not only cast *sable* Robeson as the Moor but give him star-studded support with the likes of Uta Hagen as Desdemona and her then-husband, José Ferrer, as Iago. Of course, since the Theatre Guild was producing, her credibility in the dramatic community was on solid ground. Still, she wasn't going to take the plunge pell-mell. She opened in Cambridge. Elliot Norton, the renowned Boston theater critic, said of the atmosphere on opening night, "The whole Broadway community was hiding in closets when the subject was brought up. Nobody knew what would happen when the first black actor in American history walked on to play Othello, which he had every right to play."[1] And even though he reports that "no black actor, believe it or not, had ever kissed a white actress on the American stage before that time,"[2] the republic for which it stands stood solid as Plymouth Rock nevertheless. No riots, no revulsions, no cultural trauma. So Webster moved to Princeton, then New Haven, and finally Boston! Robeson and Othello were still standing, and neither Hagen nor Ferrer got death threats. Ergo, it was time to head for *Broadway-way-way*. They opened on October 19, 1943, at the Shubert. Says Errol Hill in *Shakespeare in Sable*, "It was a stupendous hit," adding, "The barricades had been breached. Thereafter no one could argue with impunity that the theatergoing public would not accept a black actor as leading character in a racially integrated professional production of an established drama."[3] Well, Professor Hill's wishful thinking to the contrary, the "stupendous hit" did not have a repeat performance, not on a Broadway stage. Whatever "professional productions" of an established drama (read: Shakespeare) that were integrated were integrated off-Broadway or in resident theater companies. And they have been many and significant. Morris Carnovsky and Ruby Dee as Lear and Cordelia, in the American Shakespeare Festival Theatre production. Jane White as the queen and Sam Waterston as Cloten in *Cymbeline*, at the New York Shakespeare Festival. Gloria Foster and Alvin Epstein doubling in the leads in *A Midsummer's Night Dream* at the Theatre de Lys in Greenwich Village. Robeson, for all his groundbreaking triumph in a miscegenated *Othello*, didn't set a Broadway trend no matter what else he might have done. What did the critics actually think of a Moor playing the Moor? Did they accept that the Black countenance could mouth the Bard and not lose the poetry in spite of the fact that the Broadway producers were hiding in the closet? Apparently yes, they did. In fact, unlike the constant hedging in 1936, they went all out in praise of Mr. Robeson. His handling of the verse was considered first-rate: powerful at times and beautifully poignant at others. His physical presence was so dominating that it eclipsed whatever else was happening on the stage when he was on it. Lewis Nichols called the performance "electrifying." Speaking of some of the problems with the play, such as Iago's motivation being unclear and Othello's jealous rage being somewhat of a mystery, Nichols then says, "On the whole the acting is such as to make these things unimportant. Which is what they are when Mr. Robeson is on hand, with José Ferrer as Iago." He then singles out Robeson: "The news, of course, is Mr. Robeson's arrival back home in a part he played a few seasons ago in London. . . . His voice, when he is the general giving orders . . . reverberates through the house; when he is the lover of Desdemona, he is soft. His final speech about being a man 'who loved not wisely but too well' is magnificent. He passes easily along the various stages of Othello's growing jealousy. He can be alike a commanding figure, accustomed to lead, a lover willing to be led and the insane victim of his own ill judgment."[4]

An insert piece, uncredited, gave this added sense of the euphoria that gripped the theater on the night of October 19, 1943:

> Not for several seasons has a play received the tumultuous applause that was accorded last night's presentation of . . . "Othello" starring Paul Robeson. Cries of "Bravo"! Echoed through the packed Shubert Theatre. . . . At least ten curtain calls were demanded. The audience mostly wanted Mr. Robeson, who granted their wishes. . . . Miss Webster was forced to say a few words. She said that she and Paul Robeson had dreamed for many months of such a night as they had just encountered, but had never expected it to occur. Turning to Mr. Robeson, who was standing surrounded by the entire cast, she said, "Paul we are all very proud of you tonight." The theatre broke into cheers.[5]

America was at war, fighting to make the world safe for democracy. The *Times*'s headline for the twentieth of October read, "Russians Cut Nazi Escape Route; Allies Capture 8 Towns in Italy"! With a front-page picture of GIs of the Fifth Army crossing the Volturno River under fire. A proud moment for a proud country, mighty in war both at home (with an integrated *Othello*) and abroad, with the Third Reich on the run in Italy. But that was in 1943. Don't ask how many Black soldiers were lynched in 1945 or '46 or after when they returned home and were brash enough to wear their uniforms in public!

PAUL ROBESON

Robeson was heralded in his time and then vilified. The unifying effect of the public patriotism, that euphoria that comes from fighting a World War in which your country is seen as the savior, collapsed almost as quickly as Japan surrendered after the first atomic bombs fell. Robeson went from hero to villain in the twinkling of an eye. His earnings fell from $70,000 a year to $7,000 in spite of his amazing gifts in so many fields of endeavor that it seems almost surreal. Polymath, Renaissance man, or "man to behold" as in *ecce homo*, Robeson was it. He was All-American at Rutgers, but the racism of the times was such that a photograph of the team of that year (1918) had only ten players in it because Robeson was omitted. It's the only All-American team so defaced. He had his nose broken and

FIGURE 6.3. Paul Robeson as Othello in the Theatre Guild production of *Othello* on Broadway, 1943. Vandamm Studio.

his shoulder dislocated just to make the team. Once he was benched in spite of his stand-out play (his college coach called him the greatest end who ever played the game) because the opposing Southern college refused to play against a neegrow. But the athlete was also a scholar. He made Phi Betta Kappa and was one of only four students invited into Cap and Skull, a senior-year honor society for those who showed excellence in athletics, academics, the arts, and public service. The scholar was also an artist. He joined the glee club (but only informally, since membership required attending all-white mixers) and sang off campus for his

FIGURE 6.4. Uta Hagen (Desdemona), Paul Robeson (Othello), and Margaret Webster (Emilia) in *Othello*, 1943. Vandamm Studio.

supper, literally. He was also a member of the debate team. When he graduated, he was class valedictorian. When he graduated from Columbia Law School, he had already played for two professional football teams; done a stint of acting in the Torrence piece, *Simon the Cyrenian*, as Simon; met and married his wife, Eslanda "Essie" Goode; started a career as a professional singer; gone to London for a part, where Mrs. Patrick Campbell had rewritten a play just to highlight his singing; and returned to Columbia to graduate. And he sang in the chorus of an off-Broadway production of *Shuffle Along*.

After graduation, he tried his hand at law but found the racism too daunting. The secretary in a law firm he had joined refused to take dictation from a "nigger." That's when the invitation to do the lead in *All God's Chillun* came to the rescue. However, the opening was postponed, and he was offered the *Emperor Jones* revival in the meantime. His reviews in that O'Neill piece are what catapulted him into immediate stardom. When he did *Othello* in London in 1930, it was the first time that a Black actor had played the part since Aldridge. As mentioned, Peggy Ashcroft kissed him not only onstage but off. The affair was serious enough that it caused Essie to file for divorce, though they reconciled two years later. His work in *Emperor Jones* was so strong that he was given the part to play in the film. Again, another first: the first time a Black actor had a leading role in an American film. And the notices were good. *Sanders of the River* in 1935 made him an international film star, but the character was a stereotype, and the Nigerian commissioner in London said it was slanderous to his country. Robeson thought he was a good soldier, portraying a role that would enhance the image of the Black man in colonial Africa; instead, it was seen as an embarrassment and detrimental to his reputation as an artist. After that, he became much more conscious of the political implications of any role he undertook, but his activism never abated. A broadcast of a patriotic cantata led to his being dubbed America's number-one entertainer. Yet America's number-one entertainer couldn't get a booking in any hotel except the Beverly Wiltshire, even with the war supposedly bringing everybody together for the good of the country and to make the world safe for democracy. The Beverly Wiltshire had a condition: *he had to register under an assumed name.* So he spent two hours every afternoon sitting in the lobby to make sure anyone else who was Black wouldn't have the same problem. The last film he would make, *Tales of Manhattan,* is a *Green Pastures*–style segment of an anthology film that has Robeson and his "flock" receiving a "burning" coat that falls out of the sky with $43,000 in it. And oh, how de cullud folks dem did sing and praise hebben and de lawd fuh all dat moneee. After that, Robeson had had enough. He would make no more American films. Not that that stopped him from doing his patriotic duty and giving concerts to benefit the war effort.

That brings us to 1943 and the Margaret Webster *Othello.* It would have been a good time to take a well-deserved hiatus from activism to protect his acting career, especially since he would need the stage now more than ever if his refusal to do any more films was to be held to permanently. But the need to speak out would not take a back seat, and he became, if anything, even more quixotic in his quest for real justice for his people and, indeed, all peoples in *his* time and *his* place. In all fairness to him, his passion wouldn't let him look at American racism realistically any more than it would let Malcolm X or Martin Luther King do so a generation later. But they, at least, had a following and were at a point in history when such a fight's time had seemed to come. Not so Robeson. All he had was his own stirring but lonely voice. And he chose to use it at the worst of times, because once the war was over, McCarthyism and the hysteria of the Cold War would make him not only a doomed fighter but a doomed martyr as well. Doomed because his martyr's death would be a slow and agonizing one, drawn out almost as if to torture him. He met with Kenesaw Mountain Landis, the racist first commissioner of baseball, to try to convince him to let neegrows play in the white major league. Landis, predictably, said no and died shortly thereafter, leaving a genial Southerner, Happy Chandler, to say sure, bring on Jackie Robinson and his legion. The good news was but a brief respite. A Georgia mass lynching of four Black people, two married couples, known as the Moore's Ford Lynchings, was the next shocker. One of the men was a veteran who had served five years in the war and had only been back home nine months. His wife was seven months pregnant. After they killed her, they cut the fetus from her body. Robeson had a heated confrontation with Harry Truman to demand that he pass an anti-lynching bill *now* as a consequence.

Truman said the time wasn't right. "Horse meat Harry," you might remember, came from Missouri. Whereupon Robeson said, that being the case, Black people would defend themselves. Truman ended the meeting without any attempt at conciliation—that is, abruptly. So what did our Don Quixote do? He founded an organization called the American Crusade against Lynching. There's something almost beautiful about a spirit like that. So fiery, so consumed with the right of it to not be able to see the immense mountain he would have to climb to make even a dent. Poor Sisyphus. He must have been dismayed at the task Robeson was handing him. As a context in which to put the deaths of Black Americans at the hands of white Americans, consider that between August 2016 and May 2018, three hundred and seventy-eight Black Americans were killed by white police-men.[6] And there has not been one Black artist to say "I accuse" the way Robe-son did. Things are different? We're a better nation than we were? We've elected a Black president. Then why does the slaughter continue unabated generation after generation?

Henry Wallace was FDR's vice president from 1941 to 1945. In 1948, he ran for president on the Progressive Party ticket. The Progressive Party's platform sounds a lot closer to what a progressive Democrat in the twenty-first century would run on than what America thought would make it a better place to live in in 1948: desegregation, the establishment of a national health insurance system (wow), the expansion of the welfare system, and the nationalization of the energy industry. Well, Robeson couldn't resist that. He campaigned for Wallace, even going into deep red state territory, at risk to life and limb, to do so. But he was in a bind by now. The FBI had seen to it that his concert performances, which had become his chief source of income, were all canceled. No film, no theater except a tour of *Othello* after the Broadway close, so he had to travel to Europe to earn a living. With the war over, he made a passionate plea for peace at the World Congress of Partisans for Peace. What he said was, "We reject any hysterical raving that urges us to make war on anyone. Our will to fight for peace is strong." What the speech said when it came across the wires, after being altered, was "We denounce the policy of the United States government *which is similar to Hitler and Goebbels.*" The Associated Press ran the doctored version, and no one bothered to check for accuracy. Robeson flatly denied any such interpretation, but the damage was done. He was now the enemy, the outcast. Still, he was such a huge figure that he couldn't be silenced that easily. Did the experience make him take stock and think about the consequences of giving another speech? It did not.

What followed was the onslaught from which he would never recover. He was blacklisted in the mainstream press, including Black publications such as the organ for the NAACP, the *Crisis*. Then a concert he was to give in New York City was attacked because he was a "subversive." That only made the Peekskill Riots inevitable. Robeson was scheduled to sing in Peekskill in support of the Civil Rights Congress. He had performed there before without incident. But he wasn't just fighting against American imperialism. He was also attacking the Ku Klux

Klan and arguing for the decolonization of Africa and against Jim Crow legislation at home. Such was the red state thinking of America at the time that such causes were all seen as "communist" ideology. Before the concert was to start, local residents attacked the audience with baseball bats and rocks. The police, when they finally arrived, did practically nothing to intervene. Robeson was hung in effigy. The ugliness of the mob showed both anti-Black and anti-Jewish hatred. And in the aftermath of the moment, 748 people from the area applied for Ku Klux Klan membership. Youngsters ran around throwing rocks and shouting, "Dirty commie!" and "Dirty kikes!" Robeson tried to get out of the car that had brought him to the venue but was prevented from doing so. The second concert, a scant eight days later, in defiance of the racist onslaught, was a different cup of cappuccino. The hunted became an iron ring of defense, and the would-be defenders of the Republic against those "nigger commies" had to waylay what concertgoers they could as they went to their cars on their way home in order to seek their petty revenge. The likes of Pete Seeger and Woody Guthrie had the windows of their car smashed; Seeger's infant children were inside. But he kept the rocks as mementos and used them as part of the furnace he built for his cabin in Fishkill, New York. No one was ever prosecuted, and Peekskill became a cause célèbre that reached all the way to Congress. That well-known Mississippi racist John Rankin called Robeson a "nigger Communist." Congressman Vito Marcantonio, from East Harlem, protested to Speaker Sam Rayburn (Democrat–Texas) that the word be stricken from the record. Rayburn said that Rankin said *Negro*, not *nigger*. But Rankin contradicted him: "I said Nigra just as I have said since I have been able to talk and shall continue to say."[7] Rayburn said that Black people should get used to it. There were hundreds of editorials and letters to newspapers for and against. But most of the opinion was against Robeson and his supporters, blaming them for "provoking" the violence. Then eighty other cities canceled concerts that Robeson had scheduled because they were afraid of similar riots. Over the years, the riot has appeared in fiction, in an E. L. Doctorow novel, and in music, like "Hold the Line" (Pete Seeger and The Weavers), and "Let Robeson Sing" (Manic Street Preachers). The State Department denied Robeson a passport to travel and issued a "stop notice" at all ports. When Robeson asked why he wasn't allowed a passport, the official reply was "his frequent criticism of the treatment of blacks in the United States should not be aired in foreign countries." Articles appeared in the Black press denouncing him as the "Lost Shepherd," which Hoover and the FBI had reprinted and distributed throughout Africa. At least one of these articles, and maybe both, which followed the FBI's anti-Communist line, was written by Roy Wilkins, then executive secretary (the power position) of the NAACP. Robeson's response was to go global without getting on an airplane! *He went to the United Nations* and presented an anti-lynching petition titled "We Charge Genocide," which stated in no uncertain terms that the government, by its failure to pass a law banning lynching, was guilty of genocide under article 2 of the

U.N. Genocide Convention. *Wow! Wish I had his guts!* The son of a bitch put all of us armchair warriors of the sixties to shame.

The State Department wouldn't lift the travel ban, so he sang for one thousand Londoners via telephone cable. The old mountain and Mohammed trick. Tickets sold out in an hour. Still, it was impossible to hear him sing, buy his music, or see his films in America. But he continued to fight back. His "manifesto autobiography," *Here I Stand* (which I critiqued in my volume *African American Bookshelf*[8]), came out in '58 and his passport was restored in June. That led to a world tour that included London, Australia and New Zealand, Africa, and Cuba. Essie wanted them to stay in London when she got there for two reasons: he might be killed if he went back home, and even if he wasn't, he couldn't make any money. In spite of Essie's objections, he returned to America in 1963 and, for the last thirteen years of his life, lived in seclusion. Essie died in 1965, and three years later, he settled in his sister's home in Philadelphia. It's listed on the national register of historic places as the Paul Robeson House.

His last appearance on the stage in a dramatic role was as Othello, of course. And it was in Stratford-upon-Avon, not Broadway—of course. He was sixty, and his Desdemona, Mary Ure, twenty-six. It was probably his most brilliant performance ever. It was certainly his best Othello. In recordings, you can hear the complete command of the part, the informed emotion of the artist in his prime. Was this cultural treasure ever heard of or seen in the home of the brave and the land of the free? Of course not. Was there even talk of having it done in New York, as would have happened if he were white and received the accolades he received in England? Of course!!! W. A. Darlington, writing in the *New York Times*, said it was the second-best *Othello* he had ever seen in his lifetime.[9] We forgave Lindberg for being a fascist (he admired Hitler), as we forgave Joe Kennedy, JFK's father, who was ambassador to England at the time and thought Hitler was the bee's knees. So what was Robeson's problem? All of that political "activism"!—if he'd stayed home, behaved himself, and "stuck to" his acting, he would have been all right. No, don't believe it. Ken Burns's take on Jack Johnson's problem was that he committed the sin of "unforgivable Blackness." Well, hello Paul. Was Robeson a communist? You bet your pajamas he was, as was Du Bois. One reason they were such close friends. But then so was Dashiell Hammett. But Warner Bros. produced *The Maltese Falcon* three times. Hammett even went to prison because he wouldn't give up the names of his fellow Communists who had been convicted under the old interpretation of the Smith Act and had fled rather than face prison. For his refusal to divulge their whereabouts, Hammett was sent to prison for contempt of court and one of his duties was to clean toilets. We extol the heroes it suits us to, and demonize the ones we don't really consider to be part of our "ethnicity."

Robeson was a complex man, and his complexity is answerable for his talent. The private demons that drive many an actor to brilliance on the stage have been well recorded. But the Black artist does not have the luxury of living with demons, good or bad. To be acceptable, he has to be a mentor to the Black youth of America, or a Baptist preacher, or an academic who knows his place. Or some such. The man who can mesmerize us in his acting with his fire, his intensity, his grasp of the mysteries of the human experience must have burning inside him nothing more exciting than an insurance broker's imagination, because we must always think that he "knows his place." If he doesn't, then he's punishable—by death if necessary. And no artistic mumbo jumbo is going to exempt him from the taboo that "Black man no can talk white man talk. Must only talk nigger talk." Remember Gilpin. O'Neill thought him the perfect Emperor Jones, and yet he was *never* allowed to play anything else. Robeson was. But after the two O'Neill pieces and Shakespeare, he hit a wall. Then all he was able to do in film in America was Uncle Joe parts: Old Man River and the money falling from the sky in *Tales of Manhattan*—that is, when he wasn't bowing and scraping to Leslie Banks in *Sanders of the River*. But every time he did *Othello*, he was a standout. Still, the Broadway producers wouldn't come out of the closet, and Hollywood wasn't interested in *that* type of Black actor. Only Uncle Joe. This, even though Robeson proved he was good box office. John Barrymore's *Hamlet* ran for 101 performances in 1922, Gielgud's for 132 in 1936. Robeson's *Othello* almost tripled Barrymore and more than doubled Gielgud, running for a record 296 performances, and that's still a Broadway record for a classic.

There's something beyond cultural intolerance that can account for that kind of talent being blacklisted in perpetuity when all the world knows how great he was. He was a household name, and when we destroy a household name, we do more than just show our racist gene; we make it a sacred trust to keep Black people subservient in perpetuity. The culture will not tolerate greatness in a Black man unless he adheres to the Confederate code of conduct. Indeed, his greatness is in itself the ultimate test of his limitations. If he, having ascended to greatness, can be brought down, reduced to the lowliest of the low and condemned thereafter in the public perception as a traitor, then that's not just draconian punishment; that's an Inquisition-style burning at the stake, even in metaphor. Everybody remembers that Robeson was *a Communist (excoriated the nation for its racism, praised Russia for making him feel like a man) with no qualifications*. And that he could sing. But no one even knew, much less remembers, that the man who wrote *The Maltese Falcon* and *The Thin Man* (gee, wasn't it fun seeing Nick and Nora gadabouting?) went to prison because he was a Communist who wouldn't turn on his fellow travelers. And when James Stewart played Lindberg, he didn't have to denounce Hitler to appease a nation that had fought and bled to get rid of him. We wouldn't have had to marvel at Sidney Poitier making a living outside of overalls and Bill Cosby being America's father and all that has come after if we had been given permission to celebrate what Robeson was, what he achieved, what he stood for. When America lynched Paul Robeson (metaphorically, if you will), it reduced its culture to mob law, to a Deep South lynching, Northern style. It may seem as if I'm lobbying for Robeson to be treated as if he were white. Well, in a sense, he was.

White by achievement. We can't find a white artist who can match him in the variety of his experience, irrespective of that actor's greatness. That alone should have made him untouchable. But we said, "*No!* Because you Black."

There remains so much more to be said about the man than I have room for. He was a giant, but not the self-aggrandizing one that we have come to claim him to be now that he's dead and buried. That has no more value than a eulogy at a prayer meeting. He was a giant because he was an actor who did what few American actors could do: play period and contemporary and be brilliant in both, as Brando did. Olivier was never up to his Shakespeare in anything else and was often embarrassing, as when he attempted to play Tyrone in an American revival of *Long Day's Journey*. Can you see any of your favorite American actors doing period? Tracy, Bogart, Grant, Cooper? No, I'm afraid we did much more than destroy another Black man when we reduced Paul Robeson to a political footnote. We set back the advance of Black culture by fifty years and made sure that if and when we find such a man or woman once again, we will be marveling at how "groundbreaking" his or her talent is instead of seeing it as the onward march forward from Paul Robeson. Because we have made his achievements an exception not to be imitated, and in so doing, we have put his greatness in limbo. We can't deny his talent, but we certainly can put up a sign that says, "Don't celebrate it." The encomiums and the eulogizing that have come hereafter are merely a ritual burying of the dead when he's safe and sound in his grave and can cause us no more discomfort.

IN THE END, WE GOT THE RAISIN

The Little Theater Movement came to Harlem in earnest in 1940, in the basement of the 135th Street Library, in the form of the American Negro Theater. (The Little Theater Movement itself has a long history in America, going back to the first decade of the twentieth century.) The American Negro Theater trained such contemporary luminaries as Harry Belafonte, Sidney Poitier, Ruby Dee, and Ossie Davis and was led by the writer Abram Hill, who was its guiding light, and by Frederick O'Neal, who later became president of the Four A's (which includes Actors' Equity and the Screen Actors' Guild). As the forties ended and the fifties began, the Black playwright had emancipated himself from any self-conscious inhibitions when it came to talking about race in bold and no uncertain terms. And race is the theme that for the Black playwright dominated the decade that ended with *Raisin in the Sun*. Alice Childress, Loften Mitchell, Theodore Ward, William Branch, and Abraham Hill all had something to say about race that was relevant to the times. Their work can be called *journeyman* even if the term applies to the man or woman and not the work. They have spirit, and their plays are peppered with sophistication in the form of wit, sarcasm, irony, and the sadness that comes with essaying the tragedy of what it means to be Black in America. But they have also added something new to the canon. They write about the middle class for the most part, since the urban Black citizen who came of age in significant numbers in the twenties, with the Harlem Renaissance, was no longer a unique phenomenon by the fifties. Black writers, actors, and other artists of the period had grown up in a middle-class milieu that went beyond their own personal experience. So an *Emperor Jones* would have been as alien to them as *Uncle Tom's Cabin*, except as historical fact. But there's more to these plays than their newfound freedom of political thought. They show a sense of belonging to their unique Black African American culture that is profound both in its acceptance as a given and in the ease with which they handle it in their work. There is no criticism that can be laid at the door of these writers when it comes to their artistic *consciousness*. They know all the issues and have most of the answers, and they dare anyone to suggest that they can't write about what they know. But alas, that type of to-hell-with-the-consequences courage meant that they were persona non grata on Broadway—in the fifties or in any decade of the twentieth century. The surge of race pride that saw such an outpouring in the sixties never had a Broadway impact, even if one or two plays that could boast such pedigree were produced there. The mood of the rest of the twentieth century was one of muffled sound when it came to race once we had killed off Malcolm and Dr. King. Nixon's election in 1968 on the law-and-order ticket left such a pall on the political and artistic mood of the country that not even Bill Clinton's liberal appointing of Blacks to cabinet posts could put a dent in the long-extended pushback that was determined to see to it that the sixties would never happen again. When Barack Obama was elected, we were once more fulfilling our destiny of a nation of first acts, and the racists rose again in revolt like new-grown hay as soon as his eight years were up. That notwithstanding, none of the playwrights of the fifties were able to transcend their period. Most of their work has long since fallen into the out-of-print bin and can only be read in reference libraries or in Amazon's out-of-print catalogs. Very few of them are performed today or even read, except in class.

Before we take an in-depth look at these writers, the story of the American Negro Theater's eleven-year run, and its amazing Broadway success, *Anna Lucasta* needs to be discussed. Du Bois was the progenitor of the Little Theater Movement, Black style, in the twenties with his Krigwa Players, followed by the Harlem Experimental Theatre. Both were short-lived; the former was gone by 1928 and the latter by 1934. Both wanted to bring Black theater about Black people to Black people, written by Black writers, and both were housed in the basement of the 135th Street Branch of the New York Public Library. Enter Abe Hill and Fred O'Neal.

They were inspired most immediately by the Federal Theatre Project's Black unit, which had just finished presenting so many successful productions at the Lafayette a scant two years earlier. Said Hill, "[We] started with a great deal of enthusiasm, with the hope that we were going to solve all the problems . . . in our theatre. [We] had a taste of the theatre in the WPA setting. This federal program ended in 1939, leaving many [of us looking] for someplace to go. We were trying to . . . find out if we could build a theatre of our own. . . . At the first meeting . . .

we passed the hat . . . to collect money so we could send out cards to others who might be interested in our work. We collected a total of eleven cents."[10]

In the end, ANT trained over two hundred actors to become theater profession- als and played to an audience of fifty thousand people, giving a total of 325 perfor- mances, but it wasn't enough to ensure lasting success. Several villains can claim credit for ANT's demise, but two stand out: democracy and commercial success. Anyone who has worked in theater for any significant period of time knows that theatrical organizations must be run by a strong hand at the helm. ANT insisted that theirs would be a theater in which everyone would have an equal voice in all matters, most significantly in choosing the plays to be done. As Hill explains, the actors would read the scripts and if they didn't see a part for themselves, they voted not to do the play! As for villain number two, once *Anna Lucasta* became a standout commercial success (it even ran on Broadway longer than *Raisin in the Sun*), ANT became a tryout theater and their core mission of producing plays for their community became an empty one. There were other villains. *Lucasta* was getting so much press that the constant referral to "this small library basement, which is no larger than a big room, on this tiny vest pocket stage," et cetera, did not sit well with NYPL powers that be, so they had to move. Once they did that, they no longer had rent-free accommodations. In addition to having to pay rent, they also had a huge light bill that doubled the amount of the rent that they were suddenly responsible for.

So how did *Lucasta* happen, and why was it so popular? Philip Yordan, a highly successful screenwriter, wrote *Lucasta* about a working-class Polish family. Anna is a prostitute who's been shunned by her family. But when they think they can marry her off to a fairly well-to-do young man, they jump at the chance, hoping to cash in on the romance. Yordan was unable to get any producer interested in the project, so he gave it to Abram Hill for want of something better to do with it. Hill says neither he nor Fred O'Neal was intrigued at first, one reason being that it was too similar to O'Neill's *Anna Christie*. But desperate for a script, Hill gave it a second look, convinced O'Neal to go along, and decided that, with copious reworking, it had a chance. He got the English director Henry Wag- staff Gribble to come uptown and take a look at the kind of stuff they were doing. Gribble was so impressed with the acting of Fred O'Neal and the rest that he agreed. Which came as no surprise to anyone who knew ANT's work. They were thoroughgoing professionals who set a high bar for their productions. John Chapman, writing in the *Daily News*, called ANT "the finest ensemble acting in town."[11] With Gribble at the helm, they did *Lucasta* in "this tiny vest pocket stage." When they got the kind of reviews that said "money," Yordan flew in from Holly- wood to find out what all the fuss was about. By the end of the first act, he was so incensed by the changes that had been made that it was all Hill could do to keep him from walking out during intermission. By the end of the last act, though, he was beaming. His first question to Hill was whether ANT wanted to produce the play on Broadway. Hill's reply was "We are a tryout company. It would change our format if we became a first-class producer. We don't have that kind of backing. I doubt that we would want to change our status on the basis of this play."[12] Yordan's reply was "That's all I wanted to know. I brought producers with me." Then he added, "Now as far as our contract is concerned, don't worry about it. We're going to take care of you and the American Negro Theatre."[13] Yippee!!! The man who ended up producing, Jack Wildberg, however, told Hill that *he* had no contract with him or with ANT. So while Hill was scurrying around trying to find out if Yordan did intend, indeed, to take care of him, and while he was trying to get the Dramatists Guild to find the standing contract that he had governing all the other plays he'd produced, *Lucasta* was in rehearsal on Broadway with most of ANT's actors in their original parts! Why O'Neal and the others didn't force Wildberg to honor the play's obligation to both Hill as the coauthor along with Gribble, and to ANT as the original producing company, Hill doesn't say. *Lucasta*, by Hill's own account, made so much money that he "can't imagine what . . . [it] really earned. I would have to say about 25 million. Within two years the play had grossed seven million through the national company and the local company."[14] And he's talking 1944 dollars. There've been "two films and many English-speaking productions and one in Yiddish,"[15] he thinks. This is where Hill and ANT get caught in the three-card monte shuffle, trying to find out which shell has the peanut. The Dramatists Guild contract that ANT had on file stated that "American Negro Theatre got 2 percent of the Broadway production and 5 percent of subsidiary [rights] but not including any movie rights."[16] But the Guild contract couldn't be found for some strange reason, and the lawyer was out of the country but would get in touch with Hill as soon as he got back. In desperation Hill went face-to-face with Wildberg. His first offer to Hill was "I'll give you a pass so you can come into the theater anytime free of charge."[17] To placate his cast, Wildberg finally agreed to give ANT 1.25 percent, but only of the Broadway run. Under a separate agreement, Gribble and Hill were made collaborating authors with Yordan, which gave each of them 10 percent of Yordan's royalties. The fact that Yordan and Hill had the same agent further complicated matters. Apparently, the agent saw to it that Yordan was in no wise cheated even though the script that was making all that money was so indistinguishable from Yordan's original that he almost walked out of the theater the first night. So not only was ANT robbed of three-fourths of a percent of what *Lucasta* earned in New York, but they got nothing from subsidiary rights that should have been another 5 percent. Gribble got his 10 percent of Yordan's take. So Yordan, who was the original writer, of a failed script mind you, got everything that was coming to him and more. What did the American Negro Theater's Major Negro get? He had to get a lawyer just to get anything. When he walked into the lawyer's office, the lawyer asked him, "You Abe Hill?" When he said yes, the lawyer replied, "What a stupid son of a bitch."[18] In the end, the lawyer sued everybody and ended up getting Hill $25,000. Minus the lawyer's fee made it a little over $18,000 or $17,000, depending on whether they went to court. And that's for a script that Hill not only resurrected from the dead but developed, getting the eventual director involved and providing most of the leading actors who made the Broadway version such a hit. No film rights—and there were two of them. It would be interesting to know what the white boys' final take was: Yordan and Gribble. Money or the lack of has always been one of the chief ways that Black endeavor has been kept underfoot. In the case of ANT, there was a lack of vision as well. An opportunity that would have kept them going for another ten years or more was fumbled. The sudden notoriety, the changes they would have to make to continue their mission as a community theatre and at the same time become a producing company all seemed more than they were ready for. With O'Neal on a Broadway stage six nights a week, it was up to Abe Hill to make all the decisions, and it was probably more than he could handle.

All of which brings us to the major Black playwrights of the period who established their careers independently of ANT.

Theodore Ward

In addition to *Big White Fog*, Ted Ward also had his Broadway moment with *Our Lan'*,[19] which won a Theatre Guild Award, was produced off-Broadway at the Henry Street Playhouse in 1946, and then moved to the Royale and ran for forty-seven performances. Unlike *Big White Fog*, *Our Lan'* is written in a Southern vernacular that weighs heavily on it, but it is effective drama nevertheless. The mood of the play is dated, burdened as it is throughout with song. Some of the lyrics are not well known: "Ole Marster sot in de shade 'n he cried: Hoe, Boy, hoe!" Others are perennial favorites such as "Steal Away to Jesus" and "Deep River," which the romantic leads sing as the curtain line. But Ward has a great idea for his play. It opens while the Civil War is still on. A group of Black people have occupied an island off the coast of Georgia. Taking General Sherman's promise of "forty acres and a mule" as a fait accompli, they have set up a settlement, built housing, planted cotton, and hired a schoolteacher all the way from Connecticut to teach the children. The epochal idea that they, as ex-slaves, finally have their own lan' is the ethos of *Our Lan'* and its driving force. The actual facts of the case are that Lincoln agreed to the idea and Congress passed a bill that gave Black people land taken from the rebels who lost the war, but Andrew Johnson vetoed the bill. Ward builds his tension by showing the hope when they start to erect their homes and the euphoria when the news comes that the war is over and the South has been defeated. Thinking that their troubles are now over, they've sent for a cotton broker to buy the ten bales they have raised that are now ready for sale when the former owner shows up with the army to reclaim his land. Their leader, Joshua Tain, has no interest in returning to a condition of servitude, which is what having no land in the South of the 1860s will mean. The captain of the Union soldiers threatens to fire on them, and Tain tells his men to prepare to return the fire, when the captain stands down and leaves. Thinking they will prevail if they just hold on, their euphoria returns until the broker shows up. He offers them seventeen cents a pound for cotton worth thirty. Because they need money for food for the children, Tain tries to get the broker to buy only some of the cotton at seventeen, hoping to get a better price for the rest. The broker counters with five bales at fifteen. In the end, Tain has to take fifteen for all ten bales or risk not being able to sell his cotton at all. The owner and the army return. The captain now tells Tain that he can stay if he agrees to work for the owner for three years, after which he can buy the land back. When Tain asks how much the owner is offering, he's told five dollars a month! Desperate, Tain accepts the starvation wage if it means he'll eventually be able to buy the lan' after three years, but the owner says he has no intention of selling his land ever. Tain counters that he's willing to buy some of the island if he can't buy it all. The owner refuses to sell him even a plot! In spite of Tain's best efforts at a compromise, the captain says he has no choice but to fire on them if they don't either sign the contracts or leave. They refuse to sign and they refuse to leave. They worked the land, they fought for it, they slaved on it for the rebel slave master and now that they've got it, they intend to keep it. Well, the tragic ending is not difficult to foresee. Tain and his "brown-skinned" beauty are together at the end. She refuses to leave with the women and children even though she herself is pregnant. She will die enveloped in the warmth of Joshua Tain's embrace. The Broadway producers were convinced that their ending was so strong that the army's cannon going off as the lights dim would be too much for the audience to bear on top of everything else. But Ward put it back in the printed edition. A strong idea for a play of a much-neglected chapter in the long history of our travails.

William "Bill" Branch

An erudite man of letters whose professional achievements have been many and varied. I knew him well in the old days, when writing for the theater was more of a passion than a profession. Bill died in 2019. He will be sorely missed. *A Medal for Willie*,[20] his first play and arguably his best-known work, is resonant of the period between the end of the war and the beginning of the sixties. Written in 1951, it grapples with the problems of the continued racism that Black America was facing as if the war had never happened, and the only option the race had was to let the South continue its atavistic heritage of keeping the *negra* in his place. The strength of the play lies in challenging that ancient demon always gnawing at the innards of the sons and daughters of Black America without fear of reprisal. But Branch sacrifices character and a compelling narrative to this end. Willie Jackson is an eighteen-year-old Black kid from the South, who has done nothing to distinguish himself (expelled from school, hanging with the wrong crowd) before going into the army. Once there, he becomes a hero, manning a machine gun and saving the lives of his fellow soldiers and, in the process, sacrificing his own. In gratitude, he's given the Distinguished Service Cross posthumously by a grateful nation. It falls to his mother to accept the medal at the presentation ceremony. The buildup to that event is a series of disconnected scenes, each showing the racism of the town and the duplicity of honoring a Black son of the South in death who was not only not honored in life but treated as an ignorant afterthought—and not just by the white community. When the general who will present the medal arrives, the mayor tells him he can't bring any Yankee ideas with him down South, like encouraging the *nigras* so they won't know their place. The general assures him that won't happen since he, too, is a son of the South. There's a scene between the editor of the local newspaper and a reporter. The editor wants the story played up big, even calling Willie's mother Mrs. Jackson. The reporter says that would fly in the face of the taboo not to confer an honorific on anyone Black. The editor says it will probably be all right given the circumstances. He's even willing to run a picture of Mrs. Jackson shaking the general's hand. In another scene, the Black principal tells the young teacher he's chosen to take his place that once he gets promoted to his new job, he'll go around the country giving speeches about how great a segregated school system is! And there are other scenes that deliver the same message.

It finally falls to Willie's mother, when she makes her acceptance speech, to denounce the hypocrisy. Instead of accepting the medal, which is what she had initially intended to do, she throws it down like a gauntlet at their feet and walks off the stage, followed by a crying daughter and a silent, bemused, and embarrassed husband. There are several very long speeches by the villains themselves. The general has a page and a half of dialogue extolling the American way. The mayor has another running two pages praising the Southern way and how it's to its credit that it produced the likes of a Willie Jackson. So Branch does indeed pour it on, and the play isn't saved by a scene between Willie's sweetheart from the former days and a white youth who was too sensitive to go in the army but not too sensitive to molest a young Black woman who can't defend herself from his brutish advances. Needless to say, none of this challenging the racism of the times put Bill Branch or any of his confreres on Broadway. If it had, even with its structural defects, *Medal* could have provided an engaging evening of theater entertainment that would have had much more to offer than the sanitized angst that was a middle-class audience's wont.

Louis Peterson

Peterson has the distinction of being the first African American to have had a dramatic play produced on Broadway, according to one source. Langston Hughes must be turning over in his grave, since by his count, Peterson's play, *Take a Giant Step*,[21] is at least the ninth dramatic play by an African American playwright produced on Broadway before *Raisin*.[22] Peterson came from a middle-class family; both parents worked in the banking business. His academic credentials were certainly enough to supply the artist with the tools with which to sally forth. He graduated from Morehouse College in 1944 with a degree in English. He attended Yale University for a year and then got an MA in drama from New York University. He followed this up by studying acting with Sanford Meisner and at the Actors Studio. He also studied playwriting and worked closely with Clifford Odets. So

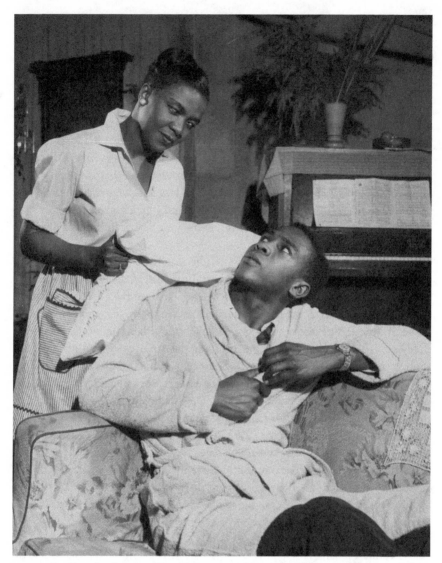

FIGURE 6.5. Dorothy Carter and Louis Gossett in *Take a Giant Step*, 1953. Friedman-Abeles.

he was well equipped to write *Take a Giant Step*, his strongest work. It was well received by the critics and ran for eight weeks at the Lyceum and was revived off-Broadway for 246 performances. It opened in 1953.

Take a Giant Step is very earnest. The hero is a high school teen, Spencer Scott, living with his parents in a white neighborhood. At school, his history teacher makes a derogatory remark about the role Black people played in the Civil War. He confronts her and walks out of class in protest—and into the bathroom to smoke a cigar. He's expelled from school for two weeks, during which time he learns who's on his side and who isn't. Both parents side with the teacher. Grandma says, "That's my boy!" He does well with his fellow classmates—the ones that are boys, that is. Since he's at the age for dating, however, he's left out of the fun and games when it comes to dating white girls. Because his parents provide him with all the material comforts, they feel justified in wanting him to crawl instead of standing up and walking, in order to survive in the nasty white world. His mother even says, "You think you can go through life being proud, well you're wrong. You're a little black boy—and you don't seem to understand it." But the mood of the play is more candy cane than raw racism. Peterson's language is one of the chief villains in this regard. When discussing his confrontation with the teacher, he asks his grandmother, "You mean I shouldn't have gotten sassy with the fruit cake?" Her reply is "Spencer, I'm not going to say one more word to you if you don't stop using language like that." Whereupon he really gets nasty. He tells her she's getting to be a "crumb," just like the whole crummy world. A young woman, a bit older than he, in trying to get him to eat something because he's mourning his grand-mother's death, calls him a "mulish critter." In the big confrontation scene with his mother, she threatens at one point to slap him. He says, "How in hell . . ." She cuts him off with "Don't use that kind of language before [sic] me." So we have a young hero who's hardly a Holden Caulfield. He's still a virgin, thanks to the racial taboo, tries to spend the night with a lady thereof, flops. Gets the older woman, who's in his family's employ, to take him over the threshold. And his grand dra-matic gesture is to politely tell his white "bros" that he wants to be left alone for a while because he has to get serious with his studies so he can, like his older brother, go to college. He seems to have taken his parents' lesson in passivity to heart. When one of his buddies, oblivious to the presence of Iggy, the Jewish kid, spouts outrageously anti-Semitic remarks, Spencer apologizes, not in front of the boys, but in private to Iggy after they've left. Oh, and he makes up with Ma. Doesn't have to with Pa since he never gets another scene after Grandma dies. And at the final curtain, he's playing the piano. After-school special or just a dis-creet reading of a coming of age story? Since the play is so kind, so sympathetic to all and sundry, let's call it the latter.

Loften Mitchell

Erudite, often scathing, often commiserating patriarch of the period (with whom I shared many a drink). In addition to his critically acclaimed, *Black Drama*, a history that covered the subject from the beginnings to the sixties, his most sig-nificant dramatic work, *Land beyond the River*, and his concert drama history of Harlem, *Tell Pharaoh*, are the most emblematic of his oeuvre. But he's probably best known for penning the book for the Broadway musical *Bubbling Brown Sugar*, which ran at the ANTA Playhouse for a little under two years in the seventies.

Based on a true story, *Land beyond the River*[23] tells the tale of a brave band of Black souls defying Southern racist bigotry in a rural county in the dreaded dark days of 1950s South Carolina. Led by their minister, Dr. Joseph DeLaine (who actually did have to escape to New York to stay alive), the men and women of

Clarendon County band together and sign a petition to sue the county for not providing equal educational facilities for their children. They want buses for the rural area and they want a new schoolhouse, since the old one is so rotted that the reverend has to close it for the children's safety. Everyone who's signed the petition is in harm's way, which results in drive-by shootings and the burning of the parson's house to the ground. The shock of seeing her house destroyed triggers a heart attack in DeLaine's wife that proves fatal. That's the heroic backdrop to the play. In the playing itself, however, Mitchell engages in a lot of strained, misplaced humor as well as folksy wisdom, mostly from an ancient named Miss Sims who lives alone in the hills. Tension in a play lives by its dialogue. At one point, DeLaine arms himself with a handgun. The white superintendent admonishes him to put the gun away. His answer: "When the Good Book mentioned turning the other cheek gun powder wasn't invented." All of the dramatic moments are handled either with similar homespun homilies or with outright sermonizing. One of the men becomes enraged when his eight-year-old son is set upon by white toughs who are grown men. In response, DeLaine does his pastoral duty and preaches to the father about love, not hate: "When I was a child I spake as a child," jumping to "And now abideth faith, hope and love. But the greatest of these is love." Trying to humanize his people so the work offers something other than "protesting" against ills real and tragic in their consequences, Mitchell makes his characters so human that he robs them of their individuality. When things get bad, they start singing. Once their spirits are lifted, it's time for a barbecue sandwich and dandelion wine. Which is fine in and of itself, but not when it acts as a cliché of how easily Black people can forget their troubles if you give 'em food. When the men try to fix the rotted floorboards in the school, they end up in fistfights that even the ministers (there are two of them) have difficulty stopping. None of this would have an unfortunate effect on the dramatic action if we were offered something other than moralizing in the way of character progression or narrative substance. But since there is nothing more, all we have to judge these good, honest, and brave people by is their all-too-familiar, stereotypical downhome pleasures and sermonizing. And that's unfortunate because their story deserved more.

Alice Childress

Childress, who supported my candidacy for membership in New Dramatists, was a charming, stylish, and well-informed theater maven whose works extended well into the sixties. She was also an accomplished actor, receiving a Tony Award nomination for her work as Blanche in *Anna Lucasta*. (The star vehicle was played by the luminous Hilda Sims.) Childress's *Trouble in Mind*[24] is a clever attempt to address the problems of Black actors struggling to get a white director to understand what's offensive about the play he wants them to perform. Even if the ending is unfortunate, it's an interesting look into what lengths Black actors have to go to just to get a part. Wiletta, the middle-aged protagonist, confronts

FIGURE 6.6. Alice Childress when she wrote *Trouble in Mind* in the midfifties. Photographs and Prints Division, Schomburg Center for Research in Black Culture, The New York Public Library.

the director who wants her to play a scene in which she sends her son out to be lynched. She asks the director if he would send his son out to be lynched. The director becomes irate and cancels the rehearsal. But Childress follows that strength with an egregiously clumsy ending to the scene. The protagonist and a minor character, onstage together, are angry at the director's racism. The minor character tells her that he's a fighting man, and Wiletta asks him if he's from

Ireland! At which point, he not only says yes but begins to spout the history of the Easter Rebellion that took place in Dublin in 1916, with names of the leaders and details of why they rebelled. In the final scene, Wiletta and the minor character are at it again. This time, she tells him she always wanted to do something grand in theater, "to stand forth at my best [on the stage] . . . and do anything I want." He, the minor character, encourages her to "say something from the Bible, like the twenty-third psalm." And the stage directions are "She comes downstage and recites beautifully from Psalm 133."

Wedding Band[25] takes place in South Carolina in 1918. Because the central story is a love affair between a Black woman, Julia, and a white man, Herman, no producer would touch it for six years. It was later filmed and shown on TV, but many stations refused to play it. Miss Childress has a strong dose of medicine to sell, but she has too many cooks spoiling the pot. We don't see Herman until scene 2 of the first act, and scene 1 lasts sixteen pages and introduces seven other characters. Herman's sister and mother don't make an entrance until the penultimate scene in the play, even though both are crucial to the ultimate dramatic effect. Again, instead of concentrating her firepower on the two lovers and the tragedy that their lives have to be because theirs is an illegal love that could get them and everyone connected with them killed, jailed, or run out of the state, she has a plethora of stories and subplots to tell before she gets to the final confrontation between Julia on one hand and the mother and daughter on the other—with poor Herman in the middle. The other characters and stories include the landlady with the most money of all the Black families who share a common backyard and who lords it over the rest; the mother with a charming daughter, whose husband is away at sea and sends her money, but it's not enough and she can't collect her allotment as his wife because they're not legally married; the older woman with an adopted son who's a soldier who can't wear his uniform at home because it might get him lynched. Unlike *Trouble in Mind*, she has tremendously strong endings for the last two scenes of the play. Herman, when he comes to visit Julia for the first time, becomes ill quite suddenly. It turns out to be the flu (the 1918 epidemic killed fifty million people worldwide). This causes great consternation all around. None of the other women want him dying in their backyard, since that means calling the police, and calling the police means the whirlwind. Herman's mother and sister, Annabelle, are summoned. Julia wants to call a doctor. Annabelle agrees, but mother won't have it. The disgrace of it being known that her son has a Black lover would be unbearable. She'd rather her son die and go to his reward, and she's quite willing to help him get there. That scene ends with Herman staggering out of Julia's house and onto the porch of one of the other women. By now he's delirious. Miss Childress gets up to one of her old tricks, injecting quotes from disconcerting sources at the worst possible time. Here, Herman begins reciting part of a speech by the granddaddy of Southern racists, John C. Calhoun, to wit, "Men are not born. Infants are born. . . . It is a great and dangerous error to suppose that all people are equally entitled to liberty." Julia becomes distraught and can't listen.

In the midst of that, he tells Julia he's dying. She tells his mother and sister to take him. Mother ends up calling her a "Black sassy nigger." She returns the compliment by using the mother's German heritage as a rejoinder: "Kraut, knuckle-eater, red neck." When they leave with Herman, Julia's rage explodes: "Out! Out! Out! And take the last ten years-a my life with you . . . and when he gets better . . . keep him home." She then throws all the bedding into the yard because Herman slept on it. She tells her woman neighbors, "I'm goin' get down on my hands and knees and scrub where they walked . . . what they touched." That's topped by the last scene: Herman has returned to die with his beloved, confessing to her, "When my mother and sister came . . . I was ashamed. What am I doin' being ashamed of us." And Julia replies, "When you first came in this yard I almost died-a shame. . . . But most times you were my husband, my friend, my lover." When Annabelle and the mother show up, Julia bolts the door, locking them out, and they leave, subdued, accepting that he will die with her, and it's where he belongs. As he gasps out the last life breaths, she's radiant in the knowledge that he's dying happily because he is dying with her. "Social dynamite," said the reviewer about *All God's Chillun's* miscegenated love. Robeson even got death threats for his 1943 Othello, from South Carolina and points all over the compass. So Ms. Childress dared to tread "where wise men never go. But wise men never fall in love." And that includes wise men of the present era. Still Alice Childress did not do her reputation or her plays any favors by overplotting and overwriting. Because of all the other stories and characters she decided to color her script with, she never gave the love tragedy, as powerful as it was, enough time to dominate the script.

The fifties was the first time that racism was confronted almost universally by the Black playwright; however, there was both a self-consciousness about it and an awkward belief that the confrontation itself was dramatic enough to make a play effective in theatrical terms. That, unfortunately, was not the case with these plays of the working and the middle class that were ubiquitous throughout the period. And that brings us to *A Raisin in the Sun.*

Like Booker T. Washington, there are probably more good reasons not to like *Raisin in the Sun*[26] than there are reasons to like it. As a dramatic reading of the state of Black America, it's a period piece; as working theater, it is highly effective and it's unquestionably a classic. But why? True, it's heartwarming and modest in its personal, emotional, and sociological read. The family wants to move into a white neighborhood. The neighborhood, instead of burning them out when they get there, want to buy them out before they even move in. The mother, as is befitting a matriarch worth her salt, is the tower of strength in the family, the rod and the rock. Her son, Walter Lee, who is a grown man in his thirties with a wife and a child and a job as a chauffeur, has let a couple of hustlers cheat him out of most of the insurance money his father left so the move will be an act of courage. Reminiscent of Torrence and his *Rider of Dreams* circa 1917? Unfortunately, yes. He's proud and angry. But it's the sort of pride and the sort of anger that sees grown men beating their chest and insisting that that's what they are: Men. And they are

FIGURE 6.7. Paul Robeson as Othello and Uta Hagen as Desdemona, in a scene from the Theatre Guild presentation of *Othello*, 1943–1944. Vandamm Studio.

not going to take it anymore! Whereupon they proceed to do just that for the rest of their lives. Instead of being a bulwark and a tower of strength, Walter Lee is a ball and chain that his mother has to drag along with the rest of the family as they try to find salvation in living, literally, in white America. He complains about his job, his condition in life, his responsibilities, his wife's not understanding him. You name it, he complains about it. But his complaints are not complaints about who we are, why we are, or how we are. They're complaints about what's wrong with *his* life that he can't do anything about because Black women don't understand him.

FIGURE 6.8. Claudia McNeil in *A Raisin in the Sun*, 1959. Friedman-Abeles.

He talks and talks and talks, and like Omar Khayyam, in the end, he goes out by the same door he came in. His sudden, belated entrance into manhood (his rite of passage coming at least fifteen years late) is made official when Mama says to his wife at the end of the play, "He finally come into his manhood today, didn't he?" And his wife agrees with her. This coup de theater has been brought about because since he was the one who lost $6,500 of insurance money, his mother gave him in trust, he's the one appointed to tell the white emissary with the filthy check that the family is going to move into the white neighborhood whether they like it or not. That's the grand act of courage that finally makes him a man. Of course, one shouldn't object to *Raisin* on grounds of it not being as socially relevant in 2020 as it was in 1959 (assuming it was even then). Social relevancy should not be a paradigm for judging a theatrical work. If a play is *universal* then it doesn't need social relevancy, and *Raisin* is universal. It's universally "I've been buked and I been scorned." But as Fannie Lou Hamer said, "I'm tired of being tired." So tired of this tired version of a Black life. So tired of its clichés, its limitations, its self-pity, its bathos. Walter Lee's problem is not that he hadn't reached his manhood. His problem is that because he's been dwarfed by the racism, the simple act of not taking payment in the family's name for agreeing to be segregated against is how he's found his manhood. But it's a low bar for 2020 or any date thereafter. When the daughter, Beneatha, and her African boyfriend, Asagai, are in the scene together (he's Yoruba, which makes him Nigerian, but the name is Zulu, which makes him South African), the dialogue and the ideas become intelligent, modern, worth one's attention—without ever really getting political. In the end, we can say that *Raisin* is a nice little play that gives some hope to the ones who still need help in feeling equal to the problems that being Black in America bring. And the family does beat with a single heart in a way that makes their suffering affecting. These are people who neither offend nor threaten. As such, they offer a window into Blackness that is relieving. There's no chance that there will be any feeling of white guilt or any fear of a cheap shot that Blacks too often have to endure whenever their lives are written about by white writers, which makes it a double win. But in the last scene of the play Asagai has the speech of a man whose dreams are worth having, a man who has a chance of making the world a better place to live in. He has the speech that ole Walter could never make.

The death of FTP and the era, short-lived though it was, that made fighting for social justice de rigueur was also the end of a time when the stage served as a forum for the best in us. A time when we were released from middle-class conventions and allowed to give free rein to wild imaginings that tear down the walls that separate us and kick away the puritanical conventions that our Mayflower past inflicts on our collective conscience. So let's have a moment of silence for that time when a play about a Black man who kills two women (one white and one Black) gets done, is praised, and does good business, as did *Native Son*. The most interesting thing we've had on our stage in recent memory is a man having sex with a goat—offstage, in Edward Albee's production of *The Goat, or Who Is Sylvia?* Usually, we dismiss our American racism with the glib question of "When did that happen?" And unless it was the day before yesterday, we smugly say, "Well, that was back then. Things like that don't happen now." But how do you excuse away the *reversal* of that argument? We had the honesty, the national fortitude to discuss the bitter hatred in our midst in forthright and forceful ways in our national theater eighty years ago, which proved how strong the democracy was then. But we can't do it now, which proves how weak our democracy has become—or should I say, how vacuous. I had one of the most powerful producers on Broadway say to me in his office after *Ain't Supposed to Die a Natural Death* closed (it opened

October 1971 at the Ethel Barrymore) that that was the end of the "brother" and the Black protest movement. Sisyphus is about to lose his gig. Instead of tradition allowing him to slog up that ole hill, the present custom seems to be to bury him headfirst before he even takes the first step. That brings us to the moment of reckoning—of where we are in the theater as the second quarter of the new century beckons. Out of it, we are mighty and mousy at one and the same time. In it, we are mostly mousy. Why can a white policeman shoot a Black man in the back eight times and still have a huge part of the citizenship support him? On the theatrical stage, that would seem to be great theater. If most people would find it abhorrent but a plurality would not, that makes it good box office. Both sides have a stake in the conflict: the ones who are against it and the ones who back the police whenever they kill anything Black that moves. Ergo, both sides would want to see the event; the ones to cheer and the ones to denounce in hopes of eradicating the evil in our gerrymandered democracy. Or take the case of the *Miscegenated Love Affair*. There are so many cases of Black and white couples in love, or married at any rate, that even celebrities are doing it for all the world to see. So what is commercial theater saying? It's all right to do it in private (read: real life), but parading it on a Broadway stage would be going too far? Male love was given full dramatic license in an Academy Award–nominated film. Surely that must have rubbed some of the electorate the wrong way. Yet it got done and was well received. Score one for enlightenment. But not good ole Black-and-white love, which has been around for over four hundred years. My oh my.

The answer to this hypocrisy is, of course, the *race neutral* ideogram in the form of Black and white characters cavorting all over the place in plot after plot and nary a sign of that ole debbil race. Or if good ole race does get a run, it comes in the form of "Black people will no longer sit in the back of the bus. We demand to be treated equally; we want to sit in the front too along with all them white people. Amen, praise the Lord, and hallelujah." That is what passes for cutting-edge race drama today. There are too many demons buried in the id of the American subconscious—or to put a finer point on, the unconscious—that make race a veritable nightmare to deal with. For over a century, Americans lynched Black people the way you'd slaughter cattle, and no one, not one single slaughterer, ever did a day in prison for it. When Black people tried to vote in the sixties, police chiefs and their minions turned water hoses on them so strong that the men, women, and children were thrown against concrete walls as if they had been shot out of a cannon. They were set upon by dogs. That's when Malcolm X said, "Shoot the dogs." Everyone in the republic with a television set saw it, and then the majority of the voting public turned it off and finished dinner. Where was the public outcry, the protest movement, the march by the thousands of decent law-abiding citizens? And what were all those violent Black men trying to do? Who were they trying to rob, to rape, to kill? Only the law that said they couldn't vote. Which was what the tea party ruckus circa 1773 was all about. Even though white men could vote even before 1776, but Black men still couldn't in

1966. One hundred and ninety years later and we still couldn't get out of the back of the bus. Then you start to pile on the heroism of the Black Quarter. Frederick Douglass beat the bejesus out of the white slave tamer sent to tame him, and the guy was a full-grown man in his forties. Douglass was just a sixteen-year-old kid, and he went on to become a giant of nineteenth-century America. Robert Smalls was pressed into service in South Carolina as the pilot of a Confederate gunboat during the Civil War. So how did he emancipate himself? Simple. He stole the boat (hello Hollywood). All 313 tons of her. He even sabotaged the loading of extra cannons and ammunition, making sure they couldn't be unloaded until the day after he made his move. How did he make his move? He posed as the captain in the early morning half-light, wearing the famous straw-hat the captain was famous for. Gave the password and sailed right past four forts loaded with cannon, including Sumter, and into the arms of the Union naval blockade waiting at anchor outside Charleston's front door. After the war, he ran for Congress and got elected to the House five times! Harriet Tubman—well, if you don't know her story, then you're ignorant. And I mean *really* know it.

So what does all this mean? It means that the dodgeball of race-neutral rules says, "Show Black and whites as equal so everyone can go home happy in the knowledge that we live in a land where we are all, Black and white together, equal." Which would be fine if that were true. Since it is not, then it's a monstrous lie that might be good for box office: it makes Black America think it's better off than it is, and it makes white America think it's more democratic than it is. But it does very little for the dramatic event. If and when we have the courage to plow into that id thing lurking back there in the inner reaches of where we think without knowing it and decide it's time to shame ourselves by letting the stinking pig of inherent bias out of the closet, then, as the psychiatrists tell us, we can begin to heal. And we won't go around pretending all Black men and women get treated the way all white men and women are treated when we know that a Black man or woman has to be a celebrity, a music icon, sports hero, or filthy rich to get treated properly. And even then the brother or sister is at risk of their Thirteenth Amendment rights being repealed. The race is being robbed not only of its humanity but its triumphs, its grandeur when we don't acknowledge how deep the hatred goes. Sure, LeBron James is king of the basketball court. But outside of it, no man is a king if he's Black. Even President Obama had to endure having his wife called a cow because protesting the insult wouldn't have been presidential for a Black president. So the richness of who we are, of what we have achieved must be buried, as in a metaphorical book burning, and all we are allowed to do onstage and on-screen is be the comedian, the second banana, the suffering young boy trying to be a man, et cetera, ad infinitum, ad nauseam. The real men, the real women can never see the light of day, and there are at least two good reasons for it. The first is white theater and film cannot match the grandeur, the pain in human suffering that Black America has had to pay for each accomplishment that litters the history of our just trying to stay alive over the centuries. (America did kill off the Native

American, so I guess that can pass for grandeur.) The second reason is simply that anything that puts the African American at the top of the dramatic heap is persona non grata on any level, personal or ideological. Since we are too good, as one eminently famous New York producer told me face-to-face in camera about my work, we don't get produced as we really are, only as we have to be in the whitewashed version, race neutral in all it's shameless, obsequious, servile, and abject knee bending. And that's where the big money is. If it's race neutral, it's grits and gravy. If it ain't, then it's "Emperor's New Clothes," pretending to be *really* about race without having the honesty to admit that it's anything but that, nor allowing us to be who we really are, to be what we've really been in this land of the free and this home of the brave since before the Mayflower.

ACKNOWLEDGMENTS

My research stretched intermittently over a period of thirty years. When I started in the late eighties, there was no internet, no computers, and no smartphones, and I was working without the benefit of a grant or paid sabbatical. In other words, I was on my own. There was interest from a publisher, but no actual advance.

I had only the researchers from the two main libraries in New York City at my disposal, the Lincoln Center Library for the Performing Arts and the Schomburg Center for Research in Black Culture in Harlem, both part of the New York Public Library system. But it was card catalogs and only card catalogs, as well as the overworked librarians, that I had to rely on. Sadly, I remember none of the names from that time.

When I got a contract from Rutgers University Press to resurrect *Macbeth in Harlem*, which was the original title of my research, I returned to my two stalwarts, Lincoln Center and Schomburg, both now splendidly refurbished with glittering arrays of computer and internet technology. But the advance in information gathering didn't make it easier for me to pick up where I had left off thirty years ago. On the contrary, much of my original data had been lost or obscured or replaced by "newness." I needed all the help I could get to put Humpty Dumpty back together again. And I got it.

John L. Calhoun, chief research librarian in the Billy Rose Theatre Division at Lincoln Center, went out of his way to give me every assistance I needed, as often as I needed it. Not to be outdone by downtown, Maira Liriano, associate chief librarian in the Research and Reference Division at Schomburg and her able assistants—Auburn Nelson, Tracy Crawford, and A. J. Muhammad—formed a fierce foursome to ferret out all the records and information they could for me. I called them "the Squad." And Alice Adamczyk, who had been there thirty years ago, even found a book that I needed without benefit of either title or author, both of which I had gotten wrong.

And downtown proved a magic casement of help from every corner. Calhoun's assistants—Annemarie van Roessel, Arlene Yu, Daisy Pommer, Carolyn Broomhead, and Jeremy Megraw—all performed feats of magic in finding information and source material that puzzled librarians whom I had reached out to in other parts of the city. The Billy Rose Collection is staffed by the very top of the profession, and that includes those in the Katharine Cornell-Guthrie McClintic Special Collections Reading Room. Carolyn Broohmead, whom I never even knew existed, appeared one day at my side to tell me that microfilm I requested was available but in another building and that she would get it for me if I wished. When I asked the reason for such unreasoning largesse, she said it was because I was using the old card catalogs, something very few writers pay attention to now.

I would be very remiss if I didn't mention Mary Yearwood and her assistant, Michael Mery, who run the photographic division at Schomburg. Michael was almost at pains to give me all the help he could in finding the images I needed and identifying old photographs that had no attribution. And Tom Lisanti, manager of Permissions and Reproductive Services at the Schwarzman building, made it possible through his patience and cut-to-the-chase approach to keep me from getting hopelessly entangled in tiffs and jpegs and what has a copyright and what doesn't.

To my dear friend Shannon Effinger, a professional writer in her own right, who graciously agreed to be my assistant and general factotum, I owe immeasurable thanks.

To all of them, I say, "I couldn't have done it without you." And I haven't even mentioned my brilliant and patient editor at Rutgers University Press, Nicole Solano, who was so sensitive to the needs of my writing style and kept her red pencil to a minimum.

NOTES

CHAPTER 1   THE BEGINNING

1. See Barbara Leaming, *Orson Welles, A Biography* (New York: Viking Press, 1985); Simon Callow, *Orson Welles: The Road to Xanadu* (New York: Viking Press, 1996); Bernice W. Kliman, *Macbeth* (Manchester: Manchester University Press, 1992).

2. Like neegrow and others used later, this is a slang term for *negro*, often used as satire.

3. Alternate title Brother Mose, RM 1777, Billy Rose Theatre Division, New York Public Library for the Performing Arts.

4. Quoted in Bernard L. Peterson, *Profiles of African American Stage Performers and Theatre People, 1818–1960* (Westport, Conn.: Greenwood Press, 2001), 237.

5. See James V. Hatch and Ted Shine, eds., *Black Theatre USA: Plays by African Americans*, vol. 1, *The Early Period, 1847–1938*, rev. and expanded ed. (New York: Free Press, 1996); Bernard Peterson, *Early Black American Playwrights and Dramatic Writers: A Biographical Directory and Catalog of Plays, Films, and Broadcasting Scripts* (New York: Greenwood Publishing, 1990) 37–39.

6. Quoted in Herbert Marshall and Mildred Stock, *Ira Aldridge: The Negro Tragedian* (London: Camelot Press, 1958), 37.

7. *National Advocate*, August 3, 1821.

8. *National Advocate*, September 21, 1821.

9. Ibid.

10. Quoted in Marshall and Stock, *Ira Aldridge*, 35.

11. Ibid., 38.

12. Ibid., 61–62.

13. Ibid., 64.

14. Ibid., 66.

15. Ibid., 67–68.

16. Ibid., 115.

17. Ibid., 120–121.

18. Ibid., 125–127.

19. Ibid., 140.

20. Ibid., 210.

21. Ibid., 230–231.

22. Ibid., 239.

23. Ibid., 244.

24. Ibid., 216.

25. Ibid., 310.

26. Ibid., 311.

27. Ibid., 312.

CHAPTER 2   THE LONG NIGHT OF THE NINETEENTH CENTURY

1. Langston Hughes and Milton Meltzer, *Black Magic: A Pictorial History of Black Entertainment in America* (New York: Bonanza Books, 1967), 16.

2. James Weldon Johnson, *Black Manhattan* (New York: Atheneum, 1977), 88.

3. Ibid., 87.

4. Eric Lott, *Love and Theft: Blackface Minstrelsy and the American Working Class* (New York: Oxford University Press, 1993).

5. "Introduction to Uncle Tom's Cabin Study Guide," BookRags, accessed on May 16, 2006, www.bookrags.com.

6. Marshall and Stock, *Ira Aldridge*, 155–156.

7. William Wells Brown, *The Escape, or A Leap for Freedom* (Boston: R. F. Wallcut, 1858).

8. Edith Isaacs, *The Negro in the American Theatre* (New York: Theatre Arts, 1947), 14.

9. Ibid., 15.

10. See Hatch and Shine, *Black Theatre USA*, vol. 1; Victor Séjour, "The Mulatto," trans. Philip Barnard, in *The Norton Anthology of African American Literature*, ed. Nellie Y. McKay and Henry Louis Gates, 2nd ed. (New York: Norton, 2004).

11. Lynne Fauley Emery, *Black Dance in the United States, 1619–1970* (Palo Alto, Calif.: National Press, 1972), 154.

12. Ibid., 147.

13. Hughes and Meltzer, *Black Magic*, 18.

14. Ibid., 18.

15. Quoted in Marshall and Stock, *Ira Aldridge*, 204–205.

16. Quoted in William Edward Farrison, *William Wells Brown Author and Reformer* (Chicago: University of Chicago Press, 1969), 190.

17. George Aiken, *Uncle Tom's Cabin* (New York: Samuel French, 192-?)

18. Traditional slave marriage consisted simply of "jumping over the broomstick" and no more.

19. Stark Young, review of *Uncle Tom's Cabin*, *New Republic*, November 18, 1936.,

20. Percy Hammond, review of *Sweet River*, *New York Herald Tribune*, May 31, 1933.

21. John Mason Brown, review of *Uncle Tom's Cabin*, *Saturday Review of Literature*, October 6, 1945.

22. Ibid.

23. Harry Birdoff, *The World's Greatest Hit* (New York: Vanni, 1947).

24. Joe Laurie Jr., "The Theater's All Time Hit," *American Mercury*, October 1, 1945.

25. Birdoff, *World's Greatest Hit*, 217.

26. Ibid., 216.

27. Ibid., 207.

28. Laurie, "Theater's All Time Hit."

29. Ibid.

30. Dion Boucicault, *The Octoroon* (London: T. H. Lacy, 1859).

31. Ibid.

32. Richard Cooke, review of *The Octoroon*, *Wall Street Journal*, January 30, 1961.

33. Ibid.

34. Thomas Dash, review of *The Octoroon*, *Women's Wear Daily*, January 31, 1961.

35. Frank Aston, review of *The Octoroon*, *New York World-Telegram and Sun*, January 28, 1961.

36. George Oppenheimer, review of *The Octoroon*, *Newsday*, February 1, 1961.

37. Walter Kerr, review of *The Octoroon*, *New York Herald Tribune*, January 28, 1961.

38. Review of *The Octoroon*, *Variety*, February 1, 1961.

39. Guy Savino, review of *The Octoroon*, *Newark Evening News*, January 28, 1961.

CHAPTER 3   NEW BEGINNINGS FOR A NEW CENTURY

1. Quoted in Rayford Logan, *The Betrayal of the Negro* (London: Collier-Macmillan, 1954), 99. Also see Clifford Mason, *The African-American Bookshelf: 50 Must-Reads From Before the Civil War Through Today* (New York: Kensington, 2003), 90.

2. Johnson, *Black Manhattan*, 171.

3. Thomas Jefferson, *Notes on the State of Virginia* (Chapel Hill: University of North Carolina Press, 1955), 139. On page 138, directly preceding the dictum on lovemaking and body odor, he also claims without any proof that orangutans (spelled "Oran-ootan") prefer Black women as sex partners over the women of their own species. This is an even more bizarre puzzler, since the orangutan is native to Asia and not Africa.

4. Robert C. Allen, *Horrible Prettiness* (Chapel Hill: University of North Carolina Press, 1991), 27.

5. Ibid., 11.

6. Douglas Gilbert, *American Vaudeville* (New York: McGraw-Hill, 1940).

7. Judy Alter, *Vaudeville—the Birth of Show Business* (New York: Franklin Watts, 1998), 19.

8. Nathan Hurwitz, *A History of the American Musical Theatre* (New York: Routledge, 2014), 64.

9. Ibid., 76.

10. Johnson, *Black Manhattan*, 109.

11. See George Alexander, "The Soprano," *American Legacy* (Summer 2007); Kwame Anthony Appiah and Henry Louis Gates Jr., eds., "M. Sissieretta Jones," in *Africana: The Encyclopedia of the African and African American Experience* (New York: Basic Civitas Books, 1999), 1065; John Graziano, "The Early Life and Career of the 'Black Patti': The Odyssey of an African American Singer in the Late Nineteenth Century," *Journal of the American Musicological Society* 53:543–596.

12. Ibid., 98.

13. Ibid., 101.

14. Ibid., 103.

15. Hurwitz, *History of American Musical Theatre*, 76.

16. Ibid., 59.

17. Ibid., 61.

18. Ibid., 63.

19. Sterling Brown, "Negro in the American Theatre," in *Oxford Companion to the Theatre*, by Phyllis Hartnoll (London: Oxford University Press, 1957), 566.

20. Jean Wagner, *Black Poets of the United States: From Paul Laurence Dunbar to Langston Hughes*, trans. Kenneth Douglas (Urbana: University of Illinois Press, 1973), 108.

21. Loften Mitchell, *Black Drama* (New York: Hawthorn Books, 1967), 42, 44.

22. Allen Churchill, *The Theatrical Twenties* (New York: McGraw-Hill, 1975), 27.

23. Ann Charters, *Nobody: The Story of Bert Williams* (London: Collier-Macmillan, 1970), 69.

24. Ibid., 71.

25. Ibid., 83.

26. Mitchell, *Black Drama*, 51.

27. Quoted in ibid., 49.

28. Churchill, *Theatrical Twenties*, 29.

29. Ibid., 24.

30. Charters, *Nobody*, 118.

31. Ibid., 147.

32. Quoted in ibid., 129.

33. Ibid.

34. *T-CLIP, Williams, Bert A., Billy Rose Theatre Division, New York Public Library for the Performing Arts.

35. Quoted in Charters, *Nobody*, 11.

36. Ibid., 148.

CHAPTER 4   THE TWENTIES

1. Johnson, *Black Manhattan*, 127.

2. Ibid., 171.

3. Ibid., 175.

4. Edward Sheldon, *The Nigger* (New York: Macmillan, 1910).

5. Brooks Atkinson, *Broadway* (New York: Macmillan, 1970), 4.

6. Susan Curtis, *The First Black Actors on the Great White Way* (Columbia: University of Missouri Press, 1998), 3.

7. Ibid., 11.

8. Ibid., 12.

9. Ibid., 25.

10. Ibid., 9.

11. Ibid., 37.

12. Ibid., 38.

13. Ibid., 163.

14. Ibid., 8.

15. Ibid., 81.

16. Ibid., 3.

17. Ibid., 23.

18. Ibid., 10.

19. Review of *All God's Chillun Got Wings*, *Journal America*, May 16, 1924.

20. Percy Hammond, review of *All God's Chillun Got Wings*, *New York Herald Tribune*, May, 16, 1924.

21. John Corbin, review of *All God's Chillun Got Wings*, *New York Times*, May 16, 1924.

22. Heywood Broun, review of *All God's Chillun Got Wings*, *New York World*, May 16, 1924.

23. Heywood Broun, review of *The Emperor Jones*, *New York World*, November 4, 1920.

24. Alan Dale, review of *The Emperor Jones*, *New York American*, November 2, 1920.

25. Broun, review of *Emperor Jones*.

26. Review of *The Emperor Jones*, *New York Times*, May 6, 1924.

27. Review of *The Emperor Jones*, *Billboard*, November 20, 1926.

28. Alexander Woollcott, review of *The Emperor Jones*, *New York World*, May 6, 1924.

29. Review of *The Emperor Jones*, *Life*, January 6, 1921, 64.

30. Burns Mantle, review of *Harlem*, *New York Daily News*, February 21, 1929.

31. Alison Smith, review of *Harlem*, *New York Morning World*, February 22, 1929.

32. Richard Lockridge, review of *Harlem*, *New York Sun*, February 21, 1929.

33. Brooks Atkinson, review of *Harlem*, *New York Times*, March 3, 1929.

34. Gilbert Gabriel, review of *Harlem*, *New York Evening Telegram*, March 4, 1929.

35. Lockridge, review of *Harlem*.

36. Smith, review of *Harlem*.

37. Percy Hammond, review of *Lulu Belle*, *New York Herald Tribune*, February 10, 1926.

38. Alexander Woollcott, review of *Lulu Belle*, *New York World*, February 10, 1925.

39. Gilbert Seldes, review of *Shuffle Along*, *Seven Lively Arts*, May 23, 1921.

40. Quoted in Johnson, *Black Manhattan*, 198.

41. Edith Isaacs, review of *Shuffle Along*, *Theatre Arts Monthly*, August 1921.

42. Eubie Blake, quoted in Mitchell, *Black Drama*, 77.

43. Quoted in Mitchell, *Black Drama*, 77.

44. Review of *Shuffle Along*, *New York Morning Telegraph*, May 24, 1921.

45. Hurwitz, *History of American Musical Theatre*, 110.

46. Ibid., 110.

47. Review of *Runnin' Wild*, *New York Times*, October 30, 1923.

48. MAG, review of *Runnin' Wild*, *New York Herald Tribune*, October 30, 1923.

49. Review of *Runnin' Wild*, *New York Sun*, October 30, 1923.

50. Alan Dale, review of *Runnin' Wild*, *New York American*, October 31, 1923.

51. Review of *Liza*, *New York World*, November 27, 1922.

52. Alexander Woollcott, review of *Liza*, *New York Herald*, November 27, 1922.

53. Heywood Broun, review of *Liza*, *New York World*, November 27, 1922.

54. Quoted in Laban Carrick Hill, *Harlem Stomp! A Cultural History of the Harlem Renaissance* (New York: Little, Brown, 2003), 22.

CHAPTER 5   THE "VOODOO" *MACBETH* AND THE FAMISHED DAWN

1. Lawrence LaMar, *New York Amsterdam News*, July 31, 1948.

2. *New York Times*, November 6, 1934.

3. *T-CLIP, (*Green Pastures*) (Marc Connelly) Billy Rose Theatre Division, New York Public Library for the Performing Arts.

4. Brooks Atkinson, review of *The Green Pastures*, *New York Times*, February 27, 1930.

5. Marc Connelly, *The Green Pastures* (New York: Farrar & Rinehart, 1929), 11–13.

6. William Bolitho, review of *The Green Pastures*, *New York World*, March 1, 1930.

7. Gilbert Seldes, review of *Scarlet Sister Mary*, *New York Evening Telegram*, November 26, 1930.

8. Whitney Bolton, review of *Scarlet Sister Mary*, *New York Morning Telegraph*, November 26, 1930.

9. Review of *Scarlet Sister Mary*, *Theater Arts*, 15 (January–June 1931).

10. Brooks Atkinson, review of *Scarlet Sister Mary*, *New York Times*, November 26, 1930.

11. Stark Young, review of *Scarlet Sister Mary*, *New Republic*, December 10, 1930.

12. John Anderson, "Baked Hampden," review of *Achilles Had a Heel*, *New York Evening Journal*, October 13, 1935.

13. "Way down south in Dixie / (Break the heart of me) / They hung my black young lover/ To a cross roads tree." Poem by Langston Hughes. MY 292.

14. The Library of Congress has a copy that I was unable to obtain in time to meet the deadline for the publication of *Macbeth in Harlem*.

15. Mason, *African-American Bookshelf*, 168.

16. Arthur Ruhl, review of *Legal Murder*, *New York Herald Tribune*, February 16, 1934.

17. John Chapman, review of *Legal Murder*, *New York Daily News*, February 16, 1934.

18. Stephen Rathbun, review of *Legal Murder*, *New York Sun*, February 16, 1934.

19. Ibid.

20. Quoted in John Houseman, *Run-Through* (New York: Simon and Schuster, 1972), 105.

21. Rudolph Fisher, *The City of Refuge: The Collected Stories of Rudolph Fisher*, ed. John McCluskey Jr. (Columbia: University of Missouri Press, 1987), 24.

22. Houseman, *Run-Through*, 198.

23. Ibid., 199.

24. Ibid., 200.

25. Ibid., 201.

26. Charles Morgan, review of *Hamlet*, *New York Times*, December 2, 1934.

27. Review of *Macbeth*, *Variety*, April 22, 1936.

28. Richard Lockridge, review of *Macbeth*, *New York Sun*, April 15, 1936.

29. Robert Garland, review of *Macbeth*, *New York World-Telegram and Sun*, April 15, 1936.

30. Percy Hammond, review of *Macbeth*, *New York Herald Tribune*, April 15, 1936.

31. Citizen Welles, "Orson Welles, Sketch Book—Episode 2: Critics," YouTube, February 21, 2013 (originally aired May 8, 1955), https://youtu.be/NL3ZoUJ-Tek.

32. John Mason Brown, review of *Macbeth*, *New York Post*, April 18, 1936.

33. Brooks Atkinson, "Harlem Boy Goes Wrong," review of *Macbeth*, *New York Times*, April 15, 1936.

34. Burns Mantle, review of *Macbeth*, *New York Daily News*, July 10, 1936.

35. Houseman, *Run-Through*, 201.

36. Ibid., 202.

37. Ibid., 209–210.

38. Hughes and Meltzer, *Black Magic*, 119.

39. Houseman, *Run-Through*, 210.

40. Hallie Flanagan, *Arena* (New York: Duell, Sloan and Pearce, 1940), 342.

41. Box 13, folder 4, Hallie Flanagan Papers, *T-Mss 1964-002, Billy Rose Theatre Division, New York Public Library for the Performing Arts.

42. Houseman, *Run-Through*, 236.

43. Brooks Atkinson, review of *Doctor Faustus*, *New York Times*, January 9, 1937.

44. Theodore Browne, *Natural Man*, Schomburg Center for Research in Black Culture, Rare Books Division; New York Public Library.

45. Theodore Browne, interview with Lorraine Brown, tape 1, side 2, page 23, FTP Collection, George Mason University, Fairfax, Va.

46. Theodore Ward, *Big White Fog* (London: Nick Hern Books, 2007).

47. Marcus Garvey was a Jamaican who came to America and created an entire Black Power movement singlehandedly. There are innumerable references to him and his work. My "Must Read #29," in *African-American Bookshelf*, 155, is a good place to start.

48. Christine Ames and Clarke Painter, *Black Empire*; *T-Mss 1966-002, American Play Company Records, Billy Rose Theatre Division, New York Public Library for the Performing Arts.

49. William Du Bois, *Haiti*, Federal Theatre Plays (New York: Random House, 1938), 52.

50. Ibid., 53.

51. Langston Hughes, "The Emperor of Haiti," in *Black Drama Anthology*, ed. Darwin Turner (Washington, D.C.: Howard University Press, 1994).

52. NCOF+ (MacEntee, G. Case of Philip Lawrence), Billy Rose Theatre Division, New York Public Library for the Performing Arts.

53. Hughes Allison, *The Trial of Dr. Beck*, New Federal Theatre Records, Schomburg Center for Research in Black Culture, Rare Books Division; New York Public Library.

54. Houseman, *Run-Through*, 463.

55. Ibid., 463–464.

56. Ibid., 466.

57. Quoted in ibid., 466–467.

58. Quoted in ibid., 473.

59. Quoted in ibid., 473.

60. Quoted in ibid., 474.

61. Quoted in ibid., 473–474.

62. Quoted in ibid., 473.

63. Brooks Atkinson, review of *Native Son*, *New York Times*, March 25, 1941.

CHAPTER 6   PAUL ROBESON AND THE FIFTIES

1. Quoted in Errol Hill, *Shakespeare in Sable* (Boston: University of Massachusetts Press, 1984), 126.

2. Ibid.

3. Ibid., 126, 128.

4. Lewis Nichols, review of *Othello*, *New York Times*, October 19, 1943.

5. Review of *Othello, New York Times*, October 19, 1943.

6. Julia Craven, "More Than 250 Black People Were Killed by Police in 2016," *Huffington Post*, May, 25, 2018.

7. *United States Congressional Record*, September 21, 1949, p 13375.

8. Mason, *African-American Bookshelf*, 187.

9. W. A. Darlington, review of *Othello, New York Times*, April 12, 1959.

10. Quoted in Loften Mitchell, *Voices of the Black Theatre* (Clifton, N.J.: James T. White, 1975), 120.

11. Ibid., 120.

12. Ibid., 137.

13. Ibid.

14. Ibid., 131.

15. Ibid.

16. Ibid., 136.

17. Ibid., 138.

18. Ibid., 140.

19. Theodore Ward, "*Our Lan'*, Playscripts," Schomburg Center for Research in Black Culture, Rare Books Division; New York Public Library.

20. William Branch, "A Medal for Willie," in *Black Drama Anthology*, ed. Woodie King (New York: New American Library, 1971).

21. Louis Peterson, *Take a Giant Step* (New York: Samuel French, 1954).

22. See Hughes and Meltzer, *Black Magic*, 199, for a detailed list of plays from the forties. The three plays from the twenties that he does mention are *Chip Woman's Fortune, Brother Mose* (or *Meek Mose*), and of course, *Appearances*.

23. Loften Mitchell, *Land beyond the River* (Cody, Wyo.: Pioneer Drama Service, 1963).

24. Alice Childress, *Selected Plays*, ed. Kathy A. Perkins (Evanston, Ill.: Northwestern University Press, 2011).

25. Ibid.

26. Lorraine Hansberry, *A Raisin in the Sun* (New York: New American Library, 1958).

SELECTED BIBLIOGRAPHY

Aiken, George. *Uncle Tom's Cabin*. French's Standard Drama. New York: Samuel French, 192-?.

Allen, Robert C. *Horrible Prettiness: Burlesque and American Culture*. Chapel Hill: University of North Carolina Press, 1991.

Alter, Judy. *Vaudeville—the Birth of Show Business*. New York: Franklin Watts, 1998.

Ames, Christine, and Clark Painter. *Black Empire*. Manuscript. Performing Arts Research Collections—Theatre. New York Public Library, New York.

Birdoff, Harry. *The World's Greatest Hit: Uncle Tom's Cabin*. New York: Vanni, 1947.

Boucicault, Dion. *The Octoroon*. London: T. H. Lacy, 1859.

Branch, William. *A Medal for Willie*. New York: New American Library, 1971.

Brown, Sterling. *Negro Poetry and Drama and the Negro in American Fiction*. New York: Atheneum, 1969.

Brown, William Wells. *The Escape, or; A Leap for Freedom: A Drama in Five Acts*. Boston: R. F. Wallcut, 1858.

Charters, Ann. *Nobody: The Story of Bert Williams*. New York: Collier-Macmillan, 1970.

Churchill, Allen. *The Theatrical Twenties*. New York: McGraw-Hill, 1975.

Connelly, Marc. *Green Pastures*. New York: Farrar & Rinehart, 1929.

Curtis, Susan. *The First Black Actors on the Great White Way*. Columbia: University of Missouri Press, 1998.

DuBois, William. *Haiti*. Federal Theatre Plays. New York: Random House, 1938.

Emmery, Lynne Fauley. *Black Dance in the United States from 1619 to 1970*. Palo Alto, Calif.: National Press Books, 1972.

Farrison, William Edward. *William Wells Brown: Author and Reformer*. Chicago: University of Chicago Press, 1969.

Gilbert, Douglas. *American Vaudeville: Its Life and Times*. New York: McGraw-Hill, 1940.

Hill, Errol. *Shakespeare in Sable*. Boston: University of Massachusetts Press, 1984.

Himelstein, Morgan. *Drama Was a Weapon: The Left-Wing Theatre in New York, 1929–1941*. Westport, Conn.: Greenwood Press, 1976.

Hughes, Langston, and Milton Meltzer. *Black Magic, A Pictorial History of Black Entertainment in America*. New York: Bonanza Books, 1967.

Hurwitz Nathan. *A History of the American Musical Theatre: No Business like It*. New York: Routledge, 2014.

Johnson, James Weldon. *Black Manhattan*. New York: Atheneum, 1977.

Laurie, Joe. "The Theatre's All-Time Hit." *American Mercury*, October 1, 1945.

Marshall, Herbert, and Mildred Stock. *Ira Aldridge: The Negro Tragedian*. London: Camelot Press, 1958.

Mason, Clifford. *The African-American Bookshelf: Fifty Must Reads From Before the Civil War Through Today*. New York: Kensington, 2004.

Mitchell, Loften. *Land beyond the River*. Cody, Wyo.: Pioneer Drama Service, 1963.

Nesteroff, Kliph. *The Comedians: Drunks, Thieves, Scoundrels and the History of American Comedy*. New York: Grove Press, 2015.

Perkins, Kathy A., ed. *Selected Plays: Alice Childress*. Evanston, Ill.: Northwestern University Press, 2011.

Peterson, Louis. *Take a Giant Step*. New York: Samuel French, Inc., 1954.

Sheldon, Edward. *The Nigger*. New York: MacMillan, 1910.

Turner, Darwin. *Black Drama in America: An Anthology*. Washington, D.C.: Howard University Press, 1994.

Wilson, Frank. *Brother Mose*. Manuscript. Performing Arts Research Collections—Theatre. New York Public Library, New York.

INDEX

Page numbers in *italics* refer to figures.

ABOUT THE AUTHOR

CLIFFORD MASON is a celebrated playwright, actor, director, and critic who has been involved in the theater for four decades and has written thirty-four plays. He is also the author of *The African-American Bookshelf: 50 Must-Reads From Before the Civil War Through Today*, a history of Black literature from colonial times to the present.